A Fail-safe Way
for You
to Receive
the Holy Spirit

A Fail-safe Way
for You
to Receive
the Holy Spirit

PAUL C. JONG

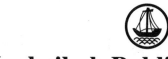

Hephzibah Publishing House

SEOUL, KOREA

Hephzibah Publishing House

48 Bon-dong, Dongjack-gu
Seoul, Korea 156-060

♠ New York Branch
   42-33 155st. 9A
   Flushing, NY 11354
   USA
♠ Website: www.pauljong.com
♠ Email addresses
   For general inquiry: service@pauljong.com
   Marketing dept.: sales@pauljong.com
   For purchase: buy@pauljong.com
   For translation: translation@pauljong.com
♠ Phone: 1-718-463-0838 (USA)
            82-016-392-2954 (Korea)
♠ Fax: 82-33-651-2954

This book can be also purchased at world's largest online store like
Amazon.com (www.amazon.com) or Barnes & Noble.com (www.bn.com).

Acknowledgments

I give thanks to the Lord, who saved us from the whispers and pressures of Satan, and I'd also like to express my heartfelt gratitude to the ministers listed below, my fellow workers and all the saints who dedicated themselves to publishing this book.

Rev. Samuel Kim
Rev. John Shin
Hyun-ah Choi
Sang-min Lee
Ross Wallace
Anthony Banks

This book is part of a follow-up series to my two previously published volumes. Again, I have attempted to prove the work of the Holy Spirit and reveal that of the devil more clearly from a clinical and biblical point of view. I hope that this book will be read by all Christians throughout the world and those suffering and lamenting after having been deceived by Satan. I also hope that ministers and even laymen will come to a greater awareness that the work of Satan continues to exist in Christianity to this day.

There was once a time when I suffered greatly after being deceived by a demon pretending to be Jesus. But the Lord saved me from the lies and agony caused by this demon by giving me the gospel of the water and the Spirit. Therefore, I give thanks to the Lord, who allowed me to do His work by revealing how Satan uses the name of Jesus to further his own work. This book is for those who are suffering under false beliefs, just as I once did. Give all glory to God... ⊠

PAUL C. JONG

Preface

The Christian faith of the world should change. In Christianity, the most frequently discussed issues are "salvation from sin" and "the indwelling of the Holy Spirit." However, few people have precise knowledge of these two ideas, despite the fact that they are the two most important concepts in Christianity. People dare to say that they believe in Jesus Christ when they are ignorant of elementary biblical knowledge of redemption and the Holy Spirit. Therefore, God has called on those of us who have received the Holy Spirit to write this book regarding the indwelling of the Holy Spirit so that people can discover answers to their questions about it.

I suffered once from the feeling of being bound by the law, even though I was a believer in Jesus Christ. However, God made me realize the beautiful gospel of the water and the Spirit and gave me the gift of the Holy Spirit. Science and technology have rapidly developed over the years, but people who know how to obtain the indwelling of the Holy Spirit are so few that I decided to write about the correct way to receive the Holy Spirit according to the Scripture.

In this book, the beautiful gospel refers to the gospel of the water and the Spirit, which grants us the indwelling of the Holy Spirit.

Do you know of the gospel of the water and the Spirit that can grant you the Holy Spirit? If you truly wish to receive the Holy Spirit, you must first obtain exact and accurate knowledge of it. Do you know the gospel that helps you receive the Holy Spirit? If you want to ask God for the indwelling of the Holy Spirit, then you must first obtain exact knowledge of it and retain faith in it. What then is the key qualification for you to receive the Holy Spirit? It is to cleanse you of all sins through the beautiful gospel of the water and the Spirit. To help you do this, I would like to pass on to you the exact knowledge of the gospel of the water and the Spirit. Only when you accept this knowledge will you receive the Holy Spirit.

The gospel of the water and the Spirit, as described in the Bible, has power equivalent to that of dynamite. When dynamite explodes, a whole building can be demolished. Likewise, the gospel blows away the sins of believers once for all. You who believe in this truth will certainly receive the indwelling of the Holy Spirit. The knowledge of the gospel of the water and the Spirit, which the Lord has given to all mankind, has brought you the blessing of the Holy Spirit. You will learn more of the beautiful gospel further on in my writings. In addition, with the indwelling of the Holy Spirit, you will live as His disciple. You, who know and believe in the gospel of the water and the Spirit, will live a peaceful and joyful life thanks to the living water arising from the indwelling of the Holy Spirit.

In contemporary society, most people are ignorant of the truth of the gospel of the water and the Spirit, and are suffering under mistaken illusions given to them by false teachers. These people gather at "Revival Meetings" and clap and rejoice in a frenzy as the preacher on stage sings fast-tempo hymns and urges people to repent. In these meetings, which sometimes take on a fanatical atmosphere, people cry out "Lord!" three times and ask God for the fullness of the Holy Spirit until their voices crack.

Those who attend such meetings tend to cry out instead of uttering prayers. When the atmosphere reaches its feverish peak, people scream out and faint in every corner. However, the preacher on stage keeps the microphone to his lips and makes the sound of the wind while he guides people ever deeper into religious fanaticism. He prays by speaking in strange tongues and jumps off stage to lay his hands on people's heads. Some people start speaking in strange tongues, and some have violent fits and faint.

Then, amidst all the excitement, fear, frenzy, and desire, the crowd starts praying in an incomprehensible language (called speaking in tongues) until they are worn out. They experience bodily convulsions, as if demons had entered their bodies. This kind of excitement and delirium make some people practically hysterical. We can call these phenomena "the syndrome of collective hysterias."

Many people are drawn into this religious fanaticism, hoping to receive the Holy Spirit. They believe that they will receive the Holy Spirit by reaching a state of frenzy and hysteria. But such fanaticism derives from Satan.

These religious fanatics are not in the least interested in His words concerning the indwelling of the Holy Spirit. Rather, they believe in their bodily experiences and the teachings of false preachers.

Examining these practices and others like them, we can see that contemporary Christianity has contracted a disease which one could describe as "the Pentecostal-Charismatic Movement" or "Neo-Pentecostalism," which comes from ancient Shaman-ism. Why have they caught this disease of fanaticism? Because they have rejected the truth that says they must receive the Holy Spirit only by believing in the beautiful gospel of the water and the Spirit.

The true gospel of the water and the Spirit is accomplished through the baptism that Jesus received from John and His blood on the Cross. Those whose faith derives from such fanaticism are under the mistaken impression that they can receive the Holy Spirit without believing in the gospel of the water and the Spirit. Their so-called faith reduces Christianity to mere shallow Shamanism. Today, these types of religious movements are spreading worldwide and many Christians are confused because they cannot tell the work of the Holy Spirit from that of demons.

"In whom does the Holy Spirit dwell?" is a question that has long been awaiting an answer from ministers and religious researchers around the world. As a result, many people have attempted to advance their knowledge and understanding of it, which has only left people confused and plagued with superstitious beliefs. This problem began with the development of the Pentecostal-Charismatic Movement in the early 19th century. This movement swept over the whole world but was the work of evil spirits and fringe groups who erroneously considered themselves Christians.

Christians throughout the world must return to His words and find the answers to their questions in the gospel of the water and the Spirit. In order to help authentic Christians, I will explain the work of the Holy Spirit in the time of the early church and also outline the relationship between "the gospel of the water and the Spirit" and "the indwelling of the Holy Spirit."

Above all, I will clarify the concept of the indwelling of the Holy Spirit in those who believe in "Jesus' baptism and His blood on the Cross."

Today, most Christians misunderstand this key concept of the indwelling of the Holy Spirit. They believe obstinately that even someone whose sins have not been forgiven can receive the Holy Spirit. According to the Bible, there can be no indwelling of the Holy Spirit without belief in the words of the gospel of the water and the Spirit. However, most people think that simply believing in Jesus, without faith in the gospel of the water and the Spirit, will enable them to receive the Holy Spirit.

We must study His words to discern whether the spirit dwelling within us is the Holy Spirit or the spirit of a demon, and also examine if the Holy Spirit can dwell within sinners as well. What do you think? If you have sin even though you believe in Jesus, do you think the Holy Spirit dwells within you? Are you sure the spirit within you is the Holy Spirit?

You must know the truth that God allows the Holy Spirit to dwell in you only when you have faith in the gospel of the water and the Spirit. Therefore, in order to receive the Holy Spirit, you must know and believe with your whole heart in the gospel of the water and the Spirit. With absolute certainty, I can tell you that this is true. If you accept the biblical truth that I am relating to you, the Holy Spirit will certainly dwell in you.

I would like to tell you to believe in the gospel of the water and the Spirit with all your heart. Then you will meet the Lord and be blessed with the indwelling of the Holy Spirit. Those who believe in the gospel of the water and the Spirit are blessed with the indwelling of the Holy Spirit. The Lord grants them every spiritual blessing in Heaven. May the Lord bless you with the indwelling of the Holy Spirit! ✉

CONTENTS

Part One — Sermons

Part Two — Appendix

SERMON 1

The Holy Spirit works
within God's Word
of the Promise

The Holy Spirit works within God's Word of the Promise

<Acts 1:4-8>

"And being assembled together with them, He commanded them not to depart from Jerusalem, but to wait for the Promise of the Father, 'which,' He said, 'you have heard from Me; for John truly baptized with water, but you shall be baptized with the Holy Spirit not many days from now.' Therefore, when they had come together, they asked Him, saying, 'Lord, will You at this time restore the kingdom to Israel?' And He said to them, 'It is not for you to know times or seasons which the Father has put in His own authority. But you shall receive power when the Holy Spirit has come upon you; and you shall be witnesses to Me in Jerusalem, and in all Judea and Samaria, and to the ends of the earth.'"

Is the indwelling of the Holy Spirit a gift from God or is it given due to efforts on one's own behalf?

It is a gift given to the person who receives the forgiveness of his sins, and contains the meaning of the fulfillment of God's promise.

Once I had the experience of receiving flames of something like the Holy Spirit through prayer. But these flames didn't last long, and soon died out in the face of accumulated sin. However, now I want to show you the truth about the Holy Spirit, which will dwell in us for eternity, not through the false Spirit easily extinguished by sin, but through the true gospel. The Holy Spirit I will now introduce to you through this message is not something that you can receive through prayers, but only through faith in the gospel of the water and the Spirit.

I want to lead you to receive [1]**the indwelling of the Holy Spirit** through this book. You will realize that the Holy Sprit inspires the message I'm delivering to you. It's God's absolute desire for us to receive the indwelling of the Holy Spirit at this time. You can learn about the indwelling of the Holy Spirit and receive it through this one book. If this book is not enough for you, I advise you to read the two books published by me previously. You will have received perfect faith before God through these books.

Many Christians are trying to receive the Holy Spirit as if He descended on Jesus' disciples on the Day of the Pentecost. Some people have earned great sums of money by exploiting this method. They pretend that the Holy Spirit is something that can be obtained through human effort. They want to have visions, perform miracles, hear Jesus' own voice, speak in tongues, heal diseases and cast out demons. However, they have sin in their hearts, and are under the influence of evil

---

[1] The Holy Spirit dwells in the hearts of the born-again, who have been forgiven for all their sins by believing the gospel of the water and the Spirit. Once He comes into a saint, He resides in him forever, and never leaves him as long as he believes in the gospel. He gives conviction to the saints, leads them to know God's will in the Bible, strengthens them to overcome the temptations and difficulties inherent in this world, and lets them bear the fruits of the Spirit in abundance. God glorifies the body of the saint as the temple of God through the indwelling of the Holy Spirit (Acts 2:38-39, John 14:16, 16:8-10, 1 Corinthians 3:16, 6:19, Galatians 5:22-23).

spirits (Ephesians 2:1-2). Even now many people continue to live without knowing that they are under the power of evil spirits. That is why Satan lures and deceives people using all kinds of methods such as wonders and miracles that are really just illusions.

Jesus ordered His disciples *"not to depart from Jerusalem, but wait for the Promise of the Father" (Acts 1:4).* The receiving of the Holy Spirit revealed in Acts is not through "experience," "devotion" or "prayers of repentance," but through "waiting for God's promise" to give the Holy Spirit to them. What we should learn from this passage is that the indwelling of the Holy Spirit doesn't happen through the desperate prayers of men. It is God's gift, which can only be obtained through complete faith in the beautiful gospel of the water and the Spirit, which the Father God and Jesus Christ gave to mankind. The true indwelling of the Holy Spirit happens through faith in the gospel that Jesus Christ gave us. God gave us truth of the water and the Spirit so that we could receive the indwelling of the Holy Spirit (1 John 3:3-5).

The phrase "the Promise of the Holy Spirit" appears many times in the New Testament. Peter says in his sermon (Acts 2:38-39) on the baptism of the Holy Spirit on the Day of Pentecost, "It is God's promise to give the Holy Spirit to those who receive the forgiveness of sins as a result of believing in the beautiful gospel."

The indwelling of the Holy Spirit is a gift given to those who receive the forgiveness of their sins, and contains the meaning of the fulfillment of God's promise. The Holy Spirit in the New Testament is not something that can be obtained through the compromise between God and men, but is a promised gift from God. Therefore, the indwelling of the Holy Spirit, as revealed in Acts, is not something that can be obtained through prayer (Acts 8:19-20).

The Holy Spirit comes upon only those who believe in the gospel of the water and the Spirit that Jesus gave us. Jesus promised His disciples to send the Holy Spirit so that they could have the indwelling of the Holy Spirit. *"For John truly baptized with water, but you shall be baptized with the Holy Spirit not many days from now" (Acts 1:5).* So His disciples waited for the fulfillment of God's promise.

By looking at the beliefs of those in the Bible who received the indwelling of the Holy Spirit, we realize that it happened not through their efforts but by the will of God. The indwelling of the Holy Spirit that came upon the disciples in Acts did not happen on the basis of human endeavor or spiritual achievement.

The coming of the Holy Spirit upon His disciples, as it was written in Acts, soon came true. It was just as Jesus had said, "not many days from now." This was the first blessing at the time of the early church. By looking at the Scriptures, we can see that God's promise was not fulfilled through fasting, prayers or self-sacrifice, but through faith in Jesus. After Jesus' Ascension, believers received the forgiveness of sins and the indwelling of the Holy Spirit at the same time.

The Holy Spirit came on Jesus' disciples suddenly from Heaven!

"When the Day of Pentecost had fully come, they were all with one accord in one place" (Acts 2:1). Jesus' disciples gathered together as they waited for the fulfillment of God's promise to send them the Holy Spirit. And Holy Spirit finally

came upon them.

"And suddenly there came a sound from heaven, as of a rushing mighty wind, and it filled the whole house where they were sitting. Then there appeared to them divided tongues, as of fire, and one sat upon each of them. And they were all filled with the Holy Spirit and began to speak with other tongues, as the Spirit gave them utterance" (Acts 2:2-4).

The Holy Spirit came on them "suddenly from Heaven." Here the word "suddenly" means that it was done not through human will. In addition, the phrase "from Heaven" explains where the Holy Spirit came from, and also counters the idea that the indwelling of the Holy Spirit can be obtained through human will or effort. The phrase "from Heaven" shows that saying the Holy Spirit could be obtained through prayers is a fraudulent claim.

In other words, saying that the Holy Spirit came suddenly from Heaven means that the indwelling of the Holy Spirit does not happen through earthly means, such as speaking in tongues or self-sacrifice. Jesus' disciples at first spoke in tongues to preach the beautiful gospel to the people from every nation. The reason for this was to allow them to preach the gospel to foreign language speaking Jews in their own language through the help of the Holy Spirit. People from every nation heard the speaking tongues of the disciples in their own language, even though most of the disciples were from Galilee.

"Then there appeared to them divided tongues, as of fire, and one sat upon each of them. And they were all filled with the Holy Spirit" (Acts 2:3-4). Here we should pay special attention to the phrase, the Holy Spirit "sat upon each of them." The disciples, waiting for the coming of the Holy Spirit in one place, already believed in the gospel of being born again of water and the Spirit.

Many Christians nowadays misunderstand this part of the passage, believing that the coming of the Holy Spirit occurs with a sound like the blowing of the wind while they are praying. However, this is a misunderstanding about the Holy Spirit that arises from ignorance and confusion. Does the Holy Spirit make such sounds when He comes upon people? No, He doesn't.

What people hear with their ears are sounds that Satan makes when he devours people's souls. He makes these sounds when he works with illusions, mimic voices and false miracles in efforts to plunge people into confusion by pretending to be the Holy Spirit. People mistake these things for evidence of the coming of the Holy Spirit. People also think that the Holy Spirit comes with a "Suihhh~" sound like that of mighty wind. They are being deluded by demons. The coming of the Holy Spirit as recorded in Acts was achieved only through faith in the beautiful gospel.

Peter's faith (1 Peter 3:21) was perfect enough to allow him to receive the indwelling of the Holy Spirit

By embossing the incidents of first Pentecost in Acts 2, God wants to emphasize the truth that the Holy Spirit came on them because they already believed in the gospel of the water and the Spirit. But people usually think of "Pentecost" as the time when the Holy Spirit comes down from heaven with some supernatural signs and tumultuous clamor.

That is why nowadays in revival meetings, it is believed that one can receive the Holy Spirit through frenetic prayers, fasting, or the laying on of hands. Phenomena such as demon possession, falling unconscious, falling into a trance for several days, or shivering uncontrollably are not works of the Holy Spirit.

The Holy Spirit is rational being and doesn't disregard man's personality. He does not behave insolently toward man because He is Person God who possesses intelligence, emotion and will. He comes on people only when they believe in the words of the gospel of the water and the Spirit (Acts 2:38).

Peter testified that the Holy Spirit had come upon the disciples as the prediction of the prophet Joel. It was the fulfillment of God's promise, which said that the Holy Spirit would fall on those who receive the remission of their sins. In other words, the indwelling of the Holy Spirit is given to those who believe in the truth that Jesus was baptized by John and crucified in order to save all mankind from their sins. Peter's sermon, along with Joel's prophecy, shows us that we need to know why Jesus was baptized and why we have to believe in it. Knowing this truth leads Christians to receive the Holy Spirit.

Do you believe in the beautiful gospel that Peter testifies to? (1 Peter 3:21) Or do you still have useless and superstitious beliefs irrelevant to the beautiful gospel? Do you try to receive the Holy Spirit through your own doing regardless of God's plans? Even if someone believes in God and offers prayers of repentance in hope of washing away their sins, there is no other way to receive the indwelling of the Holy Spirit other than by believing in the gospel of the water and the Spirit.

Are you still waiting for the indwelling of the Holy Spirit, despite having no knowledge of the gospel of the water and the Spirit? Do you know the true meaning of the baptism of Jesus and His blood on the Cross, which causes the Holy Spirit to dwell in your heart? You should know that the indwelling of the Holy Spirit is possible only when you believe in the gospel of the water and the Spirit. The true indwelling of the Holy Spirit can be allowed only to those who believe in the beautiful gospel of the water and the Spirit. We thank God for giving us His gospel of the water and the Spirit, which lets us receive the indwelling of the Holy Spirit. ⊠

SERMON 2

Can one really purchase the Holy Spirit by his own effort?

Can one really purchase the Holy Spirit by his own effort?

<Acts 8:14-24>

"Now when the apostles who were at Jerusalem heard that Samaria had received the word of God, they sent Peter and John to them, who, when they had come down, prayed for them that they might receive the Holy Spirit. For as yet He had fallen upon none of them. They had only been baptized in the name of the Lord Jesus. Then they laid hands on them, and they received the Holy Spirit. And when Simon saw that through the laying on of the apostles' hands the Holy Spirit was given, he offered them money, saying, 'Give me this power also, that anyone on whom I lay hands may receive the Holy Spirit.' But Peter said to him, 'Your money perish with you, because you thought that the gift of God could be purchased with money! You have neither part nor portion in this matter, for your heart is not right in the sight of God. Repent therefore of this your wickedness, and pray God if perhaps the thought of your heart may be forgiven you. For I see that you are poisoned by bitterness and bound by iniquity.' Then Simon answered and said, 'Pray to the Lord for me, that none of the things which you have spoken may come upon me.'"

Can a person receive the Holy Spirit through the laying on of hands?

No. He has to believe the gospel of the water and the Spirit.

Based on the main passage, I want to deliver a message on whether "one can receive the indwelling of the Holy Spirit through his own effort." The Apostles at the time of the early church received power from God and were sent to various places by Him. There are several supernatural events in Acts, one of them being the Holy Spirit's descent upon believers when the Apostles laid their hands on their heads. The Bible says, *"When the apostles laid hands on those who had not received the Holy Spirit yet even though they believed in Jesus, they received the Holy Spirit."*

Then how did they receive the Holy Spirit through the laying on of hands? At that time the words of God were still being written and the work wasn't yet completed, so God gave the Apostles special powers to do His mission. He was with the Apostles and produced many miracles and wonders through them. It was a special time, when God performed wonders and miracles that could be seen with the human eye in order to make people believe that Jesus Christ is the Son of God and the Savior. There was a necessity for God, together with the Apostles, to powerfully show the work of the Holy Spirit in order to prove that Jesus Christ is God and that He is the Son of God, the Savior. If the Holy Spirit hadn't worked through wonders and miracles at the time of the early church, no one would have believed that Jesus is the Savior.

However, it is not necessary for us to receive the Holy

Spirit through visible wonders and miracles today, because the Bible has been completed. Instead, the indwelling of the Holy Spirit now rests in faith. In other words, in believing the gospel of truth. God gives the indwelling of the Holy Spirit to those who have faith in the gospel of truth in front of God. The indwelling of the Holy Spirit only happens to those who believe in God's words, as it was fulfilled by Jesus' coming to this world and by His baptism and blood.

Nowadays, many pastors teach believers that the visible phenomena of miracles are signs of the indwelling of Holy Spirit. And they lead believers to receive the Holy Spirit in the same way. They deceive people by giving them false teachings, such as that speaking in tongues is a sign of the coming of the Holy Spirit. These pastors consider themselves to be apostles who perform great wonders and miracles, and they attract the attention of religious fanatics who want to experience God through their emotions.

This fanaticism has spread to Christians throughout the world, and many of them follow their beliefs and receive evil spirits through supernatural means. Even now, people who were influenced by religious fanaticism think that they can cause others to receive the Holy Spirit through the laying on of hands.

However, as deluded as Simon, they are like the sorcerer who appears in the main passage. They are intoxicated with self-satisfaction and corporeal greed, but all their deeds only cause confusion amongst people. This kind of false teaching deviates from the true way to receive the indwelling of the Holy Spirit before God.

Even today, many false prophets do the work of Satan through their wrongful religious practices, pretending to do the work of the Holy Spirit. True Christians must cling to the word of God, knowledge of which is the only way to receive the indwelling of the Holy Spirit. So-called Pentecostalists, who place great emphasis on physical experiences of the Holy Spirit, should discard their absurd beliefs, return to God's words and believe in the truth, which will assuredly lead them to the indwelling of the Holy Spirit.

Simon was a famous sorcerer in Samaria at that time. After seeing Jesus' disciples cause people to receive the Holy Spirit, he sought to purchase the Holy Spirit with money. People with this kind of faith inevitably became Satan's slaves, used by him to do his work. Simon wanted to receive the Holy Spirit but his desire was nothing more than greed. We can see that this kind of faith is not true Spirit-receiving faith.

Simon tried to purchase the Holy Spirit with money only in his selfish longing for His power. He was severely rebuked by God's servant, Peter, for this reason. Even though it was said that Simon believed in Jesus, he wasn't a man who had received the Holy Spirit through the remission of sins. In other words, he thought that he was able to receive the indwelling of the Holy Spirit by giving worldly things to God.

Although his outward appearances suggested that he was a believer in Jesus, his true inner thoughts were unrelated to Jesus' true words. Instead, he was filled with corporeal greed. Peter, who knew Simon's thoughts, rebuked him for trying to purchase the Holy Spirit, which is God's gift, with mere money. He told Simon that he would perish with his money.

Nowadays, false prophets possessed by evil spirits seek to deceive people by making them think that all the miracles and wonders are works of the Holy Spirit. We can often see people that admire this kind of power and arduously pray to receive the Holy Spirit. However, one should keep it in mind that no one could receive the indwelling of the Holy Spirit through prayers offered out of his worldly greed.

Are there also charismatic people around you by any chance? You should be watchful of these kinds of people. They approach others with a fanatical faith. They say that they can cast out demons and even cause people to receive the Holy Spirit through the laying on of their hands. However, they possess the power not of the Holy Spirit, but of evil spirits. Those who assert that they have received the Holy Spirit by means of the laying on of hands lead both themselves and others to receive only evil spirits.

The true indwelling of the Holy Spirit comes on those who believe in the words of the water and the Spirit (1 John 5:3-7). Even though the gospel of the water and the Spirit is clearly written in the Bible, because many people have sin in their hearts, they try to reach God through supernatural powers and experiences such as trances, speaking in tongues, clairvoyance and the casting out of demons. This is why false prophets are able to deceive so many people into believing in superstitious Christianity derived from the devil.

Peter rebuked Simon by saying; *"Your money perish with you, because you thought that the gift of God could be purchased with money! You have neither part nor portion in this matter, for your heart is not right in the sight of God. For I see that you are poisoned by bitterness and bound by iniquity. You're a son of the demon."* We should sigh with grief at the fact that there are many ministers like this these days. Most of them are charismatic people. They demand money from their flock. We should keep our distance from this kind of faith and receive the indwelling of the Holy Spirit by believing in the true gospel of the water and the Spirit (Matthew 3:15, 1 Peter 3:21, John 1:29, John 19:21-23).

Charismatic people work through the laying on of hands!

We should keep away from this kind of faith. Some people nowadays have the absurd belief that they can receive the Holy Spirit if they receive the laying on of hands from those who have obtained power. They think that since the Scriptures say that many people received the Holy Spirit when they experienced the laying on of hands from the Apostles, that they could do so as well. Some pretenders also have the absurd belief that they can give people the indwelling of the Holy Spirit through the laying on of their own hands. We should be aware of the existence of these kinds of people.

However, we should keep in mind that their faith is greatly different from that of the Apostles in the time of the early church. Nowadays the most serious challenge to the beliefs of some Christians is that they don't have faith in the true gospel of the water and the Spirit. They say that they believe in God, but they don't revere Him and instead deceive themselves and others. However, a sinner can neither receive the indwelling of the Holy Spirit nor cause others to do so. If someone says that a Spirit came on a sinner, this spirit was not truly the Holy Spirit; instead it was the spirit of Satan only pretending to be a true Spirit.

The Apostles during the time of the early church were people who knew and believed that Jesus Christ was the Savior, who took away all the sins of mankind through His baptism by John and His death on the Cross. They were able to receive the indwelling of the Holy Spirit because they believed in the truth of Jesus' baptism and His blood on the Cross. They also preached the gospel of the water and the Spirit to others, thus helping them receive the indwelling of the Holy Spirit.

But nowadays, many Christians have mistaken fanatical beliefs. Is it really possible nowadays for a sinner to receive the Holy Spirit through the laying on of hands from another sinful minister? This is absolutely nonsensical. There are people who say that even though they have sin in their hearts, they have received the indwelling of the Holy Spirit. Even if someone looks like a good shepherd in the eyes of his adherents, he cannot cause anybody to receive the indwelling of the Holy Spirit if there is sin in his heart.

Nonetheless, many people have this kind of wrong faith. This is the reason that so many false prophets are able to lead people into hell. You should know the fact that those who teach this kind of faith are false prophets. These are people who have already been captured by demons.

If a person has sin in his heart, can the Holy Spirit dwell in him? The answer is no. Then is it possible for a person who has sin in his heart to cause others to receive the indwelling of the Holy Spirit? Again, the answer is no. Then what causes charismatic people nowadays to perform miracles and wonders in Christianity, while they still have sin in their hearts? Evil spirits do so. The Holy Spirit can never dwell within a sinner. He only dwells in those with faith in the gospel of the water and the Spirit. Are you sure the spirit that came on you is the Holy Spirit?

In John 3:5, Jesus said, *"Unless one is born of water and the Spirit, he cannot enter the kingdom of God."* As such, the indwelling of the Holy Spirit can only be obtained by believing in the true gospel of the water and the Spirit. The mistake that many Christians make nowadays is to believe that one can also receive the indwelling of the Holy Spirit by receiving the laying on of hands from sinful ministers. This is a crucial mistake. Nowadays, many Christians and ministers have the faith and conviction that the indwelling of the Holy Spirit comes on them through the laying on of hands.

The relationship between true remission of sins and the laying on of hands

"The laying on of hands" is the means through which one can pass something in him on to the object. Think of it this way: If we speak into a microphone, the sound travels through the cables into amplifier and then comes out of the loud speakers so everyone can hear it. Similarly, in the Old Testament, when a sinner laid his hands on the sin offering's head, his sins passed on to the sin offering and he was thus forgiven. In the same way, God's power passes on to people when His servants lay their hands on them. In this way, the laying on of hands has taken on the meaning of "to pass, to transfer."

Charismatic people don't cause people to have the indwelling of the Holy Spirit through the laying on of their hands, instead they cause them to receive evil spirits. You must remember that a person with the power of evil spirits passes the spirits on to others through the laying on of hands. When a demon-possessed person lays his hands on the head of another, the demon in him passes on to that person, because Satan works through sinners. For this reason, everyone must believe in the gospel of the water and the Spirit if they want to receive the indwelling of the Holy Spirit. Satan rules those who are in sin, even if they believe in Jesus, if they fail to receive the remission of sins.

If someone receives the laying on of hands from a demon-possessed person, demons will also come on to him and he will also perform false miracles. We have to know that demons come to dwell in others through the laying on of hands, and that the indwelling of the Holy Spirit is only possible through the faith in the gospel of the water and the Spirit.

The laying on of hands is a method established by God of passing something on to another. But Satan causes many people to receive evil spirits through the laying on of hands. The fact that nowadays there are many people who try to purchase the power of the Holy Spirit with money is an even bigger problem.

Most Christians misunderstand the truth of the indwelling of the Holy Spirit

When asked how they can receive the indwelling of the Holy Spirit, many people answer that it's possible through prayers of repentance or fasting. This is not true. Does the Holy Spirit come on you when you offer special prayers to God? No. The indwelling of the Holy Spirit comes only on those who believe in the gospel of the water and the Spirit.

Because God is the truth, He established the law for receiving the indwelling of the Holy Spirit. Can the Holy Spirit dwell in a person who has sin in his heart? The answer is most definitely not. One cannot receive the Holy Spirit through the laying on of hands. Even if someone attends revival meetings and frantically prays to God that he might receive the power of the Holy Spirit, the Holy Spirit will remain out of his grasp. Sinners can obviously not receive the indwelling of the Holy

Spirit. Sinners can receive the true indwelling of the Holy Spirit as a gift, but only when they receive the remission of sins by believing in the gospel of the water and the Spirit.

Anyone who doesn't know the gospel of the water and the Spirit cannot receive the indwelling of the Holy Spirit. Nowadays the gospel of the water and the Spirit is spreading rapidly through Christian literature, church meetings, the Internet, and even electronic books throughout the world. Therefore, anyone who seeks the true gospel can believe in it and receive the indwelling of the Holy Spirit. If you haven't yet received the indwelling of the Holy Spirit, you should realize that to do so you must believe in the gospel of the water and the Spirit.

A prime example of false faith!

Nowadays when we examine the symptoms of people who receive false spirits we can see the actual existence of demons. "Revival meetings for the Holy Spirit" are gatherings in which people who desperately want to receive the Holy Spirit. In these meetings we see people clapping their hands and offering prayers of repentance while crying and fasting. The preacher instructs them to offer fanatical prayers by telling them that the Holy Spirit won't come on them until they do so. People then cry out, "Lord!" and start their fanatical prayers.

Can these fanatics receive the indwelling of the Holy Spirit in this manner? No. You would see people scream and fall back, and then shiver, while making strange noises at such meetings. Some are falling back and shivering on the ground here and there, and we see them scream and start to speak in tongues.

Someone throughout the meeting screams his head off and the crowd is overwhelmed with emotion. Some of them start to have fits, shaking all over and speaking in tongues. People say that these phenomena are the evidence that the Holy Spirit has come on them. But think about what happens when a demon does his work? Is this the work of the Holy Spirit? Definitely not.

Satan deceives many Christians

Nowadays, many Christians lead the kind of religious lives that Satan wants. Satan deceives people by telling them that they have to receive the laying on of hands from a powerful minister in order to receive the Holy Spirit. Many Christians tend to believe this as a formal doctrine. Satan also plants the idea into people's heads that they will receive the Holy Spirit if they pray excessively. Satan has been trying to double and triple the number of people who have this kind of faith.

Therefore many people don't know, and don't even try to learn about the gospel of the water and the Spirit. We must struggle to avoid the thoughts Satan tries to put in our heads and know and believe in the gospel of the water and the Spirit. The indwelling of the Holy Spirit only comes on those who believe in the gospel of the water and the Spirit. You must believe in this.

Christians' misconceptions about the indwelling of the Holy Spirit

First of all, there is a great misunderstanding in the beliefs of many adherents to charismatic Christianity. They try to receive the Holy Spirit with sin in their hearts. They mistakenly believe that even though they have sin in their hearts, they will be able to receive the indwelling of the Holy Spirit. However, a person without any faith in the gospel of the water and the Spirit can't receive the fullness of the Holy Spirit.

Secondly, it is said that people's arrogance hinders them from receiving the indwelling of the Holy Spirit. Then does this mean that one can receive the Holy Spirit if he doesn't behave arrogantly? Is there a person in this world who isn't the least bit arrogant? An arrogant person who can't be forgiven by God is one who adds his own thoughts to the word of God. Many people try to receive the indwelling of the Holy Spirit through their own methods, ignoring the true gospel of the water and the Spirit. However, the indwelling of the Holy Spirit comes only on those who believe in the gospel of the water and the Spirit.

Thirdly, it is said that the indwelling of the Holy Spirit comes when someone frankly confesses all his sins before God. So they are urged to confess their sins when they want to receive the Holy Spirit. But you must remember that the indwelling of the Holy Spirit does not come when someone simply confesses his sins. Most Christians nowadays eagerly long for the indwelling of the Holy Spirit and for His fullness but they can't receive the indwelling of the Holy Spirit because they still have sin in their hearts. A person with this type of rash desire will be captured by demons.

Fourthly, some say that the indwelling of the Holy Spirit can be given when we earnestly solicit God to give us the blessing. But it can't be obtained through begging. This is just mistaken thinking.

Fifthly, some identify the indwelling of the Holy Sprit with the possession of some spiritual powers. Speaking in tongues are regarded to be a common evidence of the indwelling of the Holy Spirit. But the Holy Spirit doesn't dwell in one's heart simply because he is able to cast out demons in Jesus' name or speak in strange tongues. Sin belongs to Satan. Can someone with sin in his heart truly say that he has received the indwelling of the Holy Spirit because he has possessed some strange powers? Once again, this is mischief played by demons.

The gospel of the water and the Spirit that Jesus gave us is the only true gospel that can lead us to receive the indwelling of the Holy Spirit. If you still think that you can receive the Holy Spirit and the remission of sins through other methods, you are deeply deluded. I hope that you will free yourself from your mistaken beliefs and instead come to have spiritual thoughts and authentic faith.

It is no exaggeration to say that nowadays many Christians are possessed by demons. Many Christians throughout the world come under the power of demons because they want to receive the indwelling of the Holy Spirit through special revival meetings or by receiving the laying on of hands. They go to specific people such as the superintendents of prayer houses, senior deacons, revivalists, or pastors who are said to have received the power of the Holy Spirit. They go to them in hopes of receiving the Holy Spirit through the laying on of hands. However, no one can ever receive the indwelling of the Holy Spirit through this kind of faith, no matter how arduously they believe in Jesus. In other words, there is no one except God who can cause someone to receive the indwelling of the Holy Spirit.

Like Simon, many people nowadays try to purchase the Holy Spirit. They try to receive the Holy Spirit by believing in worldly teachings, not the gospel. Most Christians throughout the world are stuck in this mind-set. The Holy Spirit only comes on those who have the necessary qualifications to receive Him. The only formula to receive the Holy Spirit is by believing in the gospel of the water and the Spirit and this is the only answer to the truth (Acts 2:38).

Receiving the Holy Spirit through the laying on of hands was only possible for a short period at the time of the early church. After this the indwelling of the Holy Spirit came on people at the same time when they came to know and believe in the gospel of the water and the Spirit. Therefore, other than the work of the Holy Spirit occurring through faith in the word of God, everything else is the work of demons. God says that demons are servants of Satan, and Satan has ingeniously worked in such a way that people cannot receive the remission of sin even if they believe in Jesus. Satan lies to people by saying that he will give them the Holy Spirit if they believe in Jesus and receive the laying on of hands. Satan expands his territory throughout the world through this kind of trickery.

We will now look at the symptoms of those possessed by demons. First, when we examine the symptoms of possession by a demon in a fortuneteller or shaman, we see that they experience trembling fits, trances and even fainting. Then their tongues get twisted and odd words come out of their mouths against their will. They speak in strange tongues.

Both sorcerers and Christians who have been possessed by demons through the laying on of hands are joint owners of this experience. When a charismatic revivalist takes out his mike and shouts, "With fire, with fire, with fire," the congregation gets excited and loses self-control. People who want to receive the laying on of hands from him come up to the front. They experience uncontrollable shaking fits and speak in tongues. These symptoms are the work of demons that are pretending to do the work of the Holy Spirit.

People who are possessed by evil spirits, which can be summoned by shamans and fortunetellers of every primitive religion, show the same symptoms as Christians who are possessed by demons through the laying on of hands. However, people misunderstand this, despite this evidence. Those Christians are plunged into deep confusion because they think they have received the Holy Spirit when they experience these kinds of symptoms.

Satan works through the Christians like a fortuneteller

Satan enables demon-possessed people to make prayers of prophecy. They prophesy by saying, "You will be a precious leader. Thousands of sheep will graze in front of you. God will train you in the future and make a precious leader out of you." To others they say delusive words such as, "You will become a precious servant of God. You will be a very dignified servant of God," in order to encourage people to follow them and live as servants of demons throughout their lives.

Fortunetellers also make prophecies about other people's futures. "You should be careful of water in the future." "You will make a lot of money." "A noble man will appear from the east and help you." These are examples of the things they say. The first symptom that shows up in demon-possessed persons is that they make false prophecies.

Then they speak in tongues that they can't even understand themselves. They experience shivering and they even show symptoms of personality disorder. If you meet a shaman or fortuneteller, can you assert that they have sound personalities? They often talk rudely to people who are much older than they are.

However, people who have the true indwelling of the Holy Spirit have received Him by believing in the biblical truth that says that Jesus cleansed all the sins of world through His baptism and death on the Cross. These people also help others know and believe in the gospel of the water and the Spirit, and help them receive the remission of sins and the indwelling of the Holy Spirit. They themselves try to live in a righteous way, and their personalities are so pleasant and sound as to lead others to the blessed faith of God and to the kind of life God wants. Now and then God reproaches them in order to keep them sacred when their minds intend to turn back to the world.

The righteous who have received the remission of all sins are definitely different from people whose personalities have been destroyed by evil spirits. True personality comes alive again if one receives the remission of sins and thereby receives the indwelling of the Holy Spirit. Additionally, the righteous are deeply worried about others under unfavorable circumstances, about what they truly need in God's words, praying for them to be delivered, and actually offering self-sacrifices to help them.

On the other hand, we can see that the personalities of demon-possessed people have been terribly destroyed. Satan controls them and bends them to his will because they think that things like shivering and speaking in tongues are the gifts of the Holy Spirit. However, these experiences are definitely not the gifts of the Holy Spirit.

There are so many ministers who are proud of their powers such as making prophecies in God's name, being capable of performing many wonders and speaking in tongues. But if they still have sin in their hearts, then their powers are decisive evidence to the fact that they are demon-possessed. Therefore, they can't give the indwelling of the Holy Spirit to others, but can only give that of demons. Also, because Satan is deceitful, the miracle they have performed runs out very easily in a short period of time.

There is a clear difference between the work of the Holy Spirit and that of a demon. Even though it may seem as if the work of the Holy Spirit offers no particular experiences or wonderful gifts in the beginning, as times go on, God's power grows in the hearts of the righteous incessantly like the rising sun in the morning.

Demon-possessed Christians

Why is it that so many people come to be possessed by demons even though they try to receive the Holy Spirit?

Because they receive demons through the laying on of hands from false prophets.

Surprisingly, we can see many believers in Jesus whose bodies and souls have gone to ruin because they received demons through the laying on of hands from false prophets. These people have nothing to do with God because their faith doesn't rest in the words of the Bible. They're busily using up their power not knowing that their services are causing many people to be Satan's servants. Why do they work so hard in performing their powers in Christianity? Because so-called powers of theirs will soon disappear if they don't use them. This is why they become very busy.

They continuously have to pray and practice wonders and signs by the name of Jesus. People who say, "I have received the gift of preaching the gospel," continuously have to preach the gospel because if they don't, their pseudo-happiness soon disappears. If these people are not loyal to the demon's gifts of speaking in other tongues, healing, or prophecy, in other words, if they are not faithful to the works of Satan, then he may make them become lingeringly sick. Just like a fortuneteller or a shaman gets lingeringly ill when he neglects the role as Satan's servant. This is why they have to use the gifts they have received from Satan ardently lest they are abandoned in misery after they have used up their powers.

I once knew someone who was a fervent believer in Jesus and looked as if he possessed many powers from God. He encouraged people to receive the fullness of the Holy Spirit and led revival meetings in which he cast out demons through the laying on of hands, also performing wonders such as speaking in tongues and healing. He became an object of envy and respect through his works of wonder. Scores of thousands of believers followed him. However, soon he began to deny Jesus saying, "Jesus Christ is a failure. He isn't the Son of God." He cursed Jesus Christ and even claimed that he was God himself.

He finally killed Jesus Christ in his heart and in the hearts of many Christians.

People like this reject the gospel of the water and the Spirit because Satan is their guide. They come to have the mistaken belief from the beginning because they have an illusion that they possess the same powers as the Apostles, to see their abilities, to make people speak in other tongues and to cast out demons through the laying on of hands. They have the firm belief that the indwelling of the Holy Spirit has come on them.

They teach people about the methods of receiving the Holy Spirit, thinking that it is possible to receive Him by offering prayers of repentance. However, this method of receiving the Holy Spirit is not based on God's words. In spite of this, they say that if a believer in Jesus speaks in tongues and makes prophecies, then this is proof of the coming of the Holy Spirit on him. Because many people don't truly understood the indwelling of the Holy Spirit, they believe that they can also receive the Holy Spirit by learning and following the teachings of false prophets. This is how Satan was able to fill Christians with the spirits of demons and reign over these people. All of these methods are the traps of Satan.

Numerous people have been possessed by demons through the teachings of false prophets. Ordinary believers lead a humdrum religious life, but demon-possessed people use the power of evil spirits and seemingly lead passionate religious lives. What are the abilities they display? They have the abilities to heal, to speak in strange tongues and lead others to be possessed by demons through the laying on of hands. We should know that the laying on of hands is a method of passing something on to others and that the demons' kingdom has been greatly expanded through this means.

Evil spirits work through human greed!

Satan works in people like Simon of the main passage. These people say that they can receive the Holy Spirit through the laying on of hands, regardless of their faith in the gospel of the water and the Spirit. Nowadays many people are deceived by Satan, and try to receive the Holy Spirit through prayers of repentance, fasting, self-sacrifice or the laying on of hands. However, they are possessed by demons and lead a cursed life.

We should be well aware that this mediator, called the laying on of hands, which many Christians receive throughout the world, facilitates the work of demons. These people who possess the same traits as Simon are false prophets before God. Even believers in Jesus, if they have sin in their hearts, can be possessed by demons. These people are capable of performing miracles through the workings of the devil. Satan leads people to receive the laying on of hands from his servants in order to facilitate their possession by demons and build his kingdom throughout the world. Nowadays, the churches of the [2]**Pentecostal-Charismatic Movement** are officially recognized

---

[2] Western Christianity began to wither away in the face of the material prosperity and mass consumption in the latter half of the 20th century At the same time, as a result of this, many Christians who were searching for a way to walk closer with Jesus were unsatisfied with the dryness of their previous churches. Others were afflicted with either a lack of, or a slow pace of spiritual growth, and yet others were frustrated with their inability to translate their faith into a personal love of Jesus.

The so-called Pentecostal-Charismatic Movement arose under these circumstances. Those who indulged in this movement seek enthusiastic experiences and practices such as speaking in tongues, prophesying, performing miracles and wonders, admiring the first Pentecostal events. In their enthusiasm, they willingly entrust themselves to so-called the dominion of the Holy Spirit, but strictly speaking most of their teachings and practices are not based on the Bible.

In the developing world, this movement has developed tremendously within the context of their needs. Their leaders have attracted developing world Christians with the blessings of wealth and health along with religious enthusiasm. Some deviation of the movement like the Neo-Pentecostalism is even reported as the movement sharing the same teachings as the New Age Movement.

as formal Christian denominations throughout the world.

This world is slowly coming to an end. If we want to be born again in the last days, we have to know how the devil works and stand firm against his schemes. We also have to be saved from our sins once and for all and receive the indwelling of the Holy Spirit as a gift by believing in the gospel of the water and the Spirit. We have to return to the truth with the perfect knowledge of how God's Spirit comes to us.

Just as God said, *"My people are destroyed for lack of knowledge" (Hosea 4:6)*, nowadays many truth seekers are destroyed when, in their ignorance, charismatic people mislead them. People say that even if so-called the Pentecostal-Charismatic churches were established in the desert, people would gather there. Why is this so? Charismatic people expand their churches by confusing others with their pseudo-powers, leading them to become demon-possessed through the laying on of hands. One of their special talents is that once people are possessed by demons through the laying on of hands, they become enthusiastic about leading a religious life.

Another special feature of charismatic people is that they donate large amounts of money to their churches and unconditionally become fanatical believers. Even numerous Christians are enthusiastic over evangelism with the power of demons, but are certainly going to hell not realizing their own destination. These people, who fervently believe the power of the devil as the evidence of their salvation, are looking forward to heaven without a single doubt. However they have sin in their hearts and are doomed to be destroyed.

If they are asked the following question, "Do you have sin in your heart, even though you believe in God?" they surely answer that it is natural of them to be in sin. They think it's impossible for a person not to have sin in his heart, even if he believes in Jesus.

People tend to think that they deserve to enter the kingdom of Heaven, even if they have sin in their hearts, because they feel comfort in believing in Jesus having the evidence of pseudo-power.

What an absurd hope this is! The reason for their firm belief is that they possess some kind of supernatural ability. They have experienced speaking in tongues, receiving visions and healing the sick, and they think and firmly believe these experiences to be the work of the Holy Spirit. Therefore they tell themselves that they have definitely received redemption and the Holy Spirit through these experiences.

Because these people have an imperfect knowledge of the words of salvation, they have no confidence in their salvation if any kind of visible ability doesn't appear to them. Therefore, these people try very hard to find visible assurances of salvation and later end up being used by Satan in his work. Because these people are trying to find God's answers through prayers of repentance or self-sacrifice rather than believing in the gospel of the water and the Spirit, they eventually receive evil spirits instead of the Holy Spirit.

The devil accuses people by whispering in their ears, "You have sinned, haven't you?" and leads them to fall into self-condemnation. There is a person I know who has now received the forgiveness of sin and the Holy Spirit. This is something that happened to him before he was born again, when he was a fervent but reckless believer in Jesus. This person even spoke in tongues and performed many miracles. Even though he cried and offered prayers of repentance all night, despite his belief in Jesus, the sin in his heart continued to torture him. This is when the whispers of Satan started. "You have sinned, so it's better for you do die than live." Satan often came to him and accused him, torturing him and reminding him of his sins. Satan led him to self-condemnation and self-judgment. However, all he could do was confess the sins in his heart. He couldn't free himself from Satan's accusation until he came to hear and believe in the beautiful gospel.

You should know that those who don't believe in the gospel of the water and the Spirit become the prey of the devil. Do you think anyone who hasn't received the forgiveness of sins has the power to reject the devil? Anyone who doesn't hold to the true gospel of the water and the Spirit will be captured and tortured by Satan. God's gospel of the water and the Spirit is absolutely necessary to casting out Satan. Therefore, everyone who believes in Jesus should believe in the gospel of the water and the Spirit, and also preach it to all the people of the world. Those who hear this should obey and believe in it.

The mystery of lawlessness is already at work in the world!

The whole world is now covered with the activities of demons. If we want to preach the gospel that leads people to receive the Holy Spirit, we have to remove the deep misunderstandings about the indwelling of the Holy Spirit.

First of all we have to make clear that it's a lie that the Holy Spirit comes through the laying on of hands. We should clearly testify that experiences such as "speaking in other tongues after receiving the laying on of hands, feeling something hot through repentance and fasting, and hearing messages directly from Jesus" are the work of the devil. Only through faith in the gospel of the water and the Spirit can people be delivered from the devil's trickery. Only by faith can we be saved from our sins through the gospel of the water and the Spirit.

We have to defeat the devil, "the father of lies," with the gospel of the water and the Spirit. Satan has bound all the people throughout the world with the bondage of self-condemnation, so we should return these people to the truth by making them realize that their misguided experiences and emotions are the trickeries of Satan.

These days, people like Samaritan Simon, who tried to purchase the Holy Spirit with money, are ministering the church. They are the blind leading the blind. They cannot show people the way to perfect salvation because they don't know the gospel of the water and the Spirit, and have sin in their hearts. So they cause Satan to dwell in the hearts of their followers by holding all-night prayer sessions, calling for prayers of repentance and using the laying on of hands. These people are actually possessed by the devil, and if we want them to return to God's word, we have to destroy the work of Satan by providing them with perfect knowledge of the water and the Spirit. If people don't know about Satan's strategies, they will have no other choice but to suffer in helplessness.

Just as I said, performing miracles such as speaking in tongues and issuing prophecies after receiving the laying on of hands are all the activities of the devil. In other words, the powers of charismatic people are manifested through the workings of the devil. We should teach them. "It is the devil who works in you if there is sin in your heart. If you think the Holy Spirit dwells in you, even though you have sin in your heart, then you have been deceived."

The faith of the Apostles and that of people who received

the laying on of hands in the main passage of Acts 8 have been placed in the same category, because both of them knew about Jesus Christ's gospel of the water and the Spirit. But the Apostles' faith was completely different from that of most Christians of today who believe merely the laying on of hands will cause them to receive the Holy Spirit.

Does a person receive the Holy Spirit through the laying on of hands by someone who has received the remission of sins? No. The Bible says that the Spirit of God was hovering over the face of the waters (Genesis 1:2). This means that in order for one to receive the remission of sins and the Holy Spirit, he has to hear and believe in the gospel of the water and the Spirit. God sends the Holy Spirit as a gift to a born-again Christian who believes in the gospel of the water and the Spirit.

We should bear in mind that it would be like opposing the gospel of the water and the Spirit, which God intended to save us from our sins, if we taught people to seek the laying on of hands in order to receive the Holy Spirit. Thinking that a person can give someone else the Holy Spirit is like challenging God, and people with this kind of faith easily fall into Satan's traps. This should never be allowed to happen.

All our sins are forgiven when we believe in the gospel of the water and the Spirit, and the Holy Spirit testifies to this. Someone who believes in the gospel of the water and the Spirit no longer has sin in his heart. This is not because he hasn't sinned, but instead because he believes in the power of the gospel of the water and the Spirit. The gospel of the water and the Spirit testifies that he has no sin in his heart, and the Holy Sprit testifies to that too. One cannot call Jesus his Savior without having the Spirit of God within him.

Demon-possessed people don't know about the gospel of the water and the Spirit, and never even make it a subject of discussion. They don't even know the gospel of the water and the Spirit, and moreover they are unable to discern the truth. They say that the Holy Spirit comes only when they perform and receive the laying on of hands. However, the Holy Spirit does never come through the laying on of hands. You should realize that the workings of the devil now exercise great influence over people in churches throughout the world with its false teachings. For this reason, it is imperative to receive the true indwelling of the Holy Spirit by believing in the gospel of the water and the Spirit. ✉

SERMON 3

Did you receive the Holy Spirit when you believed?

Did you receive the Holy Spirit when you believed?

<Acts 19:1-3>
"And it happened, while Apollos was at Corinth, that Paul, having passed through the upper regions, came to Ephesus. And finding some disciples he said to them, 'Did you receive the Holy Spirit when you believed?' So they said to him, 'We have not so much as heard whether there is a Holy Spirit.' And he said to them, 'Into what then were you baptized?' So they said, 'Into John's baptism.'"

Why does the Bible say, "From the days of John the Baptist until now the Kingdom of Heaven suffers violence, and violent men take it by force?"

Because people can take the Kingdom of Heaven by the faith in the beautiful gospel that says that Jesus blotted out all the sins of the world through His baptism by John and His blood on the Cross.

What kind of gospel did Paul preach? He preached the gospel of Jesus' baptism and His blood. Acts 19:1 says, *"And it happened, while Apollos was at Corinth, that Paul, having passed through the upper regions, came to Ephesus. And finding some disciples he said to them, 'Did you receive the Holy Spirit when you believed?'"* However, these people believed in Jesus while leaving out the meaning of Jesus' baptism. They didn't know the beautiful gospel that leads to the indwelling of the Holy Spirit. That is why Paul's question, *"Did you receive the Holy Spirit when you believed?"* was a very unfamiliar question to some disciples at Ephesus. Other people would have asked them, "Did you believe in Jesus?" But Paul asked the question in this extraordinary way so that they could receive the Holy Spirit by renewing their faith in the beautiful gospel. Paul's ministry was to preach the beautiful gospel of Jesus' baptism and His blood. Paul, Peter and John also testified to Jesus' baptism by John the Baptist.

Let's take a look at the apostles' testimony to the gospel of baptism. First Paul testified, *"Certainly not! How shall we who died to sin live any longer in it? Or do you not know that as many of us were baptized into Christ Jesus were baptized into His death?" (Romans 6:2-3)* and *"For as many of you as were baptized in to Christ have put on Christ" (Galatians 3:27).*

The apostle Peter also testified to the gospel of Jesus' baptism in 1 Peter 3:21, saying, *"There is also an antitype which now saves us — baptism (not the removal of the filth of the flesh, but the answer of a good conscience toward God), through the resurrection of Jesus Christ, who has gone into heaven and is at the right hand of God, angels and authorities and powers having been made subject to Him."*

John the Apostle also testified to this beautiful gospel in 1 John 5:5-8. *"Who is he who overcomes the world, but he who believes that Jesus is the Son of God? This is He who came by water and blood — Jesus Christ; not only by water, but by water and blood. And it is the Spirit who bears witness, because the Spirit is truth. For there are three that bear witness in heaven: the Father, the Word, and the Holy Spirit; and these three are one. And there are three that bear witness on earth: the Spirit, the water, and the blood; and these three agree as one."*

John the Baptist played a crucial role in completing the beautiful gospel. The Bible says the following about John the Baptist in Malachi 3:1-3 and Matthew 11:10-11. John the Baptist was the representative of mankind and he was the prophesied Elijah to come, as written in the Old Testament. In the Old Testament, a sin offering was killed to shed its blood after taking away the sins of a man by the laying on of his hands. In the New Testament, however, Jesus was the sin offering who took away all the sins of the world through His baptism and died on the Cross to pay the wages of sin. Jesus saved mankind because John the Baptist passed all the sins of the world on to Him through the baptism in the Jordan River.

God planned two kinds of great deeds in order to save mankind from their sins and He fulfilled them all. The first was to have Jesus come into this world through the body of the virgin Mary, and to have Him baptized and crucified to take away all the sins of the world. The second was to have John the Baptist born through Elizabeth. God caused these two events to occur in order to save mankind from their sins. This was the work planned by God in the Trinity. God sent John the Baptist into this world six months prior to Jesus, then sent Jesus Christ, the Savior of mankind, into this world to free mankind from judgment for their sins.

Jesus bore witness to John the Baptist in Matthew 11:9. *"But what did you go out to see? A prophet? Yes, I say to you, and more than a prophet."* Furthermore, when John the Baptist, who passed all the sins of the world on to Jesus, saw Him the next day, he bore witness by saying, *"Behold! The Lamb of*

God who takes away the sin of the world!" (John 1:29)

The Bible has many records of John, who baptized Jesus, and we should strive to gain better knowledge of him. John the Baptist came into the world before Jesus. His role was to fulfill the beautiful gospel, which was God's plan. The Bible says that Jesus accepted all the sins of the world from John and that John passed them on to Him to fulfill God's will.

We call him John the Baptist because he baptized Jesus. What meaning does the baptism of Jesus by John really have? The word "baptism" implies "to be washed." Since all the sins of the world were transferred to Jesus through His baptism, they have been washed away. Jesus' baptism had the same meaning as "the laying on of hands" that the sin offering received in the Old Testament. The spiritual meaning of baptism is "to pass on to," "to be washed" or "to be buried." Jesus' baptism by John was an act of redemption to take away the sins of all the people in the world.

Jesus' baptism has the same significance as the laying on of hands, which was the method of passing sins on to the sin offering in the Old Testament. In other words, the people of Israel passed their yearly sins on to the sin offering on the Day of Atonement through the laying hands on of the high priest. This sacrifice in the Old Testament had the same function as Jesus' baptism and His death on the Cross.

God appointed the Day of Atonement as the time to take away the sins of the Israelites. On the tenth day of the seventh month, the high priest passed all the yearly sins of the people onto the head of the sin offering by laying his hands on the sacrifice to atone for the sins of the people. This was the sacrificial system that God established. It was the only way to pass the sins of the people on to the sin offering, and transferring the sin by the laying on of hands was the everlasting law that God had established.

"Aaron shall lay both his hands on the head of the live goat, confess over it all the iniquities of the children of Israel, and all their transgression, concerning all their sins, putting them on the head of the goat, and shall send it away into the wilderness by the hand of a suitable man. The goat shall bear on itself all their iniquities to an uninhabited land; and he shall release the goat in the wilderness" (Leviticus 16:21-22).

In the Old Testament, a sinner laid his hands on the head of a sin offering and passed his sins on to it in order to be forgiven. And on the Day of Atonement, Aaron the high priest, as the representative of all Israelites, laid his hands on the head of the sacrifice to pass on the sins of Israel. Then the offering was killed after it took on their sins.

It has the same spiritual meaning as the baptism (*Baptisma* in Greek means "to be washed, to be buried, to pass") that Jesus received from John in the New Testament. Just as the high priest in the Old Testament laid his hands on the sin offering to pass on the sins of the people of Israel, so all the sins of humanity were passed on to Jesus through His baptism by John the Baptist. Jesus then died on the Cross to atone for our sins. This is the beautiful gospel of truth.

Just as Aaron the high priest offered the sacrifice for atonement in place of the people of Israel, John the Baptist, one of the descendants of Aaron, carried out the task as the representative of mankind by baptizing Jesus, and thereby passing all the sins of mankind on to Him. God described such a wonderful plan of His love in the Bible as follows in Psalms 50:4-5, *"He shall call to the heavens from above, and to the earth, that He may judge His people: Gather My saints together to Me, those who have made a covenant with Me by sacrifice."* Amen, Hallelujah.

History of the Church said that there was no Christmas for the first two centuries in the early church. The early church Christians along with Jesus' Apostles had only commemorated January 6th as "the Day of Jesus' Baptism" at the Jordan by John the Baptist. Why did they lay such a great emphasis on Jesus' baptism in their beliefs? The answer is the very key to the Christianity of Apostolic tradition. But I hope for you not to be confused with the water baptism of believers and the Baptism of Jesus.

The baptism of believers as it exists today has a very different meaning from the baptism Jesus received from John. Therefore, we should all have the same faith as Jesus' disciples if we want to receive the indwelling of the Holy Spirit. We should all receive the indwelling of the Holy Spirit by believing in Jesus Christ's baptism, which He received from John, and in His blood on the Cross.

If the early church thought of baptism as an extremely important ritual, it was due to their pivotal faith in Jesus' baptism, and we should nowadays also consider Jesus' baptism by John as indispensable component to our salvation. Furthermore, we must reach and keep the right faith of perfect knowledge, which says that Jesus had to be crucified due to His baptism by John. We should bear in mind that the Holy Spirit begins to dwell in us when we believe that Jesus was baptized, died on the Cross and was resurrected to become our Savior. Jesus' baptism by John and His blood on the Cross has such a special meaning in the beautiful gospel.

The fail-safe way for us to receive the Holy Spirit is to believe in the beautiful gospel of Jesus' baptism and blood. Jesus' baptism cleansed all the sins of mankind at once. It was the baptism of redemption that leads us to receive the Holy Spirit. Since some people don't realize the power of Jesus' baptism, they understand it as mere ceremony.

Jesus' baptism forms part of the beautiful gospel, which tells of how He took away all the sins of the world and accepted the judgment for them by shedding blood on the Cross. Anyone who believes in the words of this beautiful gospel becomes a member of the church, which is a possession of the Lord, and enjoys the blessings of the Holy Spirit. The Holy Spirit is a gift from God to those who have been forgiven for their sins.

With His baptism, Jesus became *"the Lamb of God who takes away the sins of the world"* well enough (John 1:29). In John 1:6-7 it says, *"There was a man sent from God, whose name was John. This man came for a witness, to bear witness of the Light, that all through him might believe."* In order to believe in Jesus as our Savior, who took away all our sins, we must understand John's ministry and testimony as it is written in the Bible. Then we will be able to believe in Jesus Christ as our Savior. In order to receive the Holy Spirit, we also need our strong faith heartened by his testimony. Therefore, to complete the beautiful gospel of truth, we must believe in Jesus' baptism by John and in His blood on the Cross.

In Matthew 11:12 it is written that, *"And from the days of John the Baptist until now the kingdom of heaven suffers violence, and the violent take it by force."* This passage is known as one of the most difficult passages in the Bible. However we have to pay attention to the phrase "from the day of John the Baptist." It surely proclaims that the ministry of John was directly connected with Jesus' ministry for our salvation.

Jesus wants us to enter the Kingdom by bold faith, as bold as violent men. We sin every day, we are fragile but He permits us to enter His Kingdom by the daring faith regardless of our wickedness. So this passage means that people can take the kingdom of heaven by the faith in the beautiful gospel that says that Jesus blotted out all the sins of the world through His baptism by John and His blood on the Cross. In other words, it means that Heaven can be taken through the bold faith in this beautiful gospel of Jesus' baptism and blood.

Jesus' baptism took away all our sins, and our faith in it guarantees that we will receive the indwelling of the Holy Spirit. We must preach this gospel to our neighbors, relatives, acquaintances, and to everyone else in the world. We must have faith in the beautiful gospel that says that the sins of the world were transferred to Jesus through His baptism. Through our faith we will obtain the bliss of redemption and the indwelling of the Holy Spirit.

Jesus' baptism took away all our sins and His blood was the judgment of the sin. We must explain to non-believers the beautiful gospel of the water and the Spirit. Only by doing so, will they come to believe in the gospel and receive the Holy Spirit. I want you to believe it. Only by having faith in Jesus' baptism by John and His blood on the Cross can man be forgiven for all his sins and receive the indwelling of the Holy Spirit.

Everyone can become a son of the Lord, in whom the Holy Sprit dwells, and one of our brothers and sisters by believing in the beautiful gospel of the water and the Spirit. You should have the same faith in the beautiful gospel as Paul had. I thank the Lord for giving us this beautiful gospel and praise Him. Amen. ✉

SERMON 4

Those who have the same
faith as the Disciples

Those who have the same faith as the Disciples

<Acts 3:19>
"Repent therefore and be converted, that your sins may be blotted out, so that times of refreshing may come from the presence of the Lord."

What kind of faith did the apostles have?

They believed in both the baptism of Jesus and His blood on the Cross.

Looking at the disciples of Jesus Christ, the extent of their faith when they had the indwelling of the Holy Spirit was clearly different from their faith when they did not. Their flesh did not look any different, but after receiving the Holy Spirit, their lives were totally changed by the light of Jesus Christ.

The town where I live has beautiful mountains and lakes. Looking at such lovely scenery, I become filled with satisfaction and wonder that I cannot but thank the Lord for such creations. The brilliance of the crystal-clear water glistening in the sun makes my heart full and the world around me seem like gold.

But there are places where such scenic beauty does not manifest itself. There are places where the sky is crystal clear, but the water under the sunlight looks more like a swamp. There is no brilliance in such a sight. Looking at a lake like this, I thank the Lord for His beautiful gospel that cleansed my sins and obtained for me the indwelling of the Holy Spirit.

As the surface of the swampy lake is not able to reflect light, so we may also be remote from the light of God and be unwittingly headed towards an unknown destiny owing to our sinful nature. But if the Holy Spirit dwells in our hearts, we will be revealed as children of God and be led to teach the gospel to other people. Because we accepted His light, we will come to shine as lights.

Likewise, after Jesus' resurrection, His disciples received the Holy Spirit and became children and apostles of the light. The light of the Holy Spirit is a great blessing to all and therefore most people wish to receive the Holy Spirit.

The Faith of the apostle Paul

What kind of faith did Paul have? Paul, in his confession of faith, said that he was educated and thoroughly trained under Gamaliel, one of the greatest teachers of the law at that time, strictly according to the law of his fathers. But he confessed that even with the law, he could not be saved from his sins and that he was, in fact, a persecutor of Jesus, our Savior. One day he met Jesus on the way to Damascus and became an evangelist of His gospel. He had faith in Jesus Christ as the Son of God, who came into this world, was baptized by John to cleanse all the sins of the world, and bled on the Cross in order to take with Him all the judgments on those sins. In other words, Paul had in his heart faith in the forgiveness of sin.

Jesus' disciples believed that Jesus' baptism by John and

His blood on the Cross was to forgive them for all their sins. Paul shared the same faith with the disciples and therefore was saved from all his sins.

Paul said in Galatians 3:27, *"For as many of you as were baptized into Christ have put on Christ,"* and confessed his faith in Jesus' baptism as his salvation. Also, Peter said in 1 Peter 3:21, *"There is also an antitype which now saves us — baptism (not the removal of the filth of the flesh, but the answer of a good conscience toward God), through the resurrection of Jesus Christ,"* and he demonstrated the beautiful gospel of Jesus' baptism through this verse. Jesus' disciples believed that His baptism by John cleansed all the sins of the world. They were forgiven for their sins, and were thus no longer under the curse of the law by believing in this truth.

They believed in both the baptism of Jesus and His blood on the Cross. It is evident that this belief was necessary to the successful qualification of the disciples. In Acts 1:21-22, it says, *"Therefore, of these men who have accompanied us all the time that the Lord Jesus went in and out among us, beginning from the baptism of John to that day when He was taken up from us, one of these must become a witness with us of His resurrection."* Becoming a disciple of Jesus began with the belief in Jesus' baptism by John.

The truth we need in order to be forgiven for our sins is faith in the baptism of Jesus and His blood on the Cross. *"For as many of you as were baptized into Christ have put on Christ"* (Galatians 3:27). Thus Paul also believed in Jesus' baptism by John and His blood on the Cross.

Let's look at Titus 3:5. *"Not by works of righteousness which we have done, but according to His mercy He saved us, through the washing of regeneration and renewing of the Holy Spirit."* Here the phrase, *"the washing of regeneration"* means that all the sins of the world were cleansed when John baptized Jesus. Likewise, if you want to be forgiven for your sins, then you need to believe in the beautiful gospel, which says that your sins were passed to Jesus through His baptism by John. The reason Jesus was crucified and bled to death is that He had taken away all our sins through the baptism He received from John. Believing in this fact is enough to obtain the indwelling of the Holy Spirit. Paul confessed that he also believed in Jesus' baptism by John and His blood on the Cross.

Let us look at Hebrews 10:21-22, it says, *"Having a High Priest over the house of God, let us draw near with a true heart in full assurance of faith, having our hearts sprinkled from an evil conscience and our bodies washed with pure water."* Here, *"washed with pure water"* refers to the baptism of Jesus by John, which cleansed all the sins of mankind.

Therefore, in both the Old and New Testaments, we can find that the core components of the beautiful gospel are His baptism and His death on the Cross. You too, must share the same faith as Paul.

Today, most Christians believe in Him in vain without knowing that when John baptized Jesus, all the sins of the world were cleansed. Some theologians argue that people themselves must be baptized in water in order to be forgiven for their sins. This assertion is probably made without knowing the true and beautiful gospel of the water and the Spirit, as it is written in the Bible. Our sins cannot be forgiven in mere ceremony when we are baptized in water. The faith in Jesus' baptism and His blood cleanse us of all our sins. Only those who believe in the beautiful gospel are forgiven for their sins. And by believing in His blood, they have paid off all their judgment. Only those who have this faith can receive the Holy Spirit.

"Let us draw near with a true heart in full assurance of faith, having our hearts sprinkled from an evil conscience and our bodies washed with pure water" (Hebrews 10:22). The writer of Hebrews tells us to draw near God with a true heart in full assurance of faith. You also should draw near Him with a true heart in full assurance of faith in the beautiful gospel.

Today, Christians sincerely hope to obtain the indwelling of the Holy Spirit. But the Holy Spirit dwells only in those whose sins have been forgiven. Many do not know this and therefore wish to receive the Holy Spirit without believing in the beautiful gospel of Jesus' baptism and His blood. Those who believe in Jesus yet do not believe in His baptism and His blood on the Cross cannot receive the Holy Spirit. The reason is that they do not have pure hearts.

Paul believed in Jesus' baptism and His blood on the Cross and therefore received the Holy Spirit. Moreover, he spread this belief and was persecuted for being a heretic. But because the Holy Spirit dwelled in his heart, he could spread the gospel of the water and the Spirit until his end. *"I can do all things through Christ who strengthens me" (Philippians 4:13).* Thanks to the indwelling of the Holy Spirit, he served God and lived under the protection of the Holy Spirit until he went up to God. Only those who have the same faith as Paul's can receive the Holy Spirit.

Let us look at Paul's faith. In Colossians 2:12, it says, *"buried with Him in baptism, in which you also were raised with Him through faith in the working of God, who raised Him from the dead."* He was forgiven for all his sins by believing in Jesus, who was baptized by John.

How has Christianity changed since ancient times?

Now, let's look at the confession of a sister who became a disciple after receiving the Holy Spirit in Jesus Christ.

"I was getting old but I could not bear a child, so in order to receive His blessing through prayer I went from one church to another. Even when I was alone at home I prayed for a child at least for one or two hours and this religious pattern became a part of my daily life.

While leading this kind of religious life on my own, I met an elderly woman. She told me that if I wanted to ask God for a child, I should try to receive the prayer of the laying on of hands from her. I heard somewhere that this woman was a messenger of God and so I allowed her to lay her hands on my head. At that moment, I had an experience that I had never felt before. My tongue started to roll and I was speaking in a different language and I felt some strange and hot energy pulling me up.

I took this experience to mean that I had received the Holy Spirit and it was His answer to my prayers. The woman who had laid her hands on my head seemed to have a gift from the Holy Spirit and could prophesy and heal. She had never received an education in God's words, but using the power of the Holy Spirit, she had helped a lot of pastors and the educated receive the Holy Spirit through the laying on of hands.

From then on, I started to attend such meetings, one of which was so called "[3]**Renewal/Revival Movement**." During

---

[3] See the next page.

one of my prayers at this meeting, I felt a shiver throughout my body and my heart burned with love for God and my neighbors. This same thing happened to others and people were fainting and speaking in tongues. There were people possessed of demons there, and the leader of this meeting cast out the demons. The purpose of this Renewal/Revival Movement was to help people experience the Holy Spirit through things such as shivering, prophesying, casting out demons, and speaking in tongues. But in spite of all these experiences, I still had sin, and the sins in my heart made me feel fear and shame.

Therefore, whenever I prayed, I prayed earnestly that I would be able to resolve the problem of sin. I confessed that I had sinned but people still regarded me as an angel. I thought I had good faith, but I was wrong. If I hadn't recognized my error, I might not have had the chance to receive the Holy Spirit.

After that, I met those who spread the gospel of the water and the Spirit and received forgiveness for all my sins by believing in God's words. Now I am truly happy. I believe in the gospel of the water and the Spirit and have received the Holy Spirit. I thank God. I wish all Christians around the world would believe in the beautiful gospel and receive the

---

[3] True renewal is a natural and necessary part of the Christian life, and it brings about spiritual maturity, evidenced by the fruit of the Spirit. But in recent years, some movements have redefined the term "renewal" in such a way that it bears no resemblance to the spiritual maturity process described in the Scriptures. Their "renewal" that produces uncontrolled emotions, is marked by all manner of suspect manifestations, and is accompanied by extra-biblical or un-biblical teachings and practices.

These are some of the problematic teachings and practices promoted within the controversial renewal and revival movements: excessive emphasis on charismatic experiences over Scripture, false manifestations, false teachings, false prophecy, false signs and wonders, etc. However, the most dangerous aspect of these movements is that they have caused many people to misunderstand the truth about receiving the Holy Spirit and put aside the beautiful gospel.

indwelling of the Holy Spirit. I thank our Lord."

Here we learned that in order to receive the Holy Spirit, we need the gospel of the water and the Spirit. If you want to be forgiven for all your sins, you must have faith in the baptism of Jesus by John. Let us look at Ephesians 4:5. *"One Lord, one faith, one baptism."* Here it says that there is only one Lord and one baptism, which we believe. We must all believe in Jesus' baptism by John and His blood on the Cross in order to receive the indwelling of the Holy Spirit. If we do not, then the Holy Spirit will never dwell in us.

Once there were some people who taught and believed that the Sanctity and Purity Movement would help them receive the Holy Spirit. However, do you think the Holy Spirit dwells in us if we join such movements? Have you received the Holy Spirit because of the Sanctity and Purity Movement? If it were possible, then you would be wise to keep the faith. But if the Holy Spirit came on you for this reason, then Jesus would not have had to come down and save us from our sins and would not have needed to be baptized by John nor be crucified on the Cross.

The receiving of the indwelling of the Holy Spirit is a gift from the faith in the gospel of Jesus' baptism and His blood, which brought you forgiveness for your sins. The indwelling of the Holy Spirit is a gift granted to those whose sins have been cleansed and forgiven by the true gospel.

These days, among those who indulge in Renewal/Revival Movement, there are some who believe that exhaustive prayers of repentance can help them receive the Holy Spirit. They say that even though a person has sin in his heart, if he prays for repentance, then he will receive the Holy Spirit.

The Pentecostal-Charismatic Movement, which has spread all over the world, started in the United States in the 1800s.

This movement came about after the Industrial Revolution, when people's ethics and morals had collapsed. The movement reached its heyday when many people's hearts were desolated due to the Great Depression. From that time, the faith based on God's words declined and a new religious movement started to rise. It was the Pentecostal-Charismatic Movement which was aimed at physically experiencing the Holy Spirit (God) – seeing the works of God with the eyes and experiencing the power of God's words with the body and mind.

But a fatal flaw in this movement is that it moves believers further away from the words of God and exists as a religion that strives for bodily blessings. As a consequence, followers of this new movement became advocates of shamanism. Even today, those who indulge themselves in the Pentecostal-Charismatic Movement believe that if one has faith in Jesus he will be rich, his illnesses will be cured, he will be prosperous in everything, he will receive the Holy Spirit and speak in tongues and have the power to heal others. The Pentecostal-Charismatic Movement has spread all around the world. This movement has become a barrier to people's faith in the beautiful gospel and their ability to obtain the indwelling of the Holy Spirit.

Modern Christianity originated in the beliefs of Luther and Calvin about 500 years ago. But within the boundaries of Christianity, the biblical study of the indwelling of the Holy Spirit is not firmly established. The problem is that from the beginning of modern Christianity, most Christians have believed in Jesus without recognizing the significance of His baptism and death on the Cross. To make matters worse, people started to stress mistaken doctrines of Christianity and emphasize bodily experiences alone. All Christians must believe the beautiful gospel that says Jesus was baptized by John to take away all the sins of the world and that He was crucified in order to be judged for those sins. This belief will cause you to receive the Holy Spirit.

Today, the reason that Christianity has become so desolate is that people tend to ignore the truth of the baptism Jesus received from John and of His blood on the Cross. Jesus tells us to know the truth. Believing in the baptism of Jesus by John and His blood on the Cross means believing in the gospel of the water and the Spirit. If you want to receive the Holy Spirit, then believe that when John baptized Jesus, your sins were passed on to Him and that His blood was the judgment and forgiveness for all your sins. Then you will receive the Holy Spirit.

Many Christians believe only in Jesus' blood as the gospel of redemption. But can those of you who believe only in His blood be freed from sin? Can you? If you think this can be so, perhaps you only have a vague knowledge of the true meaning of Jesus' baptism. In that case there is still sin in your heart. Only when you connect Jesus' baptism and blood together as one faith can you be saved from your sins and receive the Holy Spirit. The Bible says this is the only true gospel that helps us to overcome the world. *"And there are three that bear witness on earth: the Spirit, the water, and the blood; and these three agree as one"(1 John 5:8).* Therefore, we must know that it, in His desire to save us from our sins, God had John baptize Jesus and then had Him crucified.

The reason why most Christians don't have forgiveness of sins in spite of their believing in Jesus is that they don't believe in the beautiful gospel that was accomplished with Jesus' baptism by John and His blood on the Cross. Those who believe in these two things will be forgiven for their sins and the Holy Spirit will dwell in their hearts.

When people realize that their sins have been cleansed,

their hearts become peaceful and bountiful like still water. The moment the Holy Spirit dwells in someone's heart, peace like a river flows into and out of his heart. We meet our Lord by believing in this truth and walking with the Spirit as we spread the gospel of receiving the Holy Spirit. Our hearts have never had this kind of peace before. From the time we start believing in the gospel of the water and the Spirit, our lives become serene and our hearts become perfectly joyous. We cannot turn away from this beautiful gospel. The Holy Spirit is always in our hearts, prompting us to spread His word and allowing people who believe in it to receive the Holy Spirit.

Because we believed in the beautiful gospel of Jesus' baptism and His blood on the Cross, we were blessed with the Holy Spirit. Now you must have faith in the baptism of Jesus and His blood on the Cross in order to receive the Holy Spirit. It is important that people around the world start the process of believing in the word of God that Jesus was baptized by John to take away all the sins of the world and that He died on the Cross to be judged for their sins. When they do so, they will finally receive the Holy Spirit. ⊠

SERMON 5

Do you want to have fellowship with the Holy Spirit?

Do you want to have fellowship with the Holy Spirit?

<1 John 1:1-10>

"That which was from the beginning, which we have heard, which we have seen with our eyes, which we have looked upon, and our hands have handled, concerning the Word of life — the life was manifested, and we have seen, and bear witness, and declare to you that eternal life which was with the Father and was manifested to us — that which we have seen and heard we declare to you, that you also may have fellowship with us; and truly our fellowship is with the Father and with His Son Jesus Christ. And these things we write to you that your joy may be full. This is the message which we have heard from Him and declare to you, that God is light and in Him is no darkness at all. If we say that we have fellowship with Him, and walk in darkness, we lie and do not practice the truth. But if we walk in the light as He is in the light, we have fellowship with one another, and the blood of Jesus Christ His Son cleanses us from all sin. If we say that we have no sin, we deceive ourselves, and the truth is not in us. If we confess our sins, He is faithful and just to forgive us our sins and to cleanse us from all unrighteousness. If we say that we have not sinned, we make Him a liar, and His word is not in us."

What is an essential prerequisite
to having a sense of fellowship
with the Holy Spirit?

We first should know and believe
in the gospel of the water and the Spirit
and cleanse ourselves of all our
sins through faith.

If you want to have fellowship with the Holy Spirit, firstly, you must know that even a little sin in front of the Lord makes such a fellowship impossible. You might think, 'How can a man have not even a bit of sin in front of the Lord?' But if you truly wish for fellowship with the Lord then there should be no darkness in your heart. Therefore, in order to have fellowship with the Lord, you need to know that you must believe in the gospel of redemption and cleanse yourselves of all sins.

If you truly wish to have fellowship with the Holy Spirit, then you first should know and believe in the gospel of the water and the Spirit and cleanse your sins through faith. If you do not know the gospel of the water and the Spirit and do not take it into your heart, then you shouldn't even think of having fellowship with the Lord. Having fellowship with the Holy Spirit is only possible when all your sins are purged away from your heart through the gospel of the water and the Spirit.

All sins can be purged from anyone's mind with the truth of His water and the Spirit. The Lord blesses you with the Holy Spirit when you believe in the beautiful gospel of the water and the Spirit. Do you truly want to have fellowship with the Lord and the Holy Spirit? Then recognize your sins and believe in the beautiful gospel in order to purify yourself of sin. After that you can truly have fellowship with the Lord.

If you wish to have fellowship with the Lord, you must believe in the baptism Jesus received from John in the Jordan River and also believe in His blood on the Cross. If people truly wish to have fellowship with the Holy Spirit, they should know who the Holy Spirit is. The Holy Spirit is the Holy One. And therefore He can dwell only in those who believe in the beautiful gospel.

Let us look at a confession from someone whose sins were cleansed by believing in Jesus' baptism by John and in His blood, and who now has fellowship with the Holy Spirit.

"There are a lot of different people in this world and everybody lives with his own thoughts and ways. I was one just as them. I had a very ordinary life and from my childhood, I followed my mother to church and naturally came to believe in God. My father was an atheist and frequently criticized me for my beliefs, but the rest of the family all went to church. Going to church was a huge part of my life.

However, during my adolescence, seeing my bedridden father, many thoughts regarding such things as life and death, Heaven and Hell came to me. Most people said that if I believed in God I would be able to enter Heaven and become His child, but I was never sure of that. I was never sure that I'd become His child. I had learned that if I did good on earth then I could enter Heaven and so I tried to do good to the needy.

But on one side of my heart, I knew I had sinned. I might have looked like a good person to others but I couldn't but feel guilty for my sins. At that time, I made it a habit to go to church and pray, 'Please let me truly be Your child. Please let me know the truth.' While praying, I developed a new urge in my heart. Whenever I listened to the teachings of His words, I could not comprehend nor see the words. I was worn out from the emptiness of my life, my sin, death, etc.

I had thoughts such as, 'I want to be born again. If I can be born again I will not live like this.' But despite these thoughts I went to church less frequently and my adolescent years passed. I now needed to find a job but it was more difficult than I thought. I was even more distressed and no matter how hard I tried, I could not smile. Looking at myself with an empty heart, I fell into a state of depression. At that time, I heard the gospel from my elder brother.

"Repent therefore and be converted, that your sins may be blotted out, so that times of refreshment may come from the presence of the Lord"(Acts 3:19). This was exactly the gospel of the water and the Spirit. All I'd learned at previous church meetings was that Jesus died on the Cross for our sins. But this gospel told me that Jesus was baptized by John the Baptist to take away our sins and was judged for our sins on the Cross.

I had gone to church all my life and I had pretended to be a child of God but I had failed. I had tried to understand the meaning of His words but I had failed. However, after I heard the beautiful gospel of the water and the Spirit and believed in it, the sin in me and all the things that tormented me disappeared and my heart became peaceful.

I thought that if I only believed in God with enthusiasm and went to church with perfect attendance, then I would go to Heaven. But God sent me the gospel of the water and the Spirit and my sins were forgiven. He gave to me the gift of the Holy Spirit. Before I received His redemption, I didn't know about the Holy Spirit nor the notion of speaking in tongues. I just went to church and believed that if I lived earnestly and served my church, then God would bless me. But I came to realize that I could receive the Holy Spirit only when my sins were forgiven through the beautiful gospel of the water and the

Spirit.

In my previous life, I was still in sin even though I believed in God. And I lived a lukewarm kind of life, not knowing the importance of receiving the Holy Spirit. But through His servant, who preached the beautiful gospel according to the Bible, I believed and came to know that the Holy Spirit dwelt also in me.

After receiving redemption, at first I couldn't be convinced whether the Holy Spirit was in me or not. But I continuously studied His words and came to realize that in my heart a new faith was blooming and that I had received the indwelling of the Holy Spirit. Now it is true, and I feel convinced that the Holy Spirit dwells in me! When He forgave my sins, I knew that only those free of sin could become children of God and receive the Holy Spirit.

I also knew that my efforts to look perfect in His eyes or live perfectly would never allow me to receive the Holy Spirit. God comes to those who know that they are sinners and yet do not know what to do about it. He meets those who eagerly seek and need Him.

He made me see that doing good and believing in God with reckless abandon would not get me to Heaven and that Jesus Christ came into this world to save me from my sins through the beautiful gospel of the water and the Spirit. He gave me the Holy Spirit to dwell within me forever.

I thank the Lord for making me His child and blessing me with the indwelling of the Holy Spirit. If it had not been for the Lord, I would still have sin in my heart and would be condemned to an eternal life imprisonment in Hell."

Likewise, I once believed only in the blood on the Cross and could not receive the Holy Spirit even if I wanted to. At that time, I believed in Jesus but I had sin in my heart that prevented me from receiving the Holy Spirit. A sinner cannot receive the Holy Spirit in his heart. But still, many sinners try to receive the Holy Spirit even when their hearts are full of sin.

If you truly wish to receive the Holy Spirit and have fellowship with Him, you need to believe in the beautiful gospel of the water and the Spirit and obtain redemption. Are you still a sinner? Then you can hear the true gospel from those who have already received the Holy Spirit. Those who wish to have fellowship with the Holy Spirit must have a thirsty heart and trust in the beautiful gospel of the water and the Spirit.

Only the righteous can hear the words of the Holy Spirit through the church. They can live their faithful lives by hearing the beautiful gospel but sinners live their cursed lives destined for Hell without ever hearing the gospel.

Therefore, you must learn about the gospel of the water and the Spirit. Why do you need to believe in this gospel? It is necessary for you to escape from the religion of law and build your faith in the beautiful gospel based on the words of God. Jesus' disciples followed this beautiful gospel and now it belongs to those who have received the Holy Spirit. The beautiful gospel of the water and the Spirit is exactly the same as that followed by the apostles in the beginning of the early church. All Christians must receive the Holy Spirit. Only then can they become the children of God.

Those who still do not believe in the beautiful gospel of the water and the Spirit must have sin in their hearts. They cannot have fellowship with the Holy Spirit. In order to have fellowship with Him, they first need to believe in the gospel of the water and the Spirit that God gave them and receive the Holy Spirit.

The Bible repeatedly mentions the Holy Spirit

The indwelling of the Holy Spirit began after the resurrection of Jesus. Now is the day of salvation and now is the time of His boundless grace. But it is truly unfortunate if we do not receive the gospel of the water and the Spirit and if we live without fellowship with the Holy Spirit.

Do you have fellowship with the Holy Spirit? Are you prevented from having fellowship with the Holy Spirit because of your sins? Then learn about the gospel of the water and the Spirit that God gave you and believe in it. If you believe in the gospel of the water and the Spirit, the Holy Spirit will dwell in your heart and be your companion. The Holy Spirit only dwells in the hearts of those who believe in the gospel of the water and the Spirit. The Holy Spirit often reveals His will in the hearts of the righteous. Paul's ministry with the Holy Spirit was to spread the beautiful gospel.

How can you recognize someone who has received the Holy Spirit? What is the benchmark? The benchmark is whether or not he believes in the beautiful gospel of the water and the Spirit. If the person knows and believes in the beautiful gospel of the water and the Spirit, then he is a person who has the indwelling of the Holy Spirit.

The Holy Spirit does not dwell in those who do not believe in the beautiful gospel. The Holy Spirit dwells only in those who believe in the forgiveness of sin that comes from the baptism Jesus received from John and His blood on the Cross. Do you wish to have fellowship with the Holy Spirit?

Do you know what kind of gospel you need to understand in order to receive the Holy Spirit and have fellowship with

Him? The beautiful gospel is found within the faith in Jesus' baptism by John and His blood on the Cross. If you do not believe in the gospel of the water and the Spirit, your sins cannot be forgiven and therefore the Holy Spirit cannot dwell in you. The Holy Spirit demands that people should believe in the gospel of the water and the Spirit in order to receive Him.

The Holy Spirit cannot dwell within the hearts of sinners. If you want to receive the Holy Spirit, you must first believe in the beautiful gospel in order to cleanse yourself of all your sins. Also, if you wish to have fellowship with the Holy Spirit, you should be faithful in preaching the beautiful gospel. If you want to be led by the Holy Spirit, you must always love the beautiful gospel and attempt to spread it wherever you go. The Holy Spirit is with those who preach the gospel of the water and the Spirit.

The indwelling of the Holy Spirit is given only to the righteous, those who believe in the beautiful gospel. Only the righteous, those who believe in the beautiful gospel, can have fellowship with the Holy Spirit. The beautiful gospel that the Holy Spirit approves of is the gospel that was accomplished by Jesus' baptism by John and His blood (1 John 5:3-7).

Peter also believed in the beautiful gospel and said, *"There is also an antitype which now saves us — baptism (not the removal of the filth of the flesh, but the answer of a good conscience toward God), through the resurrection of Jesus Christ" (1 Peter 3:21).* In the Bible, "water" frequently stands for the baptism that Jesus received from John the Baptist.

Those who are able to receive the Holy Spirit have received redemption through the beautiful gospel and are free of all sin. Those who believe in the beautiful gospel can worship the Father in spirit and truth by the lead of the Spirit (John 4:23). The Holy Spirit helps the righteous live their lives filled with the Holy Spirit. Those who have the indwelling of the Holy Spirit can live forever praising the Lord. The Holy Spirit guarantees that we are children of God. We may live forever within the gospel of the water and the Spirit and within the Holy Spirit.

The Holy Spirit does not have fellowship with those who deceive themselves

The Holy Spirit tells sinners in 1 John 1:8, *"If we say that we have no sin, we deceive ourselves, and the truth is not in us."* The Holy Spirit cannot dwell in those who deceive themselves. The Holy Spirit reprimands sinners, saying, "Why did you not believe in the beautiful gospel accomplished by Jesus' baptism and His blood?"

We will look at a confession of a born again Christian who believed at first that he received the Holy Spirit without the evidence of Jesus' baptism and His blood. This man now believes in the gospel of the water and the blood and has received the Holy Spirit. Here, we should point out exactly in whom the Holy Spirit dwells.

"God began living in my heart when I realized the reason for my existence in this world. Looking at myself, I think my feebleness to live in this cruel world alone came out as a craving for God. I did not search for God but naturally accepted His existence for He is not visible, but He is there. Of course I asked myself, 'Is He really there?' but even the thought of it terrified me for I firmly believe that He is the Creator of all.

Those who rejected God seemed foolish, yet in some ways

much more powerful than me. They seemed like they could go through anything on their own and on the other hand I looked like a weak fool. But because I had hopes for the life after death, I looked upon God with even greater respect. I wondered whether Heaven was a place for people like me who feel they are always lacking. And that question made me wish more earnestly for the Heavenly Paradise.

My parents looked down on people with religion and my siblings went to church with no devotion. They thought my devotion to church would soon die out so they didn't stop me from going to church until I was in middle school. So I went from church to church and finally started going to a small church near my house until I was in college.

The reason I chose to attend this church was that it placed a strong emphasis on the gospel. The pastor of the church was an evangelical revivalist who apparently did nothing that would violate the words of the Bible. I had reasons for leading a religious life earnestly, even when I was stressed and oppressed by my studies.

The reason was that when people called my fellow church members heathens, I believed that my church was right and I was certain that I would go to Heaven. That certainty was based on the gospel. They said that sinners cannot enter the gates of Heaven but the people of other churches also said their hearts were full of sin. I also believed that the people of my church were sinners before I attended the church, so didn't think much of this criticism.

But those so-called evangelical revivalists were different from what I had experienced in the past. They said that if we believed in Jesus in the correct manner, we were sinless. And only those who are sinless can go to Heaven. They also said that Jesus brought us justice on the Cross and therefore we were not sinners but righteous people. I did not believe this at first, but when I thought about it, it made sense. I was young and I thought that if I wanted to go to Heaven, God would only let me in if I were sinless, for God despises sin.

This church had different beliefs than I was used to and the ritual of worship services was a little different too. But because Heaven is a place where only the chosen few can enter, it seemed that the people in this church had adopted the right beliefs. Because the church stressed Jesus' flesh and blood, every Sunday we took a bite of bread and sipped wine. Because this ceremony was based on the words of the Bible, I accepted it. But I found out later that people just took part in the ritual without understanding its true meaning.

I believed that the Holy Spirit dwelt in the hearts of believers and in the hearts of the righteous and that He heard all their prayers. So I believed that the Holy Spirit dwelt in me. I was so sure that God was my companion and I never doubted the gospel that I believed in. When I was going through hard times, I talked to God like He was right next to me. I believed that He listened to me when I told Him things that I could tell no one else. So I trusted Him and depended on Him.

I couldn't understand those who went to revival meetings to speak in tongues and I laughed at those who attended fasting prayer services. Looking at such efforts I thought, 'Why do they go through such meaningless effort to receive the Holy Spirit? The Holy Spirit comes on them only when they are sinless and stays with you always. They must be sinners. He would not come on them even with all their efforts.' I felt pity for them. I thought they were so foolish. With that in mind, I came to think that my belief in the gospel was the best and others' beliefs were all a lie.

My arrogant heart reached its peak. For 10 years I had led

a religious life of my own. But as time passed questions began to rise in my mind and in my heart. I thought, 'I am sinless due to the gospel of the blood on the Cross, but are all the other believers sinless as well? Do they really believe in this gospel too?' I didn't know why I started asking these questions. The questions just came to my mind and I could not ask anyone. This was a personal belief and should not be violated. And it would have been a rude question to ask of someone else.

But I started to ask these questions of myself. While I was in college, I started doing things that used to be restricted by religious precepts and my heart became so dark that my beliefs started to diminish. I was no longer sure of my beliefs. 'Can I call myself a righteous man? Did Jesus really cleanse me of all my sins?' Amidst all this confusion, I forced myself to think of the gospel of the Cross and I brainwashed myself with it. But the more I pressed myself, the more lost I became and I did not attend church services anymore. I used my club activities as an excuse.

Amidst all the confusion and chaos, I finally met the truth. I heard about the gospel of the water and the Spirit and it came to me like a bolt of lightning. The impact was so great that I felt like crying. But listening to the gospel, I had to admit that all that I had believed until then was false.

I had never passed on my sins to Jesus. I vaguely had believed that He had taken away my sins and that I was a sinless man, but that was not the case. Why did Jesus come to this world to be baptized? Because He wanted to show us He was as meek as a lamb? To prove that He came as a man? Or to prophesy His inevitable death? I had never dreamt that whatever vague knowledge of baptism I had was of such significance. The truth was that Jesus was baptized by John, the representative of all humankind, and with that baptism, all our sins were passed onto Him.

'Oh! That is why Jesus became God's Lamb who carried with Him all our sins!' Now everything made sense. 'Jesus was judged for my sins on the Cross. That's why I am sinless in my heart.' The moment I knew of the gospel of the water (Jesus' baptism), blood (the Cross), and the Holy Spirit (Jesus is God), the sins I'd felt in my heart vanished.

Now I am truly a sinless and righteous man and the Holy Spirit finally dwells in my heart. The belief I had in the Cross was not enough to cleanse me of the sins I'd had in my heart. If you don't know exactly how your sins were passed on to Jesus, your sins cannot be forgiven and the Holy Spirit cannot dwell in you. I thank the Lord. I was able to receive the Holy Spirit through the beautiful gospel.

Without any effort, I was forgiven through the gospel of the water and the Spirit and the Holy Spirit dwells in me now and forever. Now, I can proudly call myself a sinless man and can be proud that the Kingdom of Heaven is mine. I take this opportunity to thank the Lord for giving me such blessing without expense. Hallelujah!"

Those who receive the Holy Spirit can say that they are sinless in the presence of God. No matter how long you have believed in Jesus, if you do not believe in the beautiful gospel that God gave us, you surely have sin in your heart. People like that are deceiving themselves as well as God. These people have never met the Lord. If a sinner wishes to have fellowship with the Holy Spirit, he must first stop deceiving himself and confess that he has sinned. Only then will he be qualified to believe in the gospel of the water and the Spirit. Those who believe in this beautiful gospel deserve to receive the Holy Spirit.

What does the Holy Spirit say to sinners? He advises them

to obtain forgiveness for their sins by believing in the beautiful gospel that was accomplished by Jesus' baptism and His blood. If you say that you're not a sinner when you have sinned, then you will never receive the Holy Spirit. Those who do not believe in the beautiful gospel and say that they have not sinned deceive both God and themselves. Sinners must know of the beautiful gospel of the water and the Spirit and receive the Holy Spirit. Only then can they be delivered from God's severe judgment.

The righteous can have fellowship with the Holy Spirit by confessing their sins

I speak to those who believe in the gospel of the water and the Spirit and thus, have received the Holy Spirit. Let us look at what God has told the righteous. In John 1:9, it is said, *"If we confess our sins, He is faithful and just to forgive us our sins and to cleanse us from all unrighteousness."* This verse means that we can cleanse our actual sins from our defiled hearts by reminding ourselves of and believing in the beautiful gospel that declares Jesus took all our sins when He was baptized and He atoned for them by being crucified. The righteous need to confess their actual sins to God. Only then can they have fellowship with the Holy Spirit. The righteous should confess their actual sins and continue to believe in the beautiful gospel.

Long ago, the beautiful gospel of Jesus' baptism and His blood cleansed all our sins and therefore, the righteous should believe in this gospel and be free from all their sins. The Lord has already forgiven all their sins through the gospel of the water and the Spirit. The righteous must believe in the beautiful gospel to be free from their sins. The righteous can purify their hearts by believing in the beautiful gospel of the water and the Spirit when they are polluted with their actual sins.

Our Lord cleansed all the sins of the righteous long ago with His baptism and His blood. Therefore, those who believe are truly free from all their sins. However, the righteous should confess and admit their sins in the presence of God. And then the righteous must return to faith in Jesus' baptism and His blood, which composed the beautiful gospel, in order to be free from all their sins. Therefore, they can always lead a fresh new life accompanying the Holy Spirit. Those who can look to the Lord without concern for their weakness can have true fellowship with God thanks to the beautiful gospel of the water and the Spirit.

How can we attain a true sense of fellowship with the Holy Spirit?

There are many people who wish to have fellowship with the Holy Spirit. But they do not know how to make this wish come true, even though they believe in Jesus. All people come to receive the Holy Spirit by believing in the gospel of the water and the Spirit and start having fellowship with the Holy Spirit from that time on.

Likewise, the only way a righteous person can have fellowship with the Holy Spirit is to know and believe the truth of the gospel of the water and the Spirit. The fellowship between the righteous and the Holy Spirit cannot be achieved without the true gospel. What about fellowship with the Holy

Spirit? It is only possible by believing in the truth of the beautiful gospel.

God says that man sins throughout his life

In 1 John 1:10, it says, *"If we say that we have not sinned, we make Him a liar, and His word is not in us."* There would be no one who has not sinned in front of God. Even the Bible says, *"There is not a just man on earth who does good and does not sin" (Ecclesiastes 7:20).* All men sin in front of God. If anyone says that he has not sinned, then he is a liar. People sin throughout their lives until their dying hours and that is why Jesus was baptized by John to bear all their sins. If we did not sin, then we would not need to believe in God as our Savior.

The Lord says, *"My word is not in you"* to those who think as if they have not sinned. If a person doesn't have faith in the beautiful gospel of the water and the Spirit, then he deserves destruction. If a righteous man or a sinner says that he has not sinned in the presence of God, then he does not deserve to believe in the beautiful gospel.

The Lord gave everyone the wonderful gift of the beautiful gospel. We confessed all our sins and repented in order to receive forgiveness of sins with the beautiful gospel. We could come back to the beautiful gospel that God bestowed on us as forgiveness for our sins and believed in it in order to have fellowship with the Holy Spirit. A true sense of fellowship with the Holy Spirit is in the gospel of the water and the Spirit, and only those who have the gospel of the water and the Spirit may have fellowship with God.

Mankind was far from God because of the sins inherited from Adam and Eve. But now we, who have inherited the seed of sin, can look forward to having fellowship with God again. In order to do that, we must return to the faith in Jesus Christ's gospel of the water and the Spirit and be forgiven for the sins that have put us so far from God.

Those who believe in the beautiful gospel will be saved from all their sins and God will fill them up with the Holy Spirit. The righteous can have fellowship with God, for they have received the Holy Spirit. Therefore, those who have been cut off from God for their sins must return to the beautiful gospel of the water and the Spirit and believe in it. Only then can they begin to have true fellowship with Him.

The indwelling of the Holy Spirit comes with faith in the beautiful gospel. We must know that the indwelling of the Holy Spirit comes only through believing in the gospel of the water and the Spirit. Believing in the beautiful gospel created a new pathway to God. The Lord broke down the middle wall that separated us from Him because of both original sin and actual sins, and allowed us to have fellowship with God through our faith in the beautiful gospel of the water and the Spirit.

We must establish fellowship with the Holy Spirit once again. True fellowship with the Holy Spirit is achieved through understanding the gospel of the water and the Spirit for obedience to the faith. Fellowship with the Holy Spirit occurs when we have faith in the fact that forgiveness of our sins comes from the beautiful gospel. Those who have not received forgiveness for their sins cannot have fellowship with the Holy Spirit. In other words, no one can have fellowship with the Holy Spirit without believing in the gospel of the water and the Spirit.

If it is hard for you to have fellowship with the Holy Spirit, then you should first admit that you do not believe in the gospel of the water and the Spirit and that your sins have not been forgiven. Do you wish to have fellowship with the Holy Spirit? Then believe in the gospel that was accomplished through Jesus' baptism and His blood. Only then will you be forgiven for all your sins and as a reward will receive the Holy Spirit in your heart. This beautiful gospel can surely grant you fellowship with the Holy Spirit. ⊠

SERMON 6

Believe so that the Holy Spirit dwells in you

Believe so that the Holy Spirit dwells in you

<Matthew 25:1-12>

"Then the kingdom of heaven shall be likened to ten virgins who took their lamps and went out to meet the bridegroom. Now five of them were wise, and five were foolish. Those who were foolish took their lamps and took no oil with them, but the wise took oil in their vessels with their lamps. But while the bridegroom was delayed, they all slumbered and slept. And at midnight a cry was heard: 'Behold, the bridegroom is coming; go out to meet him!' Then all those virgins arose and trimmed their lamps. And the foolish said to the wise, 'Give us some of your oil, for our lamps are going out.' But the wise answered, saying, 'No, lest there should not be enough for us and you; but go rather to those who sell, and buy for yourselves.' And while they went to buy, the bridegroom came, and those who were ready went in with him to the wedding; and the door was shut. Afterward the other virgins came also, saying, 'Lord, Lord, open to us!' But he answered and said, 'Assuredly, I say to you, I do not know you.'"

To whom does the Holy Spirit come?

He comes to those who are forgiven for their sins by believing in Jesus' baptism and His blood.

Who are represented by the virgins that have the indwelling of the Holy Spirit?

In the passages above, there are five wise virgins and five foolish virgins. The five foolish ones ask the five wise ones to share some of their oil. But the wise told the foolish ones, *"No, lest there should not be enough for us and you; but go rather to those who sell, and buy for yourselves."* So, while the foolish ones went out to buy oil, the five wise virgins who had oil with their lamps went into the wedding ceremony. How then can we prepare oil for the Lord? The only thing we need do is to wait for Him with the forgiveness of sins in our hearts.

We can find two kinds of faith among people. One is the faith in the gospel of the forgiveness of sins. This leads to receiving the Holy Spirit. The other is simply being faithful to one's own religious creeds – indifferent to whether or not the Lord has forgiven one's sins.

To those who are faithful to their own creeds, the beautiful gospel remains burdensome. Like the foolish virgins who went out to buy oil when the bridegroom was coming, those who move from one house of worship to another in the hope of receiving the Holy Spirit are deceiving no one but themselves. Such people are ignorant of the fact that they must have faith in the beautiful gospel in their hearts prior to the Day of Judgment. They wish to receive the Holy Spirit by impressing God with their zeal. We will look at the confession of a deacon who made great efforts to receive the Holy Spirit. This confession will be helpful to you.

"I did everything to receive the Holy Spirit. I thought that if I devoted myself to my own faith fervently, I could receive the Holy Spirit and so I moved from one prayer house to another. The people at one of these prayer houses played the electric piano and drums as part of the service. The pastor who led the meeting called those who wished to receive the Holy Spirit one by one and as he slapped the person's forehead, he started speaking in tongues. He ran around with a microphone and cried "Receive fire, fire, fire" and placed his hand on people's heads, causing some of them have fits and faint. I had my doubts as to whether this practice was about receiving the Holy Spirit but I was already addicted to these meetings. Despite all this, I never succeeded in receiving the Holy Spirit.

After that experience, I went up to the mountains and tried crying and praying all night while holding onto a pine tree. I even tried praying in a cave but that didn't work either. After that, I tried praying all night long for 40 days but I never managed to receive the Holy Spirit. Then one day I was invited to a seminar on the Holy Spirit. The seminar was held once a week, and lasted for seven weeks.

The seminar was on God's love, the Cross, Jesus' resurrection, the laying on of hands, the fruit of the Spirit, and spiritual growth. At that time when the seminar program was almost over, the preacher in the seminar put his hands on my head and prayed for the Holy Spirit, and I did as he told me to. I relaxed and raised my palms to face the sky and cried out "la-la-la-la" over and over again. Suddenly, while I was crying "la-la-la-la," I started speaking fluently in a strange language. Many people congratulated me on receiving the Holy Spirit. But when I was alone at home, I was afraid. So, I started working as a volunteer worker for the seminar. I thought I should volunteer for as much work as possible so I traveled around the country to render my services. And when I laid my hands on some patients, their illness seemed to be healed, even though they relapsed soon after. And then I had visions before my eyes and found I could prophesy. Surprisingly, my prophecies always came true. From that time, I was invited to all sorts of places and treated like a celebrity. But I was still afraid. Then one day, I heard a voice say, "Don't wander around from place to place like this, instead go and help your family receive salvation." However, I didn't know what salvation was. I only knew what others had told me – that if I didn't use this gift of the Holy Spirit, He would take it away from me. On the one hand, I was afraid to use my abilities and yet I couldn't stop doing so.

One day, I heard that a female shaman wished to believe in Jesus and so I visited her with my friends. We did not inform her in advance that we would be visiting her. But the female shaman was already waiting for us outside her gate and said, "I knew you would be coming." Then she suddenly started throwing water at us and said, "There is no difference between Eastern shamanism and Western shamanism!" She called us "Jesus shamans," pointed at us and said, "This guy is frightful, but that one is not." What the female shaman said came to me like a blow to the head. I began thinking that all I had been doing was no different than what the shaman does. Nothing I ever did brought the Holy Spirit to me because I still had sin in my heart."

From this confession, we learn that receiving the Holy Spirit is beyond our abilities. Because such a faith is not based on God's gospel, those who live this kind of religious life don't have oil in their lamp.

The lamp in the Bible refers to the church and the oil refers to the Holy Spirit. The Bible implies that those who attend church, whether it is God's church or not, without receiving the Holy Spirit are fools.

The foolish ones burn their emotions and bodies day by

day. The foolish burn their feelings along with their zealous bodies before God. If we were to say that our emotions amount to 20cm and it takes one day to burn 1cm, then it would take only 20 days to consume in fire all our emotions. The emotions behind their faith gain new strength through early-morning prayers, all-night prayers, fasting prayers and revival meetings, but their emotions also burn throughout their lives. They are addicted to this never-ending process of burning their own emotions.

Their emotions are burned in the name of Jesus. They attend church and burn their emotions but their hearts are still confused and search for something else. The reason for this is that their faith comes from bodily experiences; therefore, they have a constant need to reinforce these feelings so that the flame won't die out. However, they cannot receive the Holy Spirit with this kind of faith. Burning their emotions will not lead them to receive the Holy Spirit.

All of us should prepare the proper faith to receive the Holy Spirit in the full presence of God. Then and only then will we be worthy to receive the Holy Spirit. How do we gain the faith that makes us worthy to receive the Holy Spirit? The truth lies in the beautiful gospel that was accomplished by Jesus' baptism in the Jordan and the shedding of His blood on the Cross.

God referred to us as *"A brood of evildoers" (Isaiah 1:4)*. We must admit this to ourselves. People are originally born with 12 kinds of sins (Mark 7:21-23). Human beings cannot help sinning from the day they are born until the day they die.

In John 1:6-7, it is written, *"There was a man sent from God, whose name was John. This man came to be a witness, to bear witness of the Light, that all through him might believe."* John the Baptist baptized Jesus and passed all the sins of the world on to Him, saying, *"Behold! The Lamb of God who takes away the sin of the world" (John 1:29).* We were saved from all our sins thanks to John's baptism on Jesus Christ. If John had not baptized Jesus and had not proclaimed that He was the Lamb of God who took away the sins of the world, we couldn't have known that Jesus took all our sins with Him to the Cross. Nor could we have known the way to receive the Holy Spirit. But thanks to John's testimony, we came to understand that Jesus took away all our sins and we were able to receive the Holy Spirit.

With this faith, we became brides who are completely prepared to receive Jesus, the bridegroom. We are the virgins who believe in Jesus and are fully prepared to receive the Holy Spirit.

Do you believe in the gospel of the water and the Spirit with all your heart? Do you believe that Jesus Christ took away all your sins with His baptism by John? The Bible says, *"Faith comes by hearing, and hearing by the word of God" (Romans 10:17).* We must believe that Jesus was baptized by John and died on the Cross in order to receive the Holy Spirit. We must realize that receiving the Holy Spirit can only come from believing that Jesus came to earth as a human being and was baptized by John, that He died on the Cross and was resurrected.

Even today, there are two groups of believers, just as the ten virgins in the story above were of two types. Which side are you on? You must receive the Holy Spirit by believing in the water and the Spirit. Do you attend church, but yet still find yourself waiting for the Holy Spirit to come to you? You must know the true way in which to receive the Holy Spirit.

With what beliefs can we receive the Holy Spirit? Can you receive the Holy Spirit through the ecstatic enthusiasm of

Shamanism? Can you receive the Holy Spirit in a state of coma? Can you receive the Holy Spirit by believing in fanatical religions? Do you have to pray to God for forgiveness of your sins consistently? The Bible says that when Jesus had been baptized and came up from the water, the Spirit of God descended like a dove. He was baptized in order to bear all our sins, and to tell us that He would be crucified to pay the wages of all our transgressions.

Jesus was baptized by John to bear the sin of the world and went to the Cross so that we could be saved and receive the Holy Spirit. This is the truth. Jesus was baptized by John, judged for all our sins on the Cross and resurrected. We must believe in Jesus' baptism by John and His blood on the Cross in order to receive forgiveness for our sins. We can see from Jesus' baptism (Matthew 3:13-15) that the Holy Spirit comes peacefully like a dove on those of us who are cleansed by believing in His baptism.

To receive the Holy Spirit, it is essential to believe in Jesus' baptism by John and in His blood on the Cross. The Holy Spirit comes on a person as peacefully as a dove when he believes in the forgiveness of sin. Those who have already received the Holy Spirit should know that this has been made possible due to the forgiveness of sin by faith. The Holy Spirit descends on those who believe in the forgiveness of sin with all their heart.

Jesus Christ came by the bread and wine of eternal life (Matthew 26:26-28, John 6:53-56). When Jesus came out of the water after His baptism, there was a voice from heaven, saying, *"This is My beloved Son, in whom I am well pleased" (Matthew 3:17).*

It is easy to believe in God as the Trinity. God is the Father of Jesus and Jesus is God's Son. The Holy Spirit is also God.

The Trinity is One God to us.

You must know that you will never receive the Holy Spirit by believing only in the Cross or by trying to sanctify yourself by righteous deeds. You can receive the Holy Spirit only when you believe that John baptized Jesus to put all our sins on Him, and that He was crucified to atone for all our sins. How simple and clear the truth is! It is not difficult to receive the forgiveness of sin and the Holy Spirit.

God spoke to us in simple terms. An ordinary man's IQ is around 110 to 120. His gospel is easy enough for ordinary people to understand. Even for the children at the age of 4 or 5, the beautiful gospel is never difficult for them to understand. But if God spoke to us about the indwelling of the Holy Spirit in a more sophisticated way, could we have ever understood Him? God justly forgave all our sins and gave the Holy Spirit as a gift to those who believed in it.

God tells us that we cannot receive the Holy Spirit through the laying on of hands or prayers of repentance. The Holy Spirit does not come on account of fasting or devotion or even praying all night in the mountains. What kind of faith results in the reception of the Holy Spirit within us? It is faith in the fact that Jesus came into this world, was baptized to take away all our sin, died on the Cross, and was resurrected.

Do we really have to believe in this?

Why do we have to receive forgiveness of sins and thus receive the Holy Spirit? In order to be the citizens of God's Kingdom, we need His Spirit. Therefore, to receive the Holy Spirit, we need to believe in Jesus as our Savior, in His baptism and blood, and finally, we must be forgiven for our sins.

Why does God grant the Holy Spirit to those whose sins have been forgiven? The reason is to stamp them as His people. To seal those who believe in Jesus based on God's word, He gives them the Holy Spirit as a guarantee.

So many people maintain the wrong kinds of faith. It is so easy to believe in Jesus' baptism and receive the Holy Spirit. It is easy to those of us that have already received the Holy Spirit, but it is impossible for those who have not received the forgiveness of sins. They do not know the truth and instead search for other ways to receive the Holy Spirit, such as sinking themselves into a religious coma through fanatic actions. They are so ignorant that they become confused by the seeds that Satan has sown, and fall under the influence of superstitious religions.

The Holy Spirit dwells in those who believe in Jesus' baptism and His blood on the Cross and who receive the forgiveness of sin. Only those who believe in God's salvation can confess, "I have no sin." If a person does not believe in the gospel of the water and the Spirit, then they cannot say that they have no sin. Likewise, God has granted the Holy Spirit as a pledge to His children who believe in Jesus' baptism and blood on the Cross and have received the forgiveness of sin.

Who testified that Jesus' baptism and blood took away all our sins? Jesus, His disciples, and the Holy Spirit testified so. Who planned to save all people from their sins? The Holy Father did. Who carried out this plan? Jesus Christ did. Who finally guaranteed that this plan was carried out? The Holy Spirit did.

God wanted to make us His people and therefore determined to save us from all our sins through Jesus' baptism and blood. Therefore, the Divine Trinity guarantees our ultimate salvation and approves the forgiveness of our sins.

In Matthew 3:17, it is written, *"This is My beloved Son, in whom I am well pleased."* Those who have the Holy Spirit of God are the people of God. They are His children. *"This is My beloved Son, in whom I am well pleased."* Jesus is God originally. God the Father tells us, "If you want to receive forgiveness for your sins, believe that the sins of all mankind were taken away forever by Jesus, My only begotten Son, receive the Holy Spirit, and become My children." Those who believe in this will receive forgiveness for their sins and become sons and daughters of God. He gives them the gift of the Holy Spirit to seal them as His children. We receive forgiveness for our sins only when we believe in Jesus' baptism and together with blood.

When people do not evacuate their hearts and do not believe in the gospel of forgiveness, they tend to believe that original sin is gone already but that they should nevertheless ceaselessly pray the prayers of repentance to bring forgiveness for their actual sins. If they fall victim to thoughts like this, the Bible becomes incomprehensible and confusing. Therefore, they come to have different beliefs than those of His disciples.

Some say the Holy Spirit comes on them "through prayers." But this is not strictly true from a Biblical point of view. This may sound plausible, but the Bible says that when Jesus emerged from the water after being baptized by John, the Holy Spirit descended on Him like a dove. What this proves is that if we wish to receive the Holy Spirit, we only need to believe that Jesus came into this world, was baptized by John in order to take away all the sins of the world, was judged on the Cross for them and was resurrected to become our Savior.

What does God say to us when we believe in this truth and receive the Holy Spirit? He says, "You are my son. This is My beloved son, in whom I am well pleased." God will say the same thing to those who come to believe in Jesus and be forgiven for their sins in the future. This truth is God's promise to make us His children.

But people still think that there are other ways to receive the Holy Spirit. Do you think that the Holy Spirit will come upon you through your cries and earthly efforts? God's works are dictated only by His will and He gives the Holy Spirit only to those who receive forgiveness for their sins. He says, "I had My Son baptized so that He could take away all your sins and had Him crucified to be judged for them. I appointed My Son as your Savior. If you accept the forgiveness of sin that My Son accomplished, then I shall send you the Holy Spirit."

Our Father does as He wishes. Even if a man remains on his knees all night and cries for Him until his lungs are ready to burst, God won't necessarily send him the Holy Spirit. He will only rebuke him, saying, "You have not yet accepted the true knowledge and continue to cling to mistaken beliefs. The Holy Spirit will be withheld from you as long as you refuse the true faith."

In this world, the decisions of human beings may change according to circumstances, but the law that God established for forgiving sins and granting of the Holy Spirit remains immutable. If you fall under the spell of mistaken beliefs, it is difficult to find the right path again. The Bible says that Jesus is a stumbling block to those who are disobedient (1 Peter 2:8).

People who believe in Jesus and yet do not know why He was baptized only believe in half of the gospel of redemption and will certainly fall into Hell. Therefore, when you first believe in Jesus, you should know about Jesus' baptism and His blood, of which the gospel of forgiveness of sin is composed. And if you receive the forgiveness of sin, then you will also receive the Holy Spirit.

Let us think about Jesus' life on earth. Jesus became a man and took away all the sin of this world with His baptism. He also died on the Cross and was judged for our sins in order to save us from the fires of Hell. Those who believe in Him receive the Holy Spirit as a gift.

Therefore, all of us must follow the true path in order to receive the Holy Spirit. What is needed is to think according to the words of the truth. When we do this, Jesus will keep you and bless you. Those who empty their hearts and believe in His words can live in truth by receiving the forgiveness of sin, and be led by the Holy Spirit. Moreover, they can lead others along the right path with the help of the Holy Spirit.

Believe in the redemption accomplished by Jesus' baptism and His blood. Only then can we follow Him with faith and receive the blessing of the forgiveness of sin, of eternal life and the indwelling of the Holy Spirit. Jesus is the Lord of forgiveness, who took away all the sins of the world through His baptism and death on the Cross. Jesus cleansed all our sins and gave the Holy Spirit to those who believed in the gospel of truth. You can receive the Holy Spirit by adopting the true faith. ✉

SERMON 7

The beautiful gospel that allows the Holy Spirit to dwell in believers

The beautiful gospel that allows the Holy Spirit to dwell in believers

<Isaiah 9:6-7>

"For unto us a Child is born, unto us a Son is given; and the government will be upon His shoulder. And His name will be called Wonderful, Counselor, Mighty God, Everlasting Father, Prince of Peace. Of the increase of His government and peace there will be no end, upon the throne of David and over His kingdom, to order it and establish it with judgment and justice from that time forward, even forever. The zeal of the Lord of hosts will perform this."

What allows the Holy Spirit to dwell in believers?

The beautiful gospel of the water and the Spirit

In order to receive the Holy Spirit, we need to have faith in the gospel of the water and the Spirit. Our Lord is named Wonderful, Counselor, and Mighty God. Our Lord referred to Himself as the pathway to Heaven. Jesus Christ presented everybody with the gift of the beautiful gospel.

However, in this world, there are so many people who still live in darkness. They try to escape from this darkness but because they do not know of the beautiful gospel, they can never escape from their sins. Instead they wither away from their belief in false doctrines. In contrast, for those who seek the truth, they will encounter the beautiful gospel and live the rest of their lives fulfilled with God's blessings. I believe it is God's special blessing that allows me to help them find the beautiful gospel and cleanse them of their sins.

Therefore freedom from sin would be impossible if it weren't for His blessing. If we have met the Lord and received the Holy Spirit then we are very much blessed. Regrettably, many people are not aware that God's blessing comes from faith in this beautiful gospel.

God's blessing results from believing in the beautiful gospel that was given to us by Jesus Christ, His only begotten Son. Jesus is the One who saves us from the sins of the world and blesses us with His mercy. No one else can save us from our sins and or help us erase the guilt in our hearts. Who could possibly save himself from his own sins and the pain of eternal death?

God tells us, *"There is a way that seems right to a man, but its end is the way of death" (Proverbs 16:25)*. People establish their own religions and drive themselves toward destruction and death. Many religions boast that they emphasize righteousness and show their own ways to save people from their sins but it is only the gospel of the water and the Spirit, which our Lord gave us, that can save us from all our sins. Only Jesus is the Savior who can save sinners from their sins.

In John 14:6, our Lord said, *"I am the way, the truth, and the life."* He gave His own flesh and blood to those on their way to death. He also referred to Himself as the way to true life.

God says that if one does not believe in Jesus' beautiful gospel, he cannot enter the Kingdom of Heaven.

We must believe in the gospel of the water and the Spirit, be forgiven for our sins and believe that He is our Savior in order to enter the Kingdom of Heaven.

Once in ancient Israel!

"Now it came to pass in the days of Ahaz the son of Jotham, the son of Uzziah, king of Judah, that Rezin king of Syria and Pekah the son of Remaliah, king of Israel, went up to Jerusalem to make war against it, but could not prevail against it" (Isaiah 7:1).

Israel was originally one nation. However, Israel became divided into south and north. The temple of God was in Jerusalem of Southern Judea, where Rehoboam, the son of King Solomon, ruled. Later, Jeroboam, one of Solomon's servants, established another nation in the north and so Israel became divided. From that time, faith in God deteriorated. The deterioration of faith became the source of today's heretical religions. Jeroboam thus became the originator of heretics. He amended the law of God because he needed to keep his throne and therefore, became the father of heretics. He created a different religion for His people in Israel, the Northern Kingdom and he even tried to invade Judah, the Southern Kingdom. Almost 200 years passed by, but the hostile relations between two kingdoms were unchanged.

However, God spoke through Isaiah, *"Because Syria, Ephraim, and the son of Remaliah have plotted evil against you, saying, 'Let us go up against Judah and trouble it, and let us make a gap in its wall for ourselves, and set a king over them, the son of Tabel.' — thus says the Lord God: 'It shall not stand, nor shall it come to pass. For the head of Syria is Damascus, and the head of Damascus is Rezin. Within sixty-five years Ephraim will be broken, so that it will not be a people. The head of Ephraim is Samaria, and the head of Samaria is Remaliah's son. If you will not believe, surely you shall not be established'" (Isaiah 7:5-9).*

At that time, God prophesized through Isaiah to King Ahaz, but the king had no faith in Him. Ahaz was merely worried that he wouldn't even be able to hold out against Syria's army, but hearing about the invasion of Syria and Israel in alliance with one another, he shivered in fear. But a servant of God, Isaiah, came and told him, "In less than sixty-five years, north Israel will be broken. And the evil conspiracy the two kings have plotted will never come true."

God's servant told King Ahaz to seek a sign from God. *"Ask a sign for yourself from the LORD your God; ask it either in the depth or in the height above" (Isaiah 7:11). "Hear now, O house of David! Is it a small thing for you to weary men, but will you weary my God also? Therefore the Lord Himself will give you a sign: Behold, the virgin shall conceive and bear a Son, and shall call His name Immanuel" (Isaiah 7:13-14).* This was His prophecy: That He would save His people from their sins.

Who is the enemy of God?

The enemy of humanity is sin and sin originates from Satan. And who is the Savior from our sins? The Savior is none other than Jesus Christ, the Son of God. Man has fundamental weaknesses of flesh and therefore cannot but commit sin. He is under Satan's power. A great many people still visit fortunetellers and try to live their lives exactly as these false prophets instruct them. This is direct evidence that they are under Satan's control.

The Lord gave Isaiah evidence of salvation, saying that a virgin would give birth to a Son and name Him Immanuel. It was God's plan to send Jesus in the likeness of sinful flesh of a man and have Him save sinners from Satan's oppression. In accordance with the prophecy, Jesus came into this world as a human being born of the virgin Mary.

If Jesus had not come to us, we would still have been living under the reign of Satan. But Jesus came into this world and was baptized by John and died on the Cross in order to give us the beautiful gospel that would save all sinners from their sins. Therefore, many people believed in the beautiful gospel, received forgiveness for their sins and became children of God.

Even nowadays, many theologians argue as to whether Jesus Christ is God or man. The conservative theologians say "Jesus is God," but some New Theologians retort by arguing that Jesus was Joseph's illegitimate child. What a lamentable assertion this is!

Some New theologians say that they cannot believe that Jesus had the ability to walk on water. They say, "Jesus actually walked on a low hill over the horizon and His disciples, seeing Him from far away, thought He was walking on water." Present-day doctors of divinity who belong to the schools of the New Theology aren't all great men of theology. Most of them choose to believe only what they can comprehend in the Bible.

To give another example, the Bible says that Jesus fed 5,000 people with two fish and five loaves of breads. But they remain very skeptical regarding this miracle. They explain it in the following terms. "People were following Jesus and were starving to death. So Jesus asked His disciples to gather together all the leftover food. Then a child gave Him his meal voluntarily, and all the other adults were touched and took out their own food. So after they had gathered all the food together and eaten, twelve baskets were left over." These kinds of theologians simply try to make God's words fit their own very limited understanding.

Believing in God's truth is simply having faith in the beautiful gospel God gave. Faith does not mean believing one thing just because it seems to make sense but failing to believe in something else because it doesn't. Whether we can comprehend it or not, we must trust Him and accept His words as they are written.

The fact that Jesus came to us as the Son of Man means that He was sent to save us from all our sins. Jesus, who is God, came to this earth to save us. Isaiah had prophesied that He would come to us as the Son of Man, born of a virgin.

In Genesis 3:15, the Lord God said to the serpent, *"And I will put enmity between you and the woman, and between your seed and her seed; He shall bruise your head, and you shall bruise His heel."* This means that God had planned to send Jesus, in the appearance as a man, as our Savior to save mankind from their sins.

In the Bible, it is written, *"O Death, where is your sting? O Hades, where is your victory? The sting of death is sin, and the strength of sin is the law" (1 Corinthians 15:55-56).* The sting of death is sin. When a man sins, death makes him its slave. But our Lord promised, "The seed of the woman shall bruise your head." This means Jesus would destroy the sting of the sin that Satan brought.

Jesus came into this world, was baptized to take away all the sins of the world and was crucified and judged for them. He saved from their sins all those who believe in the beautiful gospel. When Adam and Eve sinned, God promised to save mankind from Satan's power. In the modern world, the enemy of God is those who do not believe in the beautiful gospel.

Why was Jesus born in this world?

God gave us the law and the beautiful gospel to save us from our sins. Under the law of God, people became sinners in His presence. Likewise, the law was given so that people could come to know their sins. When people became slaves to sin and to the law itself, our Lord came into this world to fulfill the righteous requirements of the law.

Jesus was born under the law. He was born in the age of the law. The reason people needed the law was that they needed to know their sins in order to receive forgiveness for them. People clean the dirt from their clothes only when they realize they're dirty. Likewise, in order to recognize their sins, people should know the law of God. If there was no law, there wouldn't be any sense of sins, and Jesus would not have had to come into this world.

If you know the law of God, then you have a chance to meet Him. We knew of the law and therefore were able to learn about our sins. Only after we knew of our sin did Jesus Christ bring the beautiful gospel for us to believe in. If God did not grant us the law, then we would not be sinners and judgment would not exist. Thus, God gave us the law and presented us with the beautiful gospel to save all sinners from their sins.

The law that must exist between the Creator and His

creation is God's law of salvation. This is the law of love. God told man, *"But of the tree of the knowledge of good and evil you shall not eat"* (Genesis 2:17). This was the law God granted us, and the law became the basis of the love with which God saved us all from our sins. The law of salvation had its foundation in the forgiveness of our sins. God tells us that He is our Creator and that everything came to exist according to His will. This means that God is the Absolute Being and that people should believe in the law of salvation that was accomplished through the beautiful gospel.

The Absolute God is absolutely good. God's love for this world prompted Him to sacrifice His only begotten Son, who became the Savior of all sinners. If God made us and did not give us the beautiful gospel to save us from our sins, we would have raised complaints against Him. But God wanted to save us from our own destruction and therefore established the law of salvation. Because of the law, we were able to realize our sins and by looking at them directly, start to believe in Jesus' beautiful gospel. When we violate God's word, we are manifested as sinners before the law, and after all we sinners kneel down to beg for His mercy of forgiveness of sin before God.

Jesus was born of a woman and came into this world to save mankind from sin. Jesus came into this world as a man to fulfill God's plan for us. We believe in His beautiful gospel. Therefore, we praise the Lord.

Some complain, "Why did God make me so fragile that I fell so easily into sin and have suffered so much for my wrongdoing?" But God never wanted us to suffer. He allowed us to suffer because we were skeptical of Jesus' gospel. God gave us both suffering and the beautiful gospel so that we would have the same power as Him as His children. This was

His plan.

But the demons say, "No! No! God is a dictator! Go ahead and live as you wish. Be independent! Make your fortunes through your own efforts!" The demons also try to block mankind's belief in God. But those who choose to live apart from God are barriers to His plan for salvation. Jesus came into this world and called those who are under the power of Satan to renounce their sins. We should not live apart from God.

Man is born a sinner who is destined to Hell

There is no truth on this earth that does not change. But the beautiful gospel of Jesus is the unalterable truth. Therefore, people can depend on that truth and be delivered from the power of Satan. Mankind inherited the sins of Adam and Eve and without Christ's intervention would be doomed to the fires of Hell. Instead, thanks to His sacrifice, man was blessed with the power to become a child of God. *"Nevertheless the gloom will not be upon her who is distressed" (Isaiah 9:1).* God sent His Son to this world and glorified those who believe in the beautiful salvation.

"The people who walked in darkness have seen a great light; those who dwelt in the land of the shadow of death, upon them a light has shined" (Isaiah 9:2). Today, this word comes true to you and me. By believing in the beautiful gospel, we were blessed with eternal life, which we cannot have on this earth. Jesus Christ saved mankind from all the sins of the world and to those who believe in the beautiful gospel, He gave eternal life and the Kingdom of Heaven.

He shed the beautiful light of the gospel on those who were hopeless

Man, like a fog, exists in this world for a while but soon disappears. His life is like that of annual plants and grass. Grass retains its life force for only a few months during the year and disappears according to the Providence of God. All is vanity in our lives as meaningless as this grass. But God gave the beautiful gospel to our exhausted souls and with His righteousness, made us His children. What an amazing grace this is! Our meaningless lives became eternal lives thanks to God's love and we were also blessed with the right to become His children.

Here is the confession of a soul who was blessed with God's grace by believing in the beautiful gospel.

"I was born in a family that did not believe in God. Therefore, I was brought up thinking it beautiful for my mother to pray to the gods of heaven and earth for the well being of my family every morning with a bowl of water in front of her. As I was growing up, I did not know of my value or the reason for my existence, which made me believe that it really didn't matter whether I lived or died. Because I was unaware of my worth, I lived in solitude.

This kind of life exhausted me and so I rushed to get married. My married life was a good one. I had nothing to wish for, so I lived a quiet and serene life. Then I had a child and from that time I found that love started to appear in me. I began to lose my selfish desires but I also feared the loss of those closest to me.

Thus, I began searching for God. I was fragile and incapable and therefore, needed an Absolute Being to keep watch over my loved ones. So I started to attend church but my faith was little different from that of my mother as she prayed in front of the bowl of water — my prayer was only based on vague fears and hopes.

Once, I attended one of the small meetings held at the local church and while I was praying, tears started to fall from my eyes. I was embarrassed and tried to stop crying, but the tears continued to fall. The people around me laid their hands on my head and congratulated me for receiving the Holy Spirit. But I was bewildered. I wasn't even familiar with God's words and my faith in Him was only vague, so I had no confidence that this force was of the Holy Spirit.

The church that I attended was associated with the Pentecostal-Charismatic Movement, and many had experiences like me and almost everybody spoke in tongues. One day, I was invited to a revival meeting led by a pastor who people said had been filled with the Holy Spirit. The pastor gathered numerous people at the church and said He would heal someone's sinusitis as it was in his spiritual powers to do so. However, I thought sinusitis was an illness easily healed in hospitals, so I was more interested in how he had received the Holy Spirit. But after the pastor appeared to succeed in his attempts at healing, he began to boast that he could predict whether a high school student would succeed in his or her university entrance exam or not. A lot of people praised his powers as if they were God's.

But I could not understand him. And I could not say that whatever power the pastor had, had anything to do with the Holy Spirit. I didn't think it was important whether he could heal sinusitis or forecast someone's success on an exam. So, I could not take his apparent miracles as the works of the Holy Spirit.

The power and love of God that I had in mind was different from what I saw. For that reason, I stopped attending that church and avoided the people who believed in the pastor's powers. After that, I attended a quieter church, which I chose because I believed it dealt more with God's words. I learned of the law and through it that I was very unrighteous. God became the object of my fear and I learned that I could not look honorable in His presence and that His Spirit appeared to be neglecting me.

In Isaiah 59:1-2 it is written, *"Behold, the Lord's hand is not shortened, that it cannot save; nor His ear heavy, that it cannot hear. But your iniquities have separated you from your God; and your sins have hidden His face from you, so that He will not hear."* This appeared to fit my situation. It was impossible for me to become His child and receive the Holy Spirit because everything I did or thought was sinful.

I feared God and so consistently gave prayers of repentance. No one told me to do so, but I wanted to stand honorably in front of God. Because I was sinful, I earnestly offered even more prayers of repentance. But these prayers failed to wash away my sins. All I did was show Him my thoughts and sincerity so my sins were still in me. From that time, I began to issue complaints against God. I wished to be perfect in His eyes but I couldn't be perfect right away, so my complaints and sins piled up.

During this time of religious confusion, my father had a stroke. He suffered for 40 days in operating rooms and hospital beds before he passed away. But I could not once pray for my father. I was a sinner, so I thought that if I prayed for my father, his pain would only worsen. I was distressed at my lack of faith and I wished to follow God but couldn't, so I continued to complain and at last turned away from Him. My religious life ended like that. I thought if I believed in Him, His Spirit would dwell in me and I would find peace, but that was not the case. After that, my life became even more meaningless and I lived in fear and unhappiness.

But the Lord did not desert me. He caused me to encounter a believer who had truly received the Holy Spirit through God's words. I learned from this person that Jesus had taken our sins through His baptism by John and that He had been judged for them on the Cross. Therefore, all the sins of this world, including mine, were all forgiven. When I heard and came to understand this, I could see that all my sins were cleansed. God helped me receive forgiveness for my sins, gave me the blessing of the Holy Spirit and granted me a peaceful life. He silently led me, gave me a clear understanding of good and evil and endowed me with the power to overcome the temptations of this world. He answered my prayers and helped me live a righteous and worthwhile life. I truly thank God for giving me the Holy Spirit."

Every one of us is blessed with the Lord's grace and is capable of receiving the Holy Spirit. I thank the Lord for giving us His beautiful gospel. God blessed the righteous with such happiness. The hearts of the righteous are joyous. The Lord granted us eternal happiness. We know how precious God's salvation, love and grace are and we are thankful for them. The Lord gave us happiness through the beautiful gospel of Heaven. This is something that cannot be bought with money. God sent us the Holy Spirit as well as the beautiful gospel in order to make us jubilant and upright. The beautiful gospel is what makes our lives blessed. The Lord gave us the beautiful gospel and He is happy that the righteous ones enjoy a blessed life.

As it is recorded in Luke, Mary said, *"For with God nothing will be impossible... Behold the maidservant of the*

Lord! Let it be to me according to your word"(Luke 1:37-38).
The moment Mary believed in the beautiful words God, as
spoken by His angel, Jesus was conceived. Likewise, through
their faith, the righteous conceive the beautiful gospel in their
hearts.

*"For You have broken the yoke of his burden and the staff
of his shoulder, the rod of his oppressor, as in the day of
Midian" (Isaiah 9:4).* Satan caused all the distress, illnesses,
and oppression in our lives but we are far too weak to
overcome him. But God loves us and so He fought against
Satan and defeated him.

*"For unto us a Child is born, unto us a Son is given; and
the government will be upon His shoulder. And His name will
be called Wonderful, Counselor, Mighty God, Everlasting
Father, Prince of Peace. Of the increase of His government and
peace there will be no end, upon the throne of David and over
His kingdom, to order it and establish it with judgment and
justice from that time forward, even forever. The zeal of the
Lord of hosts will perform this" (Isaiah 9:6-7).*

God promised to glorify us as His children through the
beautiful gospel that Jesus brought. He defeated Satan in
accordance with His promise and delivered us from the power
of Satan.

The Lord came to the earth and with His power promised
to take away all the darkness of sin. So we also call our Lord,
the Wonderful one. He has done many wonderful things for us.
God's decision to come to this world as the Son of Man was
mysterious. *"Come now, and let us reason together. Though
your sins are like scarlet, they shall be as white as snow;
though they are red like crimson, they shall be as wool" (Isaiah
1:18).*

The Lord promised to save us from our sins and give us

eternal forgiveness. Jesus is referred to as the Wonderful one and, accordingly, He has done miraculous works for us. *"His name will be called Counselor, Mighty God."* God, as our Counselor, planned our salvation with the beautiful gospel and carried out His plan to save us eternally from our sins.

The foolishness of God is wiser than man. It was His wisdom for Jesus to be baptized by John and to die on the Cross in order the save us from all our sins. This is mysterious work that He did for us, but it is the law of love that saved us from all our sins. The law of love is the gospel of truth that leads us to receive the Holy Spirit through the water and His blood.

The Lord says in Isaiah 53:10, *"Yet it pleased the LORD to bruise Him; he has put Him to grief."* Jesus made His soul an offering for sin in order to do the will of God. He passed on the sins of the world to His Son, Jesus Christ, and had Him suffer the pain of crucifixion in order that He would be judged for them. This is the beautiful gospel that saved mankind from their sins once and for all. Christ offered His life for us, paid the wages of sin and blessed us with salvation.

The sacrificial system of God

How many sins did Jesus take through His baptism by John?

Past, present and future sins from the time of the beginning to that of the end

The Bible speaks of an offering that once resulted in

forgiveness for a day's sins. A sinner had to bring an animal without blemish and lay his hands on the animal's head in order to pass on his sins. Then he had to kill the sacrifice and hand its blood to the priest. And the priest took some of the animal's blood and put it on the horns of the altar of burnt offerings and poured the remainder at the base of the alter.

In this way, he could be forgiven for a day's sins. The laying on of hands was the way for a sinner to pass on his sins to the sacrifice. Those who offered their sacrifices in accordance with the sacrificial system could receive forgiveness for their sins. The sacrificial system was the way we atoned for our sins in the time before Jesus took away all sin.

God also had appointed the Day of Atonement so that the people of Israel could make atonement for the sins committed over the course of an entire year. The sacrifice took place on the tenth day of the seventh month. God appointed Aaron, the high priest, as the one who passed on the year's sins of all Israelites to the scapegoat. The ritual was carried out in accordance with God's plan. The forgiveness of sins came from His wisdom and love for mankind. This is His power.

"The horns of the altar of burnt offering" stands for "the Books of Judgment" (Revelation 20:12), where the sins of mankind are recorded. The reason the priest put the blood of the sin offering on the horns of the altar of burnt offerings was to erase the names and their transgressions written in the Book of Judgment. The blood is the life of all flesh. The sacrifice took away the Israelite's sins and the scapegoat was killed to pay the wages of sin. God had them kill a sacrificial animal to accept the judgment for their sins. This was a sign of His wisdom and love for us.

Jesus Christ came to this world as an offering for sin in

order to accomplish God's plan. Jesus took away the sins of the world through His sacrifice. If we look at the words of this promise, we see, "Yet it pleased the LORD to bruise Him; he has put Him to grief" or "He took away the sin of the world."

"For unto us a Child is born, unto us a Son is given; and the government will be upon His shoulder. And His name will be called the Wonderful, Counselor, Mighty God, Everlasting Father, Prince of Peace. Of the increase of His government and peace there will be no end, upon the throne of David and over His kingdom, to order it and establish it with judgment and justice from that time forward, even forever. The zeal of the Lord of hosts will perform this" (Isaiah 9:6-7).

The mysterious and wonderful promise was that Jesus would carry out God's will and give all believers peace by taking away the sins of the world. God's promise was a promise of love, by which He planned to bring peace to all mankind. This is what God promised us, and this is what He did.

Matthew 1:18 says, *"Now the birth of Jesus Christ was as follows: After His mother Mary was betrothed to Joseph, before they came together, she was found with child of Holy Spirit."* "Jesus" means Savior, the one who will save His people from their sins. "Christ" means the King Anointed, King. Jesus had no sins, and He is our King and Savior who was born of a virgin in order to save His people from their sins.

"'And she will bring forth a Son, and you shall call His name JESUS, for He will save His people from their sins.' So all this was done that it might be fulfilled which was spoken by the Lord through the prophet" (Matthew 1:21-22).

Jesus took all the sins of the world along with Him through His baptism

It is written in Matthew 3:13-17, *"Then Jesus came from Galilee to John at Jordan to be baptized by him. And John tried to prevent Him, saying, 'I need to be baptized by You, and are You coming to me?' But Jesus answered and said to him, 'Permit it to be so now, for thus it is fitting for us to fulfill all righteousness.' Then he allowed Him. When He had been baptized, Jesus came up immediately from the water; and behold, the heavens were opened to Him, and He saw the Spirit of God descending like a dove and alighting upon Him."*

John the Baptist appears in this passage. Why did Jesus have to be baptized by John? Jesus had to be baptized in order to take on all the sins in the world, and take them all away according to God's plan.

"The Government will be upon His shoulder" (Isaiah 9:7). Here "the government" means that Jesus is the One who has the authority and power as the Master of Heaven, as the King of the world. This is the authority granted only to Jesus Christ. Jesus did a wonderful thing to take away all the sins of mankind. This wonderful thing was for Him to be baptized by John. What Jesus meant by saying *"Thus it is fitting for us to fulfill all righteousness"* is that taking away all sins of the world was right and fitting.

Romans 1:17 says, *"For in it the righteousness of God is revealed from faith to faith."* God's righteousness is revealed in the gospel. Does the true gospel of the water and the Spirit really reveals God's righteousness? Yes! The true gospel is that Jesus Christ took away all the sins of the world through His baptism and crucifixion. The gospel of the water and the Spirit is the beautiful gospel in which the righteousness of God is revealed. How did Jesus take away the sins of the world? He took away all the sins of the world when John baptized Him in the Jordan River.

"All righteousness" is *"dikaiosune"* in Greek. This means that Jesus took away all the sins of mankind in the most just and wonderful way. It means that Jesus' cleansing of all the sins of the world was absolutely just and fair. Jesus had to be baptized by John in order to blot out the sins of the world.

God knew that Jesus' baptism was absolutely necessary in order to bring peace to mankind. Jesus could not have become our Savior, if He hadn't been baptized by John and shed His blood on the Cross. Jesus served as the sin offering in taking away all the sins of the world.

God says in Isaiah 53:6, *"All we like sheep have gone astray; we have turned, every one, to his own way. And the LORD has laid on Him the iniquity of us all."* Jesus had to accept all the sins of the world in order to do God's will. This is the reason that Jesus came as a sin offering in the flesh of a man and was baptized by John.

Jesus had to accept all the sins of mankind and be judged for them so that He could fulfill God's plan and express His undying love. When Jesus emerged from the water after His baptism, God said, *"This is My beloved Son, in whom I am well pleased"* (Matthew 3:17).

A baby was born unto us

"For unto us a Child is born, unto us a Son is given; and the government will be upon His shoulder and His name will be called Wonderful, Counselor, Mighty God, Everlasting

Father, Prince of Peace" (Isaiah 9:6). Jesus is the Son of God. Jesus is the God of Creation who created the whole universe. Not only is He the Son of the Almighty God, He is also the Creator and the King of Peace. Jesus is the God who gave happiness to mankind.

Jesus is the God of truth. He took away all our sins, saved us, and gave us peace. Is there sin in this world? No, there is no sin. The reason we can confidently say that there is no sin is that we believe in the beautiful gospel, which says that Jesus washed away all the sins of the world through His baptism and blood on the Cross. Jesus did not lie to us. Jesus paid the wages of sin with His baptism and blood. He let everyone who believed in this become His child and gave peace to us all. He made us live as His sanctified children in faith for eternity. I praise the Lord and give thanks to Him.

Behold! The Lamb of God who takes away the sin of the world!

John 1:29 says, *"The next day John saw Jesus coming toward him, and said, 'Behold! The Lamb of God who takes away the sin of the world!'"* Jesus Christ appeared again in front of John the Baptist the day after He took away all the sins of the world through His baptism. John the Baptist bore witness to Jesus by saying, *"Behold! The Lamb of God who takes away the sin of the world!"* He bore witness again in John 1:35-36, *"Again, the next day, John stood with two of his disciples. And looking at Jesus as He walked, he said, 'Behold the Lamb of God!'"*

Jesus was the Messiah who came as the Lamb of God, just

as God had promised in the Old Testament. The Messiah Jesus Christ came to us as the Wonderful One, Counselor and Mighty God, and was baptized to save us from all our sins. A baby was born unto us. He accepted all the sins of the world through His baptism by John, paid the wage of sin, and became the Prince of Peace who gives us peace and remission of all our sins. *"Behold! The Lamb of God who takes away the sin of the world"*

People once had no other choice but to die for their sins. Humans were destined to commit countless sins due to their sinful natures and eventually be condemned to Hell. They led miserable lives; not one of them could enter or even dream of the Kingdom of God due to their weaknesses. Jesus Christ, who is our God, accepted all their sins when He was baptized by John in the Jordan River and was crucified in judgment for their wrongdoing. Upon His death, Christ said, *"It is finished" (John 19:30)*. This was the cry of His witness to the fact that Jesus saved all mankind from their sins and death, and that He absolutely delivered anyone who believed in the beautiful gospel.

"Behold! The Lamb of God who takes away the sin of the world." Do you know where all the sins of the world are? Aren't they on the body of Jesus Christ? Where are all the sins and trespasses that humble us in this world? They were all transferred to Jesus Christ. Where are all our sins? They are in the flesh of the One with the principality upon His shoulder; they are in the flesh of Almighty God.

All the sins from birth to the grave!

We commit sin throughout our lives. We committed sins

from the day we were born until the day we turned 20. Where did all of those sins committed for 20 years go? They were transferred to Jesus Christ's flesh. The sins that we committed between the ages of 21 and 40 were passed on to Jesus too. No matter how many years a person lives, the sins he committed from the beginning of his life until the end were transferred to Jesus Christ. All the sins that mankind committed, starting from Adam to the last person on this earth, were transferred to Jesus. Even the sins of our children and grandchildren were already passed on to Jesus. All sins were transferred to Jesus at the time He was baptized.

Are there still sins in this world? No. Not one is left. There is no sin left in the world because we believe in the beautiful gospel that Jesus Christ gave us. Do you have sin in your heart? No. Amen! We believe in the beautiful gospel that says Jesus Christ saved us from all our sins. We praise Almighty Jesus for doing this wonderful work for us.

Jesus Christ restored our lost lives to us. Now we believe in the beautiful gospel so that we are able to live with God. Even the people who were enemies of God – the sinners who had no other choice but to hide in the dark forests – can now be saved from their sins by believing in the beautiful gospel.

The beautiful gospel teaches us that the Lord washed all our sins clean when he was baptized by John, crucified and resurrected. We became sanctified children of God by believing in Jesus' gospel. Jesus offered His own body as the offering for our sins. He, the Son of Almighty God, who never committed a single sin in this world, took away all the sins of the world and saved everyone who believes in Him. Isaiah 53:5 says, *"He was wounded for our transgressions, he was bruised for our iniquities."*

Jesus took away all the sins of the world, including both

original sin and actual sins and left out not a single transgression. He paid the wages of sin with His death on the Cross and thereby saved us from all our sins. Jesus washed away all the sins of the world through this beautiful gospel. We have found new life through Jesus. Those who believe in this beautiful gospel are no longer dead in spirit. We now have new and eternal life, for Jesus paid all the wages of our sin. We have become children of God by believing in the beautiful gospel of Jesus Christ.

Do you believe that Jesus Christ is the Son of God? Do you also believe that He is your Savior? I do. Jesus Christ is the Life to us. We found new life through Him. We were destined to die because of our sins and trespasses. But Jesus paid the wages of sin through His baptism and death on the Cross. He delivered us from our slavery to sin, from the power of death, and the bonds of Satan.

The Lord is the God who saved us from our sins and became the savior of everyone who believes in Jesus. When we look at Hebrews 10:10-12, 14 and 18, we can see that the Lord sanctified us so that there was no further need to receive the remission of sins. We enter the Kingdom of God by believing in Jesus. We were destined to die for our sins and trespasses, but we are now able to enter Heaven and enjoy eternal life by believing in Jesus' baptism and blood.

"The good shepherd gives his life for the sheep" (John 10:11). Our Lord came into this world in order to save us from the sins of the world through His baptism, His death on the Cross, and His resurrection. He also gives the indwelling of the Holy Spirit to those who have received the remission of their sins by believing in this truth. Thank you, Lord. Your gospel is the beautiful gospel, which can give believers the indwelling of the Holy Spirit. Hallelujah! I praise the Lord. ⊠

SERMON 8

Through who does the living water of the Holy Spirit flow?

Through who does the living water of the Holy Spirit flow?

<John 7:37-38>

"On the last day, that great day of the feast, Jesus stood and cried out, saying, 'If anyone thirsts, let him come to Me and drink. He who believes in Me, as the Scripture has said, out of his heart will flow rivers of living water.'"

Who can drink the living water of the Holy Spirit?

Those who believe in the beautiful gospel of Jesus' baptism and His blood at the Cross

The living water of the Holy Spirit flows out of the hearts of those who believe in the beautiful gospel. John 7:38 says, *"He who believes in Me, as Scripture has said, out of his heart will flow rivers of living water."* This means that there is true salvation and the remission of sins for those who believe in the beautiful gospel that God gave us.

When does the indwelling of the Holy Spirit take place? The indwelling of the Holy Spirit can be obtained when one hears and believes in the true gospel, which says that Jesus Christ took away all the sins of the world through His baptism by John. One can then drink the living water of the Holy Spirit. Those who believe in the beautiful gospel have the indwelling of the Holy Spirit, and can experience the feeling of the Spiritual living water freshly overflowing and moistening their dry hearts every time they're preaching or hearing God's words.

The living water of the Holy Spirit flows out of the hearts of those who believe in the gospel of the water and the Spirit, which says that the Lord came into this world in order to save all sinners from their sins. The Holy Spirit is the truth that can't be separated from the gospel of the water and the Spirit, and rests in the people who believe in God's words.

Anyone who wants to drink the living water of the Holy Spirit must receive the remission of all his sins by believing in the beautiful gospel of Jesus' baptism and His blood at the Cross. This living water of the Holy Spirit exists in the hearts of those who believe in God's words. People who believe in the gospel of the water and the Spirit have the living water of the Holy Spirit, which flows like a river, streaming through their hearts. Even at this moment, the living water of the Holy Spirit is gushing out like spring water in the hearts of those who have received the remission of their sins by believing in the beautiful gospel of Jesus Christ's baptism and His blood on the Cross.

However, there is not even a single drop of living water of the Holy Spirit flowing out of the hearts of those who don't believe in this beautiful gospel of truth. Until I believed and acknowledged the gospel of the water and the Spirit, I didn't have a single drop of Spiritual living water flowing out of my heart. At that time, even though I fervently believed in Jesus Christ, I didn't even know of the importance of the living water of the Holy Spirit because I didn't have the Holy Spirit in my heart. However, now I have the beautiful gospel of the water and the Spirit, and the living water of the Holy Spirit flowing freely out from my heart.

Now the living water of the Holy Spirit flows out of my heart, and out of the hearts of those who hear and believe in God's word. Just as Jesus said, *"If anyone thirsts, let him come to Me and drink,"* the living water of the Holy Spirit refreshes others through born again Christians who believe in the beautiful gospel of the water and the Spirit. This living water flows out of my heart together with my faith in the gospel of the water and the Spirit even at this moment, allowing others to drink from it. God lets the living water of the Holy Spirit flow out of my heart like a river. This is something familiar only to those who have the indwelling of the Holy Spirit.

Just as it's written in Revelation that no one knows except those who have received it, the indwelling of the Holy Spirit and the living water is a secret known only to those who know and believe in the beautiful gospel of the water and the Spirit. Therefore, you should know in whom the Holy Spirit dwells. You should know that the indwelling of the Holy Spirit is given only to those who believe in Jesus' gospel.

I used to believe only in the blood on the Cross

Even though I believed in Jesus' blood on the Cross for over ten years, sin was still in my heart. At that time, I had the belief that my sins were forgiven only through Jesus' blood. However, I could receive neither complete remission of sin nor the indwelling of the Holy Spirit through this kind of belief, and there was only confusion and emptiness in my life. The only sign that showed my belief in Jesus was the fact that I was attending church.

That is when I started to reconsider my beliefs. 'Had I really received the Holy Spirit?' When I first came to believe in Jesus, my heart was passionate with love for Him and even I had the gift of tongues. But what had become of me? I realized that this experience of burning emotion was not a sign of the indwelling of the Holy Spirit and that I hadn't received the Holy Spirit at all. I believed in Jesus but the Holy Spirit and the living water of the Holy Spirit were not in my heart.

It wasn't really important if my heart was hot or cold, since my faith was based on [4]**Calvinism**. The questions I really had to answer were the following:

(1) Does the Holy Spirit dwell in me? — No. I am not sure He is in me. —

(2) Is there sin in me? — Yes, there is. — There was definitely sin in me then, even though I believed in Jesus' blood on the Cross. I still had sin in my heart, even though I believed in Jesus and said prayers of repentance every day. The sin in my heart was never completely cleansed no matter how hard I tried.

'How can I receive the indwelling of the Holy Spirit?' 'How can I wash away the sin in my heart?' These were the

---

[4] A system of Christian interpretation initiated by John Calvin. It emphasizes predestination and salvation. The five points of Calvinism were developed in response to the Arminian position.
Calvinism teaches: 1) **Total depravity:** that man is touched by sin in all parts of his being: body, soul, mind, and emotions, 2) **Unmerited favor:** that God's favor to man is completely by His free choice and has nothing to do with man. It is completely undeserved by man, 3) **Limited atonement:** that Christ did not bear the sins of every individual who ever lived, but instead only bore the sins of those who were elected into salvation, 4) **Irresistible grace:** that God's call to someone for salvation cannot be resisted, 5) **Perseverance of the saints:** that it is not possible to lose one's salvation. But you can clearly discern its teachings from the gospel of the water and the Spirit, especially in regard to its doctrine of the limited atonement.

two nagging problems that I had in my mind, even after I came to believe in Jesus. I had spoken in tongues after I came to believe in Jesus and I also believed that my sins were cleansed thanks to my faith in Jesus' blood.

However, as time went on, more and more sins piled up in my heart. I was full of sin.
The prayers of repentance or fasting couldn't wash away the sins in my heart as long as I was relying on Jesus' blood alone. I worried for a long time about my actual sins. The more I worried, the more vehemently I preached the message of Jesus to others. I also attended church even more regularly and devoted myself to serving Jesus, relying on His blood.

However, as time went on, the actual sins in my heart were blocking me from having true faith. It was harder to believe in Jesus than ever before. I tried to rely more on Jesus' blood and put forth my best effort and increased my dedication to God. However, the emptiness in my heart became greater. This kind of faith left me feeling empty and lethargic, and turned me into a hypocritical Christian who only cared about outward appearances. Thinking to myself, 'Believing in Jesus is like this for everyone, it's not just me!' I tried to deny that my faith was misguided. However, the blood of Jesus and the prayers of repentance still couldn't wash away all my actual sins.

Then by what faith could my actual sins be cleansed? My actual sins could be washed away only through my belief that all my sins were transferred to Jesus when He was baptized in the Jordan River. This is what is written in Matthew 3:13-17. Then why were my actual sins not washed away by Jesus' blood? I didn't know and believe in the beautiful gospel, which contains the meaning of John's baptism on Jesus.

Does this mean that all the sins of the world were washed away through Jesus' baptism? Yes, that's right. The Bible bears witness to this by saying, *"One cannot enter the kingdom of God unless he is born again of water and the Spirit" (John 3:3-5)*. Jesus came into this world and accepted all the sins of the world through His baptism by John.

I was still doubtful about this and compared the Old and New Testaments to clarify this. The result was that I found out it was indeed true. All the sins of the world were passed on to Jesus when He was baptized, and all my sins were also passed on to Him at that time. I became sanctified through my faith in these words. I came to realize that this was the word of truth as it is written in the Bible and it is the most beautiful gospel in the world.

In addition, I realized why my sins were not blotted out through my faith in Jesus' blood alone. The reason was that I couldn't pass my actual sins on to Jesus when I didn't know the truth of His baptism in the Jordan River. I had finally met the truth. I learned that Jesus came into this world for me, and that He took away all the sins of the world through His baptism, and was later crucified to deliver us from all the sins of the world. I also learned and believed in the truth that the purpose of Jesus' baptism and His blood on the Cross was to take away all the sins of the world. Now I am righteous thanks to my belief in the beautiful gospel Jesus gave us, and because all my sins had been forgiven.

It was not the doctrines of the church that blotted out my sins, it was Jesus' baptism and His blood on the Cross that did so. This truth was in the beautiful gospel. I was saved from all my sins and became righteous not through my belief in Jesus' blood alone, but through my faith that Jesus' baptism and His blood on the Cross are of my salvation.

One more thing I need to give thanks for is that God's Holy Spirit came upon me after I started to believe in the beautiful gospel. Now the Holy Spirit dwells in me together with the words of Jesus' baptism by John and His blood on the Cross.

I thank the Lord who gave me this beautiful gospel and who let me preach the same beliefs as those of Jesus' Apostles. God gifted me with the Holy Spirit, even though the only thing I did was to believe in the beautiful gospel. Now I can deliver this message with great honor and conviction to all the people in the world. Assuredly I can tell them that believing only in Jesus' blood won't blot out all their sins!

But I can tell them that all their sins will surely be washed away only if they believe in the beautiful gospel, which tells of the baptism of Jesus by John and His blood on the Cross. I don't have even the slightest shame in front of God as I preach this beautiful gospel. I can now honorably preach this beautiful gospel of being born again of water and the Spirit to all the people of the world. I give thanks to the Lord. I thank the Lord who let me drink the living water of the Holy Spirit by giving me the gospel of the water and the Spirit.

Clinical tests show that the true gospel is that of the water and the Spirit

Have you really received remission of your sins and the indwelling of the Holy Spirit? How can you tell if the gospel is really true? Once I performed tests on people who were about to believe in the beautiful gospel given us by Jesus. To one person I only preached the message of Jesus Christ's blood on the Cross. I also told him that there should be no sin in Jesus Christ. To another person I preached the beautiful gospel of Jesus' baptism by John and His blood on the Cross. The result was that the person who received remission of his sins by believing only in Jesus' blood said that he had to continuously be forgiven for his actual sins. But the person who believed in the beautiful gospel of Jesus' baptism and blood, on the other hand, said that he had now become a perfect sinless person.

He said that he had no sin in his heart because he believed in the truth that Jesus took away all his sins and was judged for them. He was able to receive the Holy Spirit from God because he believed in the beautiful gospel, which says that Jesus' baptism by John washed away all the sins of the world.

The reason that this man could say that he had no longer had sin in his heart was because he had received the Holy Spirit in his heart through his belief in the beautiful gospel. The Holy Spirit gave him the conviction to say he had no sin in his heart. God gives the indwelling of the Holy Spirit to all those who believe in Jesus' baptism by John and His blood at the Cross. In whom does the Holy Spirit dwell? The Holy Spirit is given as a gift to those who believe in the beautiful gospel of Jesus' baptism by John and His blood on the Cross.

Just seeing the superficial phenomena on the Day of the Pentecost has caused many people to misunderstand the truth about receiving the Holy Spirit and put aside the beautiful gospel. People think that if they desperately pray and seek the Holy Spirit, they will be able to receive the indwelling of the Holy Spirit. For a long time, Christians around the world didn't have even the slightest idea of the truth, which said that one could receive the Holy Spirit only by believing in the beautiful gospel of Jesus' baptism and blood. However, now many servants of God, who have received the indwelling of the Holy Spirit through their belief in the gospel of the water and the Spirit, have preached the gospel with the help of the Holy Spirit. As a result, many people throughout the whole world have learned to accept this beautiful gospel and receive the indwelling of the Holy Spirit.

God allows people who believe in this beautiful gospel to experience the indwelling of the Holy Spirit. In the Bible, it says, *"And it shall come to pass in the last days, says God, that I will pour out of My Spirit all fresh" (Acts 2:17).* However, one should know that trying to receive the indwelling of the Holy Spirit without knowing the beautiful gospel is a mistake. There is no other way to receive the indwelling of the Holy Spirit than to believe in Jesus' baptism by John and His blood on the Cross.

Since God says that one can enter the Kingdom of Heaven only when he is born again of water and the Spirit, and only the born again possess the gift of the Holy Spirit, there is no doubt that everyone needs the indwelling of the Holy Spirit in order to enter the Kingdom of Heaven. How can you think of receiving the Holy Spirit or entering Heaven without believing in the beautiful gospel of the water and the Spirit? There is no way to Heaven other than by believing in the beautiful gospel. You can receive the Holy Spirit only by believing in the gospel of Jesus' baptism and His blood. Just like we pay money when we buy things, we receive the indwelling of the Holy Spirit when we believe in the beautiful gospel.

I want to tell you that if you truly want to receive the indwelling of the Holy Spirit, you must first know and believe in the gospel of the water and the Spirit. Then you will have the experience of receiving the Holy Spirit. You can only receive the indwelling of the Holy Spirit by believing in the beautiful gospel of the water and the Spirit. God wants to present you with the indwelling of the Holy Spirit.

I believe in the beautiful gospel and as time passes, I feel even more strongly that this beautiful gospel that God gave me is the most beautiful and precious thing in the world. I feel thankful to God. Do you feel the same way? We realize that those of us who have received the Holy Spirit have been greatly blessed by God.

I am giving you the message of how you can receive the indwelling of the Holy Spirit by believing in the beautiful gospel. People can qualify themselves to receive the indwelling of the Holy Spirit only by accepting this blessed beautiful gospel of being born again of water and the Spirit.

In John 7:38, Jesus says, *"He who believes in Me, as the Scripture has said, out of his heart will flow a river of living water."* This means that people who receive the remission of all their sins by believing in the beautiful gospel that Jesus Christ gave them have the indwelling of the Holy Spirit. The living water of the Holy Spirit will flow like a river out of their hearts. People who believe in this beautiful gospel will experience the flowing out of the Spiritual living waters.

Even though I was a devout believer in Jesus before I was born again through the gospel of the water and the Spirit, there was no living water of the Holy Spirit flowing out of my heart. However, after I came to believe in the beautiful gospel of the water and the Spirit, the living water began to flow freely out of my heart just as it is written in the Bible. Even at this moment, the living water of the Holy Spirit flows together with the gospel of the water and the Spirit that God gave me. The living water of the Holy Spirit flows in abundance from my heart all year round. I began to do the work of an evangelist, preaching the beautiful gospel, after I received the indwelling of the Holy Spirit.

My confession of faith after believing in the beautiful gospel and receiving the indwelling of the Holy Spirit

It was just before the end of autumn in my early twenties. That autumn especially made me think of the inevitability of my death. My life that year was marked by confusion, emptiness and darkness due to the sins in my heart. I was moving in the wrong direction, with no idea which way to turn. My body was getting ill along and the emptiness in my heart was growing.

Because of my sins, I was in total despair and I wasn't even sure of the cause. I had no other choice but to wait for God's judgment at the sudden end of my life and beg for the remission of my sins. "Oh Lord, I want to receive the remission of my sins through my faith in You before I die. Also, please heal the sickness in my body!" I prayed and prayed.

Just then, new hope started to pour out from deep down in my desperate heart. My heart was filled with longing for God, and was as hot as a fireball. It wasn't despair, it was new hope that was burning like a raging fire in my heart. From that day on I began a new religious life, believing that Jesus died on the Cross to save me from my sins.

Not long after that, I had the experience of speaking in tongues. Later I continued to shed tears as I thought about the blood Jesus had shed on the Cross. I was thankful that He had shed His blood on the Cross for me.

After that incident I abandoned my old life and got a new job that allowed me to keep the holy Sunday. At that time, my heart was full of love for Jesus, and overflowed with the endless gratitude whenever I felt that Jesus had shed His blood on the Cross to save me from my sins. My religious spirit began to grow, but it was solely based on the words of Jesus' blood on the Cross.

However, as time went on, my religious life began to be plagued by suffering due to my weaknesses and actual sins. All my actual sins hadn't been completely washed away because my belief was in Jesus' blood on the Cross alone. I tried to wash away my actual sins through prayers of repentance. However, the prayers I offered in hopes of achieving God's forgiveness could not completely wash away my actual sins. It was all because I couldn't keep God's laws. My actual sins began to pile up.

Even though my sins weren't completely washed away through my prayers of repentance, I had no other choice but to continue to say these prayers. I believed that every time I sinned, I could wash away my sins through prayers of repentance and by thinking about Jesus' blood on the Cross. The more I continued with my religious life, the more my actual sins were piling up due to my weaknesses. My suffering was only increasing because of these sins.

I was becoming a Pharisaic Christian, and I was appointed a deacon and later an evangelist regardless of the burden of my sins. I went out to preach the gospel whenever I felt the pain of my actual sins, thinking this was the only way to cleanse my soul. But my actual sins were not washed away through this kind of faith based on doctrine and self-sacrifice.

I even had the experience of getting caught by Satan. I fell into condemnation due to my actual sins and even felt the urge to die for my transgressions. "You have sinned, haven't you?" Satan continued to condemn and torment me with my sin.

My faith was on the verge of collapse. I realized that I couldn't wash away my actual sins through faith in Jesus' blood and prayers of repentance alone, and eventually found myself in a state of frustration.

Studying Calvinism in a theological seminary, I became interested in the reason for Jesus' baptism by John. I asked many professors why Jesus Christ was baptized by John in the Jordan. But their answers used to be the stereotyped ones, such as that He was baptized to show His modesty or to announce that He was the Son of God. However, these answers were not enough to quench my curiosity.

The truth of Jesus' baptism by John caused me to recognize the beautiful gospel

After my time in the seminary, my sins were still not washed away, and I suffered under their weight more than ever before. Then one day I came to understand why Jesus was baptized and why He said that all righteousness would be fulfilled through this deed. It was the beautiful gospel that said that all my sins were passed on to Jesus through His baptism in the Jordan River. God helped me realize this truth through His written words.

After reading and rereading God's words, in which the beautiful gospel is recorded, I finally recognized the truth that all my sins were transferred to Jesus through His baptism by John and that He was judged for them on the Cross.

This was when I realized that the indwelling of the Holy Spirit had truly come to me. All the sins in my heart were completely forgiven after I understood and believed in this beautiful gospel. The sins that plunged me into frustration and despair were completely washed away by the power of the beautiful gospel. Those sins that were never blotted out in spite of my endless self-sacrifices and prayers of repentance completely vanished at once. I sincerely give thanks to the Lord.

I speak the truth when I say that all the sins of the world could not be washed away only through Jesus' blood on the Cross. Jesus' baptism by John also led to the remission of sin. Now everyone should understand and believe that all his sins were washed away thanks to the beautiful gospel of the water and the Spirit. I have the indwelling of the Holy Spirit deep in my heart because I believe in the beautiful gospel of the water and the Spirit, and the word of God's Witness, which He has testified of His Son, was enough to drive out all the sins from my heart. I received the Holy Spirit like a dove as a result of my belief in the beautiful gospel.

From that day on, the Holy Spirit worked in my heart, enabling me to do my spiritual work, in other words, to preach the beautiful gospel. Now there is no sin in my heart. Jesus' baptism by John and His blood on the Cross bore witness to the remission of my sins and led me to receive the indwelling of the Holy Spirit. Hallelujah! I praise the Lord. The Holy Spirit silently fell on me like a dove and began to dwell in me from the day I came to believe in the gospel of the water and the Spirit. He began to work in my heart sometimes like a dove, other times like a blast furnace.

Now you can also receive the indwelling of the Holy Spirit if you accept and believe in the beautiful gospel of the water and the Spirit. Don't you want to receive the Holy Spirit and praise the Lord by believing in the beautiful gospel of the water and the Spirit together with me? Don't you want to work with me in preaching the beautiful gospel of the water and the Spirit to the whole world? The beautiful gospel of the water and the Spirit will sanctify you and give you the indwelling of the Holy Spirit. The righteousness of God is revealed in the gospel from faith to faith. That is why the indwelling of the Holy Spirit is given only through faith in the beautiful gospel of the water and the Spirit.

The wonderful things the Holy Spirit has done for me

After I received the indwelling of the Holy Spirit, I began to work at a new church in order to preach the beautiful gospel. The Holy Spirit enabled me to powerfully preach the beautiful gospel.

It was at this time that the following incident took place. In the city where I lived, there was a tailor who did business with foreign buyers. This person was a deacon. He once stopped by a local hotel to do business with someone and he saw our poster there. He was attracted by the invitation, and tried to contact me. He met with me and said he had lived in sin for a long time. After five hours of counseling on the gospel of the water and the Spirit, he finally recognized the truth of the remission of sins. He came to be born again, and also received the indwelling of the Holy Spirit at that time.

Here is another story that occurred when I went out to look for a church building. I found a wonderful and specious building. But at that time I had an insufficient amount of money to rent it as our church building. It seemed impossible for me to rent the building on account of the great shortage by my estimate. However, the Holy Spirit in me said, "Be strong and confident." Surprisingly I was able to obtain the church building and do His work thanks to the help of the Holy Spirit. The Holy Spirit made me preach the beautiful gospel of the water and the Spirit from that time on. The Holy Spirit dwelling in my heart is with me even at this moment, prompting me to preach the beautiful gospel to all people. And I see those who hear and believe in this beautiful gospel receive the indwelling of the Holy Spirit.

I thank the Holy Spirit who gave me the ability to preach this beautiful gospel. I know that even my whole lifetime would be insufficient to write about all the things the Holy Spirit has done for me. The Holy Spirit lets me live with the living water flowing freely out of my heart. I give thanks to Him who dwells in me.

The Holy Spirit planted the church that walks with Him through the gospel of the water and the Spirit

Once I went out in the wilderness to preach the beautiful gospel. At that time, God led me to a small town and I met a small group of people who were looking for God. God led me to preach the beautiful gospel to them, which caused them to have the indwelling of the Holy Spirit. They also received the Holy Spirit by listening and believing in the beautiful gospel. The Holy Spirit led them to become my co-workers, and I came to preach this beautiful gospel to the whole world together with them from then on.

At that time they were just a small group of people, not belonging to any religious denomination. They wanted to live according to God's words, but desperately used to cry out to God for forgiveness of their sins because of their slavery to sin. The Holy Spirit led me to this group of people and prompted me to preach this beautiful gospel. I could see that the Holy Spirit had prepared both them and me to meet each another. God led me to preach the beautiful gospel of the water and the Spirit starting with the sacrificial system as it is written in Leviticus, and the people received the Holy Spirit through the words of the beautiful gospel.

God established the church of the Holy Spirit together with those believers in the beautiful gospel. The Holy Spirit appointed them Jesus' disciples through the beautiful gospel. Now more and more sheep have begun to receive the Holy Spirit and to enter the church.

The Holy Spirit led me to start up a mission school and raise disciples. He helped me to teach God's words to the people and helped them to learn to obey by faith and serve as God's workers. He allowed works of the beautiful gospel to occur everywhere they went, and God planted His churches through them. The Holy Spirit has been leading His servants to preach the beautiful gospel of the water and the Spirit. The Holy Spirit led the righteous, who received the remission of sin, to unite with the church and be blessed to live a righteous life in this world.

Satan has been deceiving people since time immemorial and he will continue to do so. Satan tells people that they can receive the Holy Spirit through prayers of repentance, fasting or the laying on of hands. This is not true at all. People cannot receive the Holy Spirit through prayers of repentance or the laying on of hands. They can receive the Holy Spirit only when they are forgiven for all their sins by believing in the gospel of the water and the Spirit, which God gave us. This is the true meaning of the indwelling of the Holy Spirit. The Holy Spirit has continuously led Jesus Christ's disciples to preach the beautiful gospel of the water and the Spirit in order to help people receive the indwelling of the Holy Spirit.

The Holy Spirit has led us to do literature ministries worldwide

Just like Paul left the beautiful gospel in his epistles, the Holy Spirit dwelling in my heart has been the catalyst for me to preach and spread the beautiful gospel of the water and the Spirit in writing. This is the reason that we publish Christian books containing the beautiful gospel, which leads believers to receive the Holy Spirit. At first we started with small tracts of only a few pages, but soon our books containing the beautiful gospel spread throughout the world.

The Holy Spirit dwelling in me led more and more people to enter the church after receiving the remission of their sins by reading the books and believing in the beautiful gospel. Furthermore, He led us to preach the beautiful gospel in various foreign languages. He led us to preach the beautiful gospel in about 150 countries around the world, including the United States.

The Holy Spirit prompted the church to pray for the world mission and has led us to translate the beautiful gospel into various languages and preach it through literature ministries so that many different nationalities could hear and believe in it. The Holy Spirit led me to work together with new disciples in other countries and preach the beautiful gospel together with them there. I give thanks to the Holy Spirit.

The Holy Spirit filled me with enthusiasm to preach the gospel in Russia. The Holy Spirit led us to pray and gave us the chance to meet truth-seeking Russian evangelists and to preach the beautiful gospel to them. That was when they first heard the beautiful gospel. They then received the Holy Spirit just like us, after hearing and believing the beautiful gospel of the water and the Spirit.

One of them, a professor of a national university in Moscow, offered this confession to me after hearing the beautiful gospel of the water and the Spirit.

"I had believed in God for 6 years, but I believed without really understanding Him. However, after hearing about the beautiful gospel of the water and the Spirit, I had a strong faith and tranquil comfort in my heart. I really thank the Lord. I had thought until then that I had led a religious life through the right kind of faith. My religious life consisted only of believing in the blood of Jesus, who died for our sins. However, I had no idea that God had cleansed all my sins.

I then met the born again pastors and heard about the beautiful gospel which God gave us, and learned that I was still a sinner. I tried to find out more about the beautiful gospel and also about what being righteous means. I realized that all my sins were passed on to Jesus when He was baptized. It was the beautiful gospel. I realized that not only original sin, but also my daily sins and all my future sins were transferred to Him through His baptism. I gained the great happiness of being born again by hearing and believing in this gospel of truth."

Many Russians, including this professor, received the Holy Spirit by hearing and believing in the beautiful gospel of the water and the Spirit. Now the church of the Holy Spirit has been planted there, and more and more people have come to believe in the beautiful gospel through the work of the Holy

Spirit. God did all these things, and therefore I give special thanks to the Holy Spirit.

The Holy Spirit dwelling within me made me a born-again Christian, just like all those who believe in the beautiful gospel of the water and the Spirit, and now I preach the beautiful gospel to the world. He let our books on the beautiful gospel be continuously translated not only into English, but also into many other languages throughout the world. He made us preach this beautiful gospel throughout the world. I give thanks to the Holy Spirit. You too can also receive the indwelling of the Holy Spirit. God wants you to have the indwelling of the Holy Spirit.

Many people try to receive the Holy Spirit by calling out His name and offering desperate prayers to God. However, trying to receive the Holy Spirit without the beautiful gospel of the water and the Spirit, which Jesus gave us, is a mistake. Saying that one can receive the Holy Spirit without Jesus' beautiful gospel of the water and the Spirit is false teaching.

Did Jesus' disciples receive the Holy Spirit without believing in the beautiful gospel that Jesus gave them? No, absolutely not. You should know that nowadays the Holy Spirit dwells in those who believe in the beautiful gospel of the water and Spirit, and the living water of the Holy Spirit flows out of their hearts. Even right at this very moment, the living water of the Holy Spirit flows out of my heart together with the beautiful gospel. Hallelujah, I thank the Lord. ✉

SERMON 9

The gospel of His baptism that made us clean

The gospel of His baptism that made us clean

<Ephesians 2:14-22>
"For He Himself is our peace, who has made both one, and has broken down the middle wall of separation, having abolished in His flesh the enmity, that is, the law of commandments contained in ordinances, so as to create in Himself one new man from the two, thus making peace, and that He might reconcile them both to God in one body through the Cross, thereby putting to death the enmity. And He came and preached peace to you who were afar off and to those who were near. For through Him we both have access by one Spirit to the Father. Now, therefore, you are no longer strangers and foreigners, but fellow citizens with the saints and members of the household of God, having been built on the foundation of the apostles and prophets, Jesus Christ Himself being the chief cornerstone, in whom the whole building, being fitted together, grows into a holy temple in the Lord, in whom you also are being built together for a dwelling place of God in the Spirit."

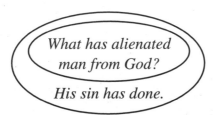

What has alienated man from God?

His sin has done.

The adopted child due to poverty

Half a century has passed since the end of the Korean War. But it left tremendous wounds among the Korean people. In the aftermath of the Korean War, many young children were adopted to foreign countries. Even though the United Nations forces came to Korea and helped us enormously at that time, but many children were left fatherless after the soldiers left.

Many of the UN soldiers who had wives and children here left their families behind when they returned home. Many of these children were then again abandoned to orphanages by their mothers and then sent away for adoption to foreign countries. It was actually very fortunate that these young people could find foster parents and be brought up very well.

These adopted children realized that they looked quite different from their parents and their neighbors as they grew older, and they learned that they were adopted from a far away country called Korea. 'Why did my parents abandon me? Did they send me away to this country because they hated me?' With their young minds, these children just couldn't understand what had happened.

Their curiosity and hatred toward their real parents began to grow in tandem with a longing to meet them. 'I wonder what my parents look like? How could they abandon me? Did they do it because they hated me? No, there was probably a reason for this.' They probably had many misunderstandings and sometimes even felt extreme hatred. And at other times they likely resolved not to think about it anymore. Before they were even aware of it, time had passed and the children grew up to be adults. They got married, had children and formed families of their own.

I became interested in these children through a program on

one of the local TV networks. In this program, a TV reporter interviewed a woman now living in Germany who had been adopted. This woman was in her twenties at that time and was studying theology. At first, the woman very much tried to avoid meeting the reporters because she didn't want anyone else to become aware that she was adopted. The reporter persuaded her to understand that submitting to an interview would help stem the tide of adoptions to foreign countries. The woman agreed.

One of the reporter's questions was, "What would you say if you could meet your real parents? What are you most curious about?" The woman answered, "I just can't understand why they had to put me up for adoption. I want to ask them if they hated me." Her birth mother saw the woman's interview on TV, contacted the broadcasting station, and said that she wanted to meet her daughter. This is how the two came to meet.

The mother went very early to the airport and waited for her daughter's arrival. When the young woman emerged from the exit, her mother could only stand there and weep.

These two people had never met face to face. The first time the mother saw her grown-up daughter was when she appeared on TV. Even though they spoke different languages, they could talk with their hearts, and through the emotional looks they exchanged. They touched each other's faces while the mother begged for forgiveness for what she had done. All she could do was cry and repeat that she was very sorry.

The mother brought her daughter home and they ate together. Of course, the daughter only spoke German and the mother only Korean so they couldn't communicate verbally. But somehow the fact that they were mother and daughter allowed them to make themselves understood. They had many wordless conversations and expressed themselves through gestures, touching each other's faces and talking with their eyes and their hearts.

By the time she returned to Germany, the daughter knew that her birth mother loved her. The same reporters that had conducted the previous interview spoke to her once again before her departure. "There was no need for me to ask why my mother had given me up for adoption. My mother is poor even now. Wealthy people in this country are so rich that they drive foreign cars, but my mother is still living in poverty." She went on to say, "Even though I didn't ask my mother that question and didn't receive an answer from her, I could see that she sent me away to save me from poverty. That is why I didn't feel the need to ask her that question, and why all doubts and hatred are now gone."

People become alienated from God due to the sin in their hearts

Why do we become separated from God, and why can't we draw near to Him? The woman who was put up for adoption learned that her birth mother sent her away to save her from poverty. Is the same true of God? God created us in His own image. What could have separated us from Him? The answer is that Satan tempted man to commit sin, and sin separated him from God.

Originally, God created man in His own image and dearly loved His creation. Men were made as an object for God's love and possessed more nobility than any other creation. However, a fallen angel named Satan worked to alienate man from God. Satan tempted man not to believe in God's words, and made him eat the fruit of the tree of the knowledge of good and evil.

Man was thus separated from God due to his sin. Man was disobedient to God. Man did not eat the fruit of the tree of life, which gives eternal life and which God allowed, but instead ate the forbidden fruit that gave him knowledge of good and evil. The result was that man was separated from God.

Previously the object of God's love, man disobeyed and became separated from Him out of arrogance. Due to the sin that came to dwell in his heart, man was eventually alienated from God. After that, man lived apart from God for a long time and complained, "Why did God abandon us after He made us? Why did He let us commit sin? Why does He send us to hell after making us weak? It would have been better if He hadn't made us in the first place." We lived with many questions, as well as curiosity, doubts and hatred before we were born again.

When I saw the adopted woman on a TV program, I realized that the relationship between man and God is the same as the relationship she had with her real mother. No tribulation, misunderstanding, curse or sin of any kind could separate man from God under any circumstances. Also, I could understand that even though the relationship between God and man is based on love, it was still possible for misunderstandings to occur.

Just as the mother hadn't sent her daughter away out of hatred, so God separated Himself from man not out of hatred but because of sin. There is no reason for God to hate man and no reason for men to hate God. We love each other. The reason that man remains separated from God is that he became a sinner after succumbing to Satan's trickery.

God has embraced us through Jesus

"But now in Christ Jesus you who once were far off have been brought near by the blood of Christ. For He Himself is our peace, who has made both one, and has broken down the middle wall of separation, having abolished in His flesh the enmity, that is, the law of commandments contained in ordinances" (Ephesians 2:13-15). The Lord was baptized by John and took away all the sins of the world in order to abolish the law of commandments. He then shed His blood on the Cross in order to save man from his sins and allow him to be embraced by God. God has now embraced those who were cleansed by Him.

Have you ever imagined a world without water? Not long ago, I attended a Bible meeting in Inchon City, one of the largest ports in Korea where the tap water didn't work at that time for a few days and I thought, 'People can't live without water.'

If God would make this world waterless for a month, it would be impossible to live in the cities due to the odor, filth and all-pervasive thirst. We should understand the value of water, which God gave us. Just as water is an absolute necessity for humans, the baptism that Jesus received from John in the Jordan River is equally indispensable.

If Jesus had not come into this world to be baptized by John, then how could believers in Jesus receive the remission of sins? Just as people cannot live without water, everyone in this world would have died from their sins if John hadn't baptized Jesus.

However, since Jesus' baptism took away all our sins, we can now feel confident in the knowledge that our hearts have been cleansed and we have been blessed with salvation. Jesus' baptism is crucial to our faith. Furthermore, His baptism is absolutely necessary for us to receive the indwelling of the Holy Spirit.

Peter, one of Jesus' disciples said, *"There is also an antitype which now saves us — baptism, through the resurrection of Jesus Christ" (1 Peter 3:21).* Peter's statement says that Jesus was baptized by John the Baptist and shed His blood in order to save us from our sins. Jesus' baptism, which washed away all the sins of the world, is the true gospel.

Now let's look at the passage about the laver of bronze written in Exodus 30:17-21. *"Then the LORD spoke to Moses, saying: 'You shall also make a laver of bronze, with its base also of bronze, for washing. You shall put it between the tabernacle of meeting and the altar. And you shall put water in it, for Aaron and his sons shall wash their hands and their feet in water from it. When they go into the tabernacle of meeting, or when they come near the altar to minister, to burn an offering made by fire to the LORD, they shall wash with water, lest they die. So they shall wash their hands and their feet, lest they die. And it shall be a statue forever to them — to him and his descendants throughout their generations.'"*

In the tabernacle there was a laver of bronze, which was set between the tabernacle of meeting and the altar, and which contained water for washing. If this laver had not been in the tabernacle, how dirty the priests offering the sacrifices would have been.

How much blood and dirt would stain the priests who were offering so many daily sacrifices for the people and laying their hands on the sin offerings and then killing them? If there hadn't been the laver in the tabernacle, the priest would have gotten very dirty.

This is why God prepared the laver for them so they could draw near to Him with clean hands. Sinners passed on their sins by laying their hands on the head of the sin offerings, and then the priests sacrificed them to God on their behalf. God prepared the laver of bronze so that the priests could enter the holy place, and so that they could wash with water, lest they die. Even a priest could not enter the holy place while stained with an animal's blood. That is why priests washed away all the dirt with the water in the laver in order to draw near to God after offering sacrifices for the people.

Jesus' baptism washed away all the sins of the world

Through Jesus' baptism by John in the Jordan River, all the sins of the world were transferred to Him. And His total submersion in the water symbolized His death and His emergence from the water represented His resurrection. In other words, Jesus was baptized by John to take all the sin of the world, paid the wages of sin and died on the Cross. His death was to pay the price for our sins and His resurrection gave us eternal life.

If we didn't believe that Jesus took away all our sins through His baptism, our hearts would be full of sin. In that case, how could we possibly draw near to God? The gospel of the remission of sins is not a doctrine of one denomination but the truth of God.

We cannot lead our faith without perfect knowledge, in other words, we can't overcome the world if we don't really care whether Jesus was baptized by John. Just as all living things need water in order to sustain their lives, we need the remission of sins and the water of Jesus' baptism in order to live by faith and enter the Kingdom of Heaven. Jesus had to be baptized, die on the Cross and resurrect in order to save us from our sins. This is the gospel of the water and the Spirit, which we must believe with all our hearts.

Even though Jesus was crucified to death on the Cross, He had done nothing to deserve such punishment. He came into this world to wash away our sins, was baptized at age 30, and became our Savior through His death on the Cross at age 33. God wanted to make mankind His children no matter how fragile and sinful we were. That's why Jesus was baptized. God gave us the remission of sins and the gift of the Holy Spirit at the same time.

"Unless one is born again of water and the Spirit, he can neither see the kingdom of God nor enter it" (John 3:3-5). You have to know and believe that Jesus was baptized in order to wash away all our sins. Even if one is a born-again Christian, if he doesn't meditate on the truth that Jesus Christ took away all the sins of the world through His baptism, his heart will soon become soiled. Because we are corporeal beings, we are liable to be soiled by sin even in daily life. That's why we always have to live by faith, meditating on Jesus' baptism, His blood, and His resurrection. This faith upholds us until the day we enter the Kingdom of Heaven.

Jesus had no choice but to be baptized and die for our sins, so we must believe that by doing so He brought us salvation. There is nothing more we have to do than believe in this beautiful gospel in order to be delivered from all the sins of the world.

We give thanks to the Lord, who gave us the gospel of the water and the Spirit. The greatest gift God gave us was to send His only begotten Son to save us from all our sins through His baptism and blood.

The reason we couldn't draw near to God and were forced to live apart from Him was that we had sin in our hearts. Jesus was baptized by John to take away all the sins of the world and died on the Cross in order to break down the wall that was separating God and man. The relationship between God and man was restored by His baptism and blood. We thank Him for these gifts. The love of the physical parent toward their child is great, but it is incomparable to God's love, by which Jesus saved us sinners.

Jesus' baptism and blood are both important. If there were no water in this world, would any living thing survive? Without Jesus' baptism, there would be no one without sin in his heart. If Jesus had not been baptized and if He had not died on the Cross, no one would have received the remission of sins. Fortunately, Jesus was baptized and made the ultimate sacrifice for us. Even though we are lacking and fallible, we can receive the Holy Spirit by believing in His baptism and blood on the Cross.

People who believe in Jesus Christ's baptism and death on the Cross can draw near to God, pray and praise Him. We are now able to praise the Lord and worship Him because we have become His children. This is God's grace and blessing. The gospel of the baptism of Jesus and His blood on the Cross is truly wonderful. We can all receive salvation and the indwelling of the Holy Spirit by believing in this beautiful gospel. ⊠

SERMON 10

Walk in the Spirit!

Walk in the Spirit!

<Galatians 5:16-26, 6:6-18>

"I say then: Walk in the Spirit, and you shall not fulfill the lust of the flesh. For the flesh lusts against the Spirit, and the Spirit against the flesh; and these are contrary to one another, so that you do not do the things that you wish. But if you are led by the Spirit, you are not under the law. Now the works of the flesh are evident, which are: adultery, fornication, uncleanness, lewdness, idolatry, sorcery, hatred, contentions, jealousies, outbursts of wrath, selfish ambitions, dissensions, heresies, envy, murders, drunkenness, revelries, and the like; of which I tell you beforehand, just as I also told you in time past, that those who practice such things will not inherit the kingdom of God. But the fruit of the Spirit is love, joy, peace, longsuffering, kindness, goodness, faithfulness, gentleness, self-control. Against such there is no law. And those who are Christ's have crucified the flesh with its passions and desires. If we live in the Spirit, let us also walk in the Spirit. Let us not become conceited, provoking one another, envying one another."

"Let him who is taught the word share in all good things with him who teaches. Do not be deceived, God is not mocked; for whatever a man sows, that he will also reap. For he who sows to his flesh will of the flesh reap corruption, but he who sows to the Spirit will of the Spirit reap everlasting life. And let us not grow weary while doing good, for in due season we shall reap if we do not lose heart. Therefore, as we have opportunity, let us do good to all, especially to those who are of the household of faith. See with what large letters I have written to you with my own hand! As many as desire to make a good showing in the flesh, these would compel you to be circumcised, only that they may not suffer persecution for the cross of Christ. For not even those who are circumcised keep the law, but they desire to have you circumcised that they may boast in your flesh. But God forbid that I should boast except in the cross of our Lord Jesus Christ, by whom the world has been crucified to me, and I to the world. For in Christ Jesus neither circumcision nor uncircumcision avails anything, but a new creation. And as many as walk according to this rule, peace and mercy be upon them, and upon the Israel of God. From now on let no one trouble me, for I bear in my body the marks of the Lord Jesus. Brethren, the grace of our Lord Jesus Christ be with your spirit. Amen.''

What should we do to walk in the Spirit?

We should preach and follow the beautiful gospel.

The apostle Paul wrote about the Holy Spirit in his epistle to the Galatians. In Galatians 5:13-14 he said, *"For you, brethren, have been called to liberty; only do not use liberty as an opportunity for the flesh, but through love serve one another. For all the law is fulfilled in one word, even in this: 'You shall love your neighbor as yourself.'"*

In brief, the message is that since we have been saved and freed from sin by believing in the beautiful gospel, we must not take this liberty as an opportunity to indulge ourselves in the lust of the flesh, but through love we must serve one another and follow the beautiful gospel. As God has saved us from all our sins, it is fitting for us to preach the gospel. Paul also said *"If you bite and devour one another, beware lest you be consumed by one another" (Galatians 5:15).*

Walk in the Spirit to be filled with the Holy Spirit

In Galatians 5:16 Paul said, *"I say then: Walk in the Spirit, and you shall not fulfill the lust of the flesh."* And in verses 22-26 he said, *"But the fruit of the Spirit is love, joy, peace, longsuffering, kindness, goodness, faithfulness, gentleness, self-control. Against such there is no law. And those who are Christ's have crucified the flesh with its passions and desires. If we live in the Spirit, let us also walk in the Spirit. Let us not become conceited, provoking one another, envying one another."* Here, Paul tells us that if we walk in the Spirit, we will bear the fruit of the Spirit. The Holy Spirit requires us to walk in the Spirit. But we live in the flesh.

We human beings are born with flesh that cannot bear the fruit of the Spirit. Even if we try to walk in the Spirit, our nature can't be changed. That is why only those who receive the indwelling of the Holy Spirit by believing in the beautiful gospel can walk in the Spirit and bear the fruit of the Spirit.

When the Bible tells us to walk in the Spirit, it means we should preach the beautiful gospel so that others can also be forgiven for their sins. If we live for this beautiful gospel, we will bear the fruit of the Spirit. In other words, it is not a matter of changing human nature. When we walk with this beautiful gospel, we can bear the fruit of the Spirit, namely love, joy, peace, kindness, goodness, faithfulness, gentleness and self-control. The fruit of the Spirit helps us save others from their sins to have eternal lives.

The lusts of the flesh vs. the desires of the Spirit

Paul said, *"The flesh lusts against the Spirit, and the Spirit against the flesh; and these are contrary to one another, so that you may not do the thongs that you wish" (Galatians 5:17).* Since we, who have been redeemed, possess the lust of the flesh and the Spirit at the same time, these two elements are always at odds with one another. The result is that neither one can completely fill our hearts.

The Spirit leads us to wish, from deep in our hearts, to preach the beautiful gospel and serve the Lord. It makes us zealous to engage in spiritual works. It helps us save people from their sins by preaching the beautiful gospel of God.

But on the other hand, our desires stir up the lust of the flesh so that we cannot walk in the Spirit. This is the eternal conflict between the Spirit and the lusts of the flesh. When a person is consumed with the lusts of the flesh, he ends up making provisions for the flesh. The flesh sets its desire against the Spirit. They are in opposition to one another, so that we may not do the things that we wish.

Then what is involved in walking in the Spirit? And what kinds of things are pleasing to God? God said that preaching and following the beautiful gospel is the life of walking in the Spirit. He gives the hearts to walk in the Spirit to those who have the indwelling of the Holy Spirit, so that they can lead a spiritual life. The commandment God gave us to bear the fruit of the Spirit by walking in the Spirit was an admonition and an order for us to save others from their sins by preaching the beautiful gospel. Walking in the Holy Spirit means living a life that is pleasing to God.

In order to walk in the Spirit, we need to have the indwelling of the Holy Spirit first of all. We first have to believe in the beautiful gospel that God gave us if we wish to receive the Holy Spirit that dwells in us. If we do not believe in the beautiful gospel deep in our hearts, we will neither receive the indwelling of the Holy Spirit nor obtain salvation from sin, which means we won't be able to walk in the Spirit.

The Spirit gives us the desire to preach the beautiful gospel, to serve the Lord and bring glory to God. This desire comes from a heart that is dedicated to God and to preaching the beautiful gospel to the entire world. It also comes from a heart that is willing to do whatever it takes to preach the beautiful gospel. Those who believe in the beautiful gospel and receive the Holy Spirit after they are forgiven for their sins are able to walk in the Spirit and dedicate themselves to preaching the gospel. This is their spiritual inheritance from above.

Those who have the indwelling of the Holy Spirit come to obey the Holy Spirit and walk in the Spirit, even though they still have the lusts of the flesh because the Holy Spirit dwells in them. Paul said, *"Walk in the Holy Spirit."* What he meant by this is that we must preach the beautiful gospel of the water and the Holy Spirit that Jesus gave us so that we can help others to be forgiven for their sins.

Sometimes while walking in the Spirit, we walk according to the flesh. The lust of the flesh and the desire of the Spirit fight against each other in our lives, but what we have to know and recognize clearly is that those who have the indwelling of the Holy Spirit should live the life walking in the Spirit. Only in this way will we be able to live lives filled with the blessings of God. If those who have the indwelling of the Holy Spirit refuse to bear the fruit of the Spirit, they end up perishing by bearing the fruit of the flesh. Their fruit is perishable and miserable. Therein lies the reason for us to live by walking in the Spirit.

We have heard "Walk in the Spirit," but some of us might think "How can I do so, when I can't feel the Holy Spirit inside me?" Some of us think we could only recognize the indwelling of the Holy Spirit if God appeared and spoke directly to us. But this is a misunderstanding. The Spirit gives us the desire to live for the beautiful gospel of the water and the Spirit.

There may be times that we are sure He dwells within us but cannot feel Him because we are walking according to the flesh. Some may even think He is sleeping inside us. They are the ones who have received the Holy Spirit but still walk with the flesh.

These people only comfort their own flesh and act as it dictates, but suffer in the end due to the incremental requirements of the flesh. Even the ones who have the indwelling of the Holy Spirit tend to live according to the lusts of their flesh, because they think it is natural to do so. But those who submit to the flesh eventually become slaves to the flesh.

The Lord tells us to live according to the Spirit. This means serving the beautiful gospel. It also means that we must devote ourselves entirely to the beautiful gospel of the water and the Spirit. Rejoicing in the gospel and living by it is to live according to the Spirit. We have to live like that by learning what it means to walk in the Spirit. Are you walking in the Spirit?

Can a person who doesn't have the indwelling of the Holy Spirit walk in the Spirit?

Those who are not born again do not know what it means to walk in the Spirit. Thus, many people try to receive the Holy Spirit and long for it in their own way. They think the action of desiring the Holy Spirit is the same as being filled with the Holy Spirit.

For instance, when people gather in certain chapels for service, the minister prays aloud and everyone starts to cry out the name of the Lord. Some of them speak in tongues as if they were filled with the Holy Spirit, but no one, not even themselves, can understand what they are saying. Meanwhile, some of them fall on the ground and their bodies begin to quiver in ecstasy. They surely have been possessed by demons but they think they have received the Holy Spirit. Then comes the uproar when the people shout, "Lord, Lord!" They call out to the Lord, shed tears and clap their hands. This phenomenon is usually called "being filled with the Holy Spirit."

The minister speaks in tongues while banging the pulpit, and people scream out "Lord! Lord!" They love this kind of atmosphere and some even say that they saw a vision of the tree of the knowledge of good and evil in the Garden of Eden and Jesus' face during their unholy trance. They misconceive those things as ways to receive the Holy Spirit, to be filled with Him and to walk with Him. Their misguided deeds result from their misconceptions about the word of God and the Holy Spirit.

"Walk in the Spirit." This is what God says to those who are born again. It means doing the things that are pleasing to

Him. Paul compared the deeds of the flesh to the fruit of the Holy Spirit. He said, *"The fruit of the Holy Spirit is love, joy, peace, longsuffering, kindness, goodness, faithfulness, gentleness, self-control" (Galatians 5:22-23).*

To "walk in the Spirit" means to preach the beautiful gospel and save others from their sins. If we do so, we will be able to bear the fruit of the Spirit. The fruits of the Spirit are love, joy, peace, longsuffering, kindness, goodness, faithfulness, gentleness and self-control, and we will be able to bear this fruit only when we live by the beautiful gospel. If one serves and preaches the beautiful gospel, sacrificing himself for it, then he can live a spiritual life filled with the Holy Spirit.

As a fruit of the Spirit, "goodness" means doing good deeds. It also means virtue. Maintaining virtue for the beautiful gospel and doing something for the benefit of others is the goodness. The highest good in the sight of God is to preach the gospel for the benefit of others.

And "kindness" is to feel compassion for people. He who is gracious to others serves the gospel with patience and kindness will be at peace. He who walks in the Spirit is happy to see the work of the Lord accomplished, loves to do His work, loves others and is faithful in all things. Although no one gave them a compulsory obligation to do so, he who has the indwelling of the Holy Spirit is faithful in His work until it is accomplished. He is gentle and maintains self-control. He has the fruit of the Spirit. The person who has the Holy Spirit within him has to walk in the Spirit. Only if he does so, will he be able to bear the fruit of the Spirit.

You can also bear the fruit of the Spirit if you walk in the Spirit. But if you do not, you will end up walking with the lusts of the flesh. The Scriptures say in Galatians 5:19-21, *"Now the works of the flesh are evident, which are: adultery, fornication, uncleanness, lewdness, idolatry, sorcery, hatred, contentions, jealousies, outbursts of wrath, selfish ambitions, dissensions, heresies, envy, murders, drunkenness, revelries, and the like; of which I tell you beforehand, just as I also told you in time past, that those who practice such things will not inherit the kingdom of God."*

The works of the flesh are evident

The works of the flesh are evident. The first work of the flesh is *"adultery,"* which means to engage in an improper relationship with the opposite sex. The second is *"fornication."* The third is *"uncleanness."* The forth is *"Lewdness,"* which means to be lustful. The fifth is *"idolatry,"* which means to serve idols rather than God. The sixth is *"sorcery."* The seventh is *"hatred."* If a person without the Holy Spirit walks according to the flesh, he cannot but show his hatred for others according to his sinful nature. The eighth is *"contentiousness."* This means quarrelsomeness with our friends or family. The others are *"jealousies, outbursts of wrath and selfish ambitions."* All of these are characteristic of people who walk with the flesh.

The tenth is *"dissent."* When a person walks only according to the flesh, it is impossible for him to do the work of the church and eventually he will end up leaving the church of his own accord. The eleventh is *"heresy."* He who walks in the flesh does so to satisfy his own will. But that life is so different from the will of God that he eventually turns away from the beautiful gospel. Heresy means diverging from the biblical truth. No one who has faith in the word of God and walks in the Spirit comes to turn away from the will of God.

"Envy, murders, drunkenness, revelries, and the like" are also works of the flesh. Those who walk only according to the flesh practice such things in the end. That is why the Lord says, *"Walk in the Spirit."* We, who are born again, have to walk in the Spirit.

Those who are not born again have nothing but the lusts of the flesh in their hearts. That is why they come to engage in "fornication, uncleanness, licentiousness, and idolatry." False ministers who are not born again practice "sorcery" on their followers to persuade them to donate a lot of money. They give important responsibilities and high position of the church to those who donate the most. Those who live by the flesh show their "hatred" for others. They divide churches into many denominations, boast of their own denomination and censure others as heresies. "Contentions, jealousies, outbursts of wrath, selfish ambitions, dissensions, heresies and envy" are all in the hearts of those who have not been born again. It will be the same for us the saints if we walk only according to the flesh.

The Spirit makes born again Christians bear the fruit of the Holy Spirit

Those who are born again must live to preach the beautiful gospel. As it is too hard for us to follow the Lord alone, we must do the work of serving the beautiful gospel by joining God's church. We have to pray together and devote our energies to becoming someone who walks by the beautiful gospel of the Spirit. People who walk in the Spirit live to preach the gospel of the water and the Spirit. In other words, walking according to the flesh means to live a life only for oneself while walking in the Spirit means working to save the souls of others. Many born again Christians lead this kind of beautiful life. They live for the good of others.

There are huge numbers of people around the world who haven't ever heard the beautiful gospel. We love the people in Africa and Asia. We love everyone in Europe and America as well as in isolated islands. We should show our love by introducing them to the gospel of the water and the Spirit.

We must walk in the Spirit. There is no law against this. *"The fruit of the Spirit is love, joy, peace, longsuffering, kindness, goodness, faithfulness, gentleness and self-control. Against such there is no law" (Galatians 5:22-23).* Is there any law that can be against this? No. This is the law of the Spirit that we must obey. Paul told us to walk in the Spirit. Just as our Lord gave His life for us sinners, we must preach the gospel to others. Saving others from their sins is walking in the Spirit. We should walk in the Spirit.

Paul said in Galatians 5:24-26, *"And those who are Christ's have crucified the flesh with its passions and desires. If we live in the Spirit, let us also walk in the Spirit. Let us not become conceited, provoking one another, envying one another."* We must live to save the lost souls if we are to live in the Spirit. We should do the work of the Spirit and walk with Him. The Holy Spirit that God gave us leads us to live with Jesus Christ in our hearts. The Holy Spirit is the King of love. God uses us as vehicles for His love.

Paul said, *"Those who are Christ's have crucified the flesh with its passions and desires"(Galatians 5:24).* He also said that those who are born again have died together with Jesus Christ. Those who are really born again have died with Jesus already. We do not realize it, but we died with Jesus Christ when He was crucified to pay for our sins. In other words, the fact that Jesus Christ was crucified means you and I died with Him on the Cross. His death was our death and His resurrection symbolizes our guaranteed resurrection. You and I live and die in Jesus Christ through our faith. We need to have faith. Our faith leads us to walk in the Spirit.

God has given us the power to walk in the Spirit. Therefore, we who have been forgiven for all our sins should walk in the Spirit. Those who have received the Holy Spirit must be thankful that their sins were forgiven and dedicate themselves to preaching the beautiful gospel for the salvation of the lost. Even though one is forgiven for his sins and born again, he will be separated from the church of the Lord and unable to serve Him if he lives according to the lusts of the flesh. You and I should live by the gospel of the water and the Spirit until the Day of our Lord Jesus Christ.

Never become conceited but live by the fullness of the Holy Spirit

Paul said, *"Let us not become conceited, provoking one another, envying one another."* What is conceit? It is to walk according to the lusts of the flesh. There are a lot of people in this world who live for their own conceit. Many people accumulate money, contend for supremacy, love worldly beauty and live for the here and now. There is no fidelity in these, and they will decay and disappear as time goes by. That is why people who walk according to the flesh are called conceited. Even if people have riches, is there real peace and satisfaction in their hearts? The fruit of the flesh eventually decays. Earthly things are of no use to the souls of others and are only for oneself. They are only good for one's own flesh.

The Bible says, *"There is one who scatters, yet increases more; And there is one who withholds more than is right, but it leads to poverty" (Proverbs 11:24).* Those who are not born again try to withhold money too much. Because worldly things are everything to them, they do not have room inside them to care for others. That is why they only want and care about their own lives. But it says in the Bible that there is one who withholds more than is right, but it leads to poverty. People walk according to the lusts of the flesh, but the results are the same as coming across a burglar and ending up dead. All of these things are the results of conceit.

Those who love to follow the desires of the Spirit

Paul wanted to live a life in the Spirit. And he did so. He taught us to live well through God's word. He said in Galatians 6:6-10, *"Let him who is taught the word share in all good things with him who teaches. Do not be deceived, God is not mocked; for whatever a man sows, that he will also reap. For he who sows to his flesh will of the flesh reap corruption, but he who sows to the Spirit will of the Spirit reap everlasting life. And let us not grow weary while doing good, for in due season we shall reap if we do not lose heart. Therefore, as we have opportunity, let us do good to all, especially to those who are of the household of faith."*

Paul advised those who know God's word to share all good things with their teachers. What he meant by "good things" was to please the Lord by saving the lost souls through a life of walking in the Spirit and preaching the gospel. Those who are born again should join those who teach and walk in the Spirit having the same mind, love and the same judgment.

"Share in all good things with him who teaches." Good things means to save others from their sins through the church. Paul told us to do everything in the same mind, in the same prayer and in the same devotion. We must do the work of the Lord together.

Paul said, *"Do not be deceived, God is not mocked; for whatever a man sows, that he will also reap."* Here, "to mock" means to "deride and sneer." So *"Do not be deceived, God is not mocked"* means do not deride and sneer at God. For instance, one must not take the words of God lightly, translating them into his own words and failing to believe in them. Paul said, *"For whatever a man sows, that he will also reap."* This means that he who sows the flesh will reap corruption, but he who sows the Spirit will reap everlasting life.

What will we reap if we live by the beautiful gospel of the water and the Spirit? We will receive everlasting life and salvation for our sins. We will reap the fruits of the Spirit by leading the souls of others to redemption for their sins and eternal life through the blessings of God.

But what about people who live for their own flesh? They reap corruption and there is nothing but death in the end. There is nothing left of them after their death. Man is born with empty hands and dies with empty hands.

If he does the work of saving others from their sins, they will reap the fruit of the Spirit and have everlasting life. But if he keeps walking according to the lusts of the flesh, he ends up reaping corruption. Then he will reap curses and pass the curses on to others. Therefore, Paul, who knew everything about living by faith, advised us not to walk according to the flesh.

"And let us not grow weary while doing good, for in due season we shall reap if we do not lose heart." Paul was a servant of God who walked in the Spirit. When people see in the Bible that he walked in the Spirit, some may think the Holy Spirit would have ordered him directly to do things like, "Paul, go to the left and meet someone" or "You should avoid the man." But this is untrue.

He walked in the Spirit by preaching the gospel of salvation to others and helping to save their souls. Paul also served the Lord by joining with those who also walked in the Spirit. Among Christians, there are people who do not walk in the Spirit but walk according to the lusts of the flesh. They did not welcome Paul but opposed and even slandered him. Paul said he didn't want anything to do with those who fought against and slandered the disciples of Jesus Christ.

If you want to walk in the Spirit, you have to live by the gospel. The circumcised prosecuted Paul. In Galatians 5:11 it says, *"And I, brethren, if I still preach circumcision, why do I still suffer persecution? Then the offense of the Cross has ceased."* The circumcised were those who championed the practice of circumcision, saying, "Even if one is born again by the faith in Jesus, he has to be circumcised. If he is not circumcised in the flesh of his foreskin, he is not a child of God." Why did they prosecute him? Paul believed that redemption and the blessing of everlasting life came from only faith in the baptism of Jesus and His blood on the Cross. This is what he preached.

The faith that makes people righteous comes from learning the truth and preaching it. Paul considered the truth of the water and the Spirit to be very important. He believed that those who knew the truth could walk in the Spirit and that there was no need to be circumcised. This is what he preached. But the circumcised believed that circumcision was an essential part of a person's faith in salvation. However, there is no gospel other than that handed down by God and therefore we must not add to it nor subtract anything from it.

When Paul walked in the Spirit, he was ignored and persecuted by his fellow Jews. *"As many as desire to make a good showing in the flesh, these would compel you to be circumcised, only that they may not suffer persecution for the Cross of Christ. For not even those who are circumcised keep the law, but they desire to have you circumcised that they may boast in your flesh. But God forbid that I should boast except in the Cross of our Lord Jesus Christ, by whom the world has been crucified to me, and I to the world. For in Christ Jesus neither circumcision nor uncircumcision avails anything, but a new creation"* (Galatians 6:12-15). And Paul said to the circumcised, *"As many as desire to make a good showing in the flesh, these would compel you to be circumcised, only that they may not suffer persecution for the Cross of Christ."*

Paul reproached those who walked according to the lusts of the flesh. They walked according to the lusts of the flesh in deed and there were many people like them. But Paul ended his relations with them. Paul said, *"But God forbid that I should boast except in the Cross of our Lord Jesus Christ."* Jesus Christ was baptized by John to take away all the sins of the world and died on the Cross to save Paul and all the people as many as The Lord our God calls. Paul said, *"By Jesus Christ the world has been crucified to me, and I to the world. For in Christ Jesus neither circumcision nor uncircumcision avails anything, but a new creation."* Paul, who was dead to the world, lived through Jesus Christ again.

We are actually dead in Jesus Christ. But sometimes we forget this truth. We must believe it. If we do not have the faith in this truth, we are bound by the lusts of the flesh and by our families, and this prevents us from walking with the Lord. Our flesh is so weak that even our families can't help us follow Him. Only the Lord can help us. But now we are crucified to the world. How can a dead man help earthly people in earthly affairs? People who are dead in this world cannot own the things of the world.

Jesus was resurrected. His resurrection allowed us to be born again to a new spiritual life. Here we have new work, new family, new hope. We are the born again people. We, as the soldiers of heaven, have a responsibility to preach the word of God. Paul confessed that he became a man by helping others achieve salvation not through physical means but using spiritual methods. He said he had already died and was born again through Jesus Christ. Let's struggle to be the kind of people who dare to give the same confession of our beliefs.

Paul said in Galatians 6:17-18, *"From now on let no one trouble me, for I bear in my body the marks of the Lord Jesus. Brethren, the grace of our Lord Jesus Christ be with your spirit. Amen."* Paul bore the marks of the Lord Jesus. He didn't take care of his health for the Lord in order to walk in the Spirit. He couldn't even write, as he gradually lost his sight. So not a few of Pauline Epistles were recorded by his companions like Tertius while he was speaking God's words. Even though he was physically weak, he was happy to be able to walk in the Spirit and said, *"Even though our outward man is perishing, yet the inward man is being renewed day by day"* (2 Corinthians 4:16).

Paul advises us to be the kind of people who walk in the Spirit. He also says, "Walking in the Spirit means living for the gospel." You and I must bear it in mind that what walking in the Spirit means. We must not pursue objects of vanity and instead serve and live for the gospel. Let's walk in the Spirit by faith for the rest of our lives.

Now by believing in the gospel of the water and the Spirit, the real Spirit is in our hearts. God will gladly respond if we pray in accordance with the gospel. To bear the fruit of the Spirit means to walk in the Spirit and redeem souls. You can bear the fruit of the Spirit, namely love, joy, peace, longsuffering, kindness, goodness, faithfulness, gentleness and self-control, when you walk in the Spirit and live for the gospel. To preach the gospel of the water and the Spirit, we must suffer, remain tolerant, exercise kindness and do good to for the lost.

The fruits of the Spirit come into bearing for those who save the lost souls by doing good and preaching the gospel that causes them receive the indwelling of the Holy Spirit. This is what it takes to bear the fruits of the Spirit and walk in the Spirit. ✉

SERMON 11

To maintain your life
full of the Holy Spirit

To maintain your life full of the Holy Spirit

<Ephesians 5:6-18>

"Let no one deceive you with empty words, for because of these things the wrath of God comes upon the sons of disobedience. Therefore do not be partakers with them. For you were once darkness, but now you are light in the Lord. Walk as children of light (for the fruit of the Spirit is in all goodness, righteousness, and truth), finding out what is acceptable to the Lord. And have no fellowship with the unfruitful works of darkness, but rather expose them. For it is shameful even to speak of those things, which are done by them in secret. But all things that are exposed are made manifest by the light, for whatever makes manifest is light. Therefore He says: 'Awake, you who sleep, arise from the dead, and Christ will give you light.' See then that you walk circumspectly, not as fools but as wise, redeeming the time, because the days are evil. Therefore do not be unwise, but understand what the will of the Lord is. And do not be drunk with wine, in which is dissipation; but be filled with the Spirit."

What do we have to do in order to maintain our lives full of the Holy Spirit?

We have to abandon ourselves, take up the cross, and deny our evil thoughts, devoting ourselves to preaching the gospel.

In order to "maintain a life full of the Holy Spirit," we must devote ourselves to preaching the gospel. To live a life full of the Holy Spirit, we must first receive the blessing that makes the Holy Spirit dwell in our hearts. To receive the indwelling of the Holy Spirit we must have this kind of faith, that is, we must believe in the gospel of the water and the Spirit that God gave us. By having this faith, we will receive the blessing that makes the Holy Spirit dwell in us.

Do those who have the indwelling of the Holy Spirit want a life full of the Holy Spirit? Of course they do. But why is it that some of them cannot live this life? The reason is that their own problems take precedence over the works of God, meaning that they cannot walk with Him. To maintain a life full of the Holy Spirit, we must learn and believe in the words of God. First of all, let's look in the Bible to find out what kind of life and faith we must have.

What is the reason that some people cannot live a life full of the Holy Spirit?

First, we can say that it is because they cannot abandon themselves. The Bible said that only those who abandon themselves could walk with the Lord. Since achieving a life full of the Holy Spirit is not possible through one's own power, everyone must have faith of the indwelling of the Holy Spirit in order to abandon himself. Even for those who have the indwelling of the Holy Spirit, it is difficult for them to abandon their selves without having some concern for the Kingdom of God. Thus for a life full of the Holy Spirit, we must serve the gospel of the water and the Spirit. Only then can a person abandon himself and live as a servant of righteousness.

In Matthews 16:24-26 it says, *"Then Jesus said to His disciples, 'If anyone desires to come after Me, let him deny himself, and take up his Cross, and follow Me. For whoever desires to save his life will lose it, but whoever loses his life for My sake will find it. For what profit is it to a man if he gains the whole world, and loses his own soul? Or what will a man give in exchange for his soul?'"*

The reason that some people who are born again cannot live a life full of the Holy Spirit is that they failed to deny the lusts of their flesh. Even people who have the indwelling of the Holy Spirit can follow the Holy Spirit only when they give up the lusts of their flesh. There are many aspects of the life of the flesh that we must give up in order to follow the Lord. The Lord said, *"Let him deny himself, and take up his Cross, and follow Me."*

To be carnally minded is death, but to be spiritually minded is life and peace. People who wish to walk in the Spirit must abandon the life of the flesh. Only those who dare to make this sacrifice can maintain a life full of the Holy Spirit. This is the truth of the fullness of the Holy Spirit.

Which do you want to follow, the Lord or the world? According to your choice, a life full of the Holy Spirit or a life of the lust is yours. If you really want to live a life full of the Holy Spirit, the choice is yours. God saved us from all our sins and gave us the gift of the indwelling of the Holy Spirit. But it is up to you to decide whether you live a life full of the Holy Spirit. In other words, the life full of the Holy Spirit is not predestined or fated by God. The life full of the Holy Spirit depends only on the wills of those of us who believe in the beautiful gospel of the water and the Spirit.

You must have the will to live a life full of the Holy Spirit

If you have the will to live a life full of the Holy Spirit, God will allow it. He will help and bless you. But if you do not want it, you must give up the life full of the Holy Spirit.

You can receive the indwelling of the Holy Spirit only by faith in the gospel of the water and the Spirit and not by your will. But to live and maintain a life full of the Holy Spirit is totally dependent on your will.

Therefore, if you want a life full of the Holy Spirit, you must examine your own will and ask for God's help. If we really want lives full of the Holy Spirit, God will bless us and fulfill our desires. But to achieve our goal, we must deny the lusts of the flesh.

Second, to live a life full of the Holy Spirit, we must take up our own crosses. We must live and walk by the will of God even in difficult situations. This is what it means to live a righteous life full of the Holy Spirit.

And third, the Lord said, *"For whoever desires to save his life will lose it, but whoever loses his life for My sake will find it. For what profit is it to a man if he gains the whole world, and loses his own soul? Or what will a man give in exchange for his soul?"* This means following the Lord is relevant to our lives. Indeed, if we follow Him, our spirit and flesh will prosper but if we do not follow Him and choose to live lives of our own, our spirit and flesh will perish.

Why can't we have lives full of the Holy Spirit? The reason is that we don't deny our thoughts, namely the lusts of the flesh. When we follow Jesus, the Spirit strengthens our inner selves and therefore He can lead us with greater forcefulness.

In Ephesians 5:11-13 it says, *"And have no fellowship with the unfruitful works of darkness, but rather expose them. For it is shameful even to speak of those things which are done by them in secret. But all things that are exposed are made manifest by the light, for whatever makes manifest is light."* Christians must have no fellowship with the unfruitful works of darkness. But when we indulge ourselves in the unfruitful works of darkness, God tells us to expose them. We should be reproached with our works of darkness, for it is shameful even to speak of those things that are done by them in secret. But all things that are exposed are made manifest by the light.

Who is capable of exposing and talking about all these shameful things? If others, your brothers or sisters and the servants of God cannot expose them, you must expose them on your own. It is said that all things that are exposed are made manifest by the light. Therefore we must admit our evil deeds to be not right, and be led by the Holy Spirit to expose the unfruitful works of darkness by ourselves or through our leader.

In this world, all things that are exposed end just as they are rebuked but in the world of God, all exposed things are made manifest by the light, for whatever makes manifest is light. Since we are far from perfect, we commit many sins unconsciously in this world. However, when we shed the light of the words of God on ourselves, we become conscious of certain sins and are able to admit them. And so it is that we come to give endless thanks to God.

Because Jesus took away all our sins and iniquities, and all the righteousness of God was fulfilled when He was baptized in the Jordan River, we are able to be manifest by the light through the righteousness of God. The billions of sins that humanity has committed were transferred to Jesus when John baptized Him. He is the Lamb of God who took away the sins of the world, died on the Cross to be judged for them, and was resurrected. Jesus forgave all the sins of humanity and when He said, *"It is finished" (John 19:30),* all of mankind was saved. We become sanctified through our faith in what Jesus Christ did. Since our sins are forgiven, we can come into the light again and follow God righteously.

God told us to redeem the time

Paul said that if we want to live a life full of the Holy Spirit, we must redeem the time. In Ephesians 5:16-17 it says, *"Redeem the time, because the days are evil. Therefore do not be unwise, but understand what the will of the Lord is."* If we want to live a life full of the Holy Spirit, we must redeem the time and not be unwise. We should understand what the will of the Lord is and do it. We must decide which is more worthwhile: the life faithful to our flesh or that devoted to God.

After we are born again, the Holy Spirit dwells within us. If we receive the indwelling of the Holy Spirit, it means our Master is the Lord and He is our King. Only He is our Savior and we must admit Him absolutely to be our God. He is our only Master. He is the Master who made me, forgave all my sins and blessed me. And He is the King that has dominion over my life and death, blessings or curses. We must admit that the Lord is the Master Himself and God so we should obey Him throughout our lives.

Let's see what it says from Philippians 2:5-11 *"Let this mind be in you which was also in Christ Jesus, who, being in the form of God, did not consider it robbery to be equal with*

God, but made Himself of no reputation, taking the form of a bondservant, and coming in the likeness of men. And being found in appearance as a man, He humbled Himself and became obedient to the point of death, even the death of the Cross. Therefore God also has highly exalted Him and given Him the name which is above every name, that at the name of Jesus every knee should bow, of those in heaven, and of those on earth, and of those under the earth, and that every tongue should confess that Jesus Christ is Lord, to the glory of God the Father."

Paul said, *"Let this mind be in you."* He said this was the heart of Jesus Christ. What Paul said was that *"this mind"* is of Jesus, who was God the Creator and came into this world to save His people from their sins according to the will of His Father. The Lord came to this world and took away all the sins of the world through His baptism by John. And when He died on the Cross, the sins of the world were extirpated with Him. He was then resurrected after three days and became our Savior.

The reason why Jesus Christ, the Creator, came to this world was to save us. He showed His love for us through His baptism and blood on the Cross. All creation must kneel before Him and appreciate His love that gave us forgiveness of sin by lowering Himself as a creature even though He is the Creator. That is why all the creatures should confess that He is their true Savior. He made us confess that He is not only the Lord of all creation but also the Lord of the utmost righteousness to us.

We, who believe in God and have the indwelling of the Holy Spirit, must believe that 'God is the only real Master to me' and have the love of Jesus Christ in our heart. We must have faith that our master is not ourselves but Jesus Christ, who created and saved us from all our sins. And we must also have faith that He is the Master who makes us live a blessed new life and prepares everything for us and works for us.

There are many people who do not want to exchange masters after being born again. There are many who have the indwelling of the Holy Spirit but insist that they are the masters of themselves. The life full of the Holy Spirit is the life of following God. This kind of life cannot be gained in one day but is possible only when we believe that Jesus is the Master of our lives and the One that created us and all other creations in the universe. We need to have faith in order to serve Jesus our Lord, Master and God, who has saved us from our sins and gave us everlasting life in the Kingdom of Heaven.

We need to bear the truth in our minds. Many people live their lives as masters of themselves. They protect and maintain dominion over their own lives. But now is the time to change masters. We've now become the ones who know God, and so our essential Master is the Lord.

All of us have sin in our hearts and should be condemned to hell for our wrongdoing. But we found God through our faith in the gospel of the water and the Spirit. God loves us so much that He came into this world, took away all our sins by being baptized by John and dying on the Cross to become our real Savior. And through our faith in God, we were delivered from all our sins. In other words, we received the indwelling of the Holy Spirit.

The Bible says, *"Now if anyone does not have the Spirit of Christ, he is not His" (Romans 8:9).* When we received His redemption, that is, the indwelling of the Holy Spirit, we became the children of God. The Holy Spirit is God to us and we must walk in the righteousness of God under the instruction of the Holy Spirit. To live so, we must give up mastery over ourselves. After we met Jesus and are delivered by Him, we must make Him our one and only Master.

We must hand the thrones in our hearts to Jesus

We cannot follow the Lord if we consider ourselves masters of our own lives. When God orders us to serve Him, we will say "Yes" without delay if we are not our own masters. Otherwise, we might say "Why should I do it for you?" The person who is his own master will refuse to do what God wants him to do, thinking, "He should ask me as a favor to do what He wants." To such a person, God's instructions are nothing but idle and bothersome words.

However to be filled with the Holy Spirit, we must obey His order. We cannot be cows that are dragged to the slaughter, but rather we must volunteer to follow God. We must follow God, our Savior, who leads us along the righteous path. God is the Lord, who blessed us with salvation. If we serve Him as our Master and keep His rules, we can be filled with the Holy Spirit. If you and the members of your family hand your kingship to Jesus and place Him above all else, you will have grace and blessings in your lives.

You may have seen pictures like the one in which a man who is sailing against a strong windstorm and Jesus is standing right behind him. When it seems that we are managing the challenges in our lives and doing the work of the Lord, it is actually our Lord Jesus Christ who is leading us and holding our hands. It is Almighty God who oversees our lives. He saved us. He protects us from Satan, leads us and has dominion over our lives.

Since He became our Master, He is able to supervise and bless us. But if we do not acknowledge Him as our Master, He cannot perform the role. As He is the God of personality, He does not force us to obey His will. Even though He is Almighty God, He does not do anything for us unless we volunteer to serve Him as our Master and ask for help.

Cast all things on Him

Cast all things on to Him so that He can fulfill His mastery over us. Serve Him and admit that He is our Master. Since we are far from perfect, we must cast all things on Him and pass all responsibility on to Him. Once we cast our families, daily lives and everything else on Him, we will receive the wisdom from God and become able to live as He wants, managing all the problems with the faith and power that God has given us.

Our problems then become those of our Master, which means that if we just follow Jesus the Almighty God, He will take responsibility for us. We will be able to live a life full of the Holy Spirit and enjoy the peace that resides in Him. As faithful Christians, we must kneel down before God, admit and serve Him as our Master.

Let's see what it says in Philippians 3:3 about what kind of faith we must have to live a life full of the Holy Spirit. *"We are the circumcision, who worship God in the Spirit, rejoice in Christ Jesus, and have no confidence in the flesh."* What it means by 'the circumcision' here is the ones who worship God in the Spirit, rejoice in Christ Jesus, and have no confidence in the flesh.

To live as the circumcision means to cut off all the sin in our hearts and pass it on to Jesus Christ, who was baptized by

John. Those who are led by the Spirit owe their lives to the Spirit. They serve God and rejoice in Christ Jesus saying, "Jesus has led me to live this glorious life. He made me righteous and blessed me. He gave me all the grace I needed to serve Him." We need to live like this. This is the life full of the Holy Spirit. Paul said, *"Therefore, whether you eat or drink, or whatever you do, do all to the glory of God" (1 Corinthians 10:31).*

In Philippians 3:13-14 it says, *"Brethren, I do not count myself to have apprehended; but one thing I do, forgetting those things which are behind and reaching forward to those things which are ahead, I press toward the goal for the prize of the upward call of God in Christ Jesus."* God told us to forget those things that are behind us in the past, and reach forward to those things that are ahead. We must press toward our goal. Regardless of our righteous deeds or wrongdoings, we must forget those things that are behind us and try to reach forward to those things that are ahead and press toward our goal. This goal is to serve His will holding on to Jesus Christ by believing in Him.

We are far from perfect, so we are apt to fall down when we feel the lure of the flesh. However by looking up to God and having faith, we can dispose of all our weaknesses and iniquities. When Jesus Christ was baptized by John and died on the Cross, all our sins were transferred to Him. When He became our Savior through the resurrection, we were given new lives thanks to our belief in Him. Therefore, we must dispose of all those things that are behind us, reach forward to those things that are ahead and press toward our goal.

To maintain a life full of the Holy Spirit

We must reach forward to those things that are ahead and press toward the higher goal. I hope you can forget all past things as quickly as possible if they burden you. There are many things that can't be done because of our weaknesses, but those are of no concern because what is important lies in the future. As the future is more important, we must hand our kingship to Jesus Christ through faith and be led by Him. We must let Him decide how we will live in the future and do what is pleasing to Him.

We have to live as the disciples did

We can lead a life full of the Holy Spirit only if we become strong in our faith in the remission of sin. This is very important. Let's look at 2 Timothy 2:1-10. *"You therefore, my son, be strong in the grace that is in Christ Jesus. And the things that you have heard from me among many witnesses, commit these to faithful men who will be able to teach others also. You therefore must endure hardship as a good soldier of Jesus Christ. No one engaged in warfare entangles himself with the affairs of this life, that he may please him who enlisted him as a soldier. And also if anyone competes in athletics, he is not crowned unless he completes according to the rules. The hardworking farmer must be first to partake of the crops. Consider what I say, and may the Lord give you understanding in all things. Remember that Jesus Christ, of the seed of David, was raised from the dead according to my gospel, for which I suffer trouble as an evil-doer, even to the point of chains; but the word of God is not chained. Therefore I endure all things for the sake of the elect, that they also may obtain the salvation which is in Christ Jesus with eternal glory."*

Just as Paul said to Timothy, the Holy Spirit says to us, *"Be strong in the grace that is in Christ Jesus. And the things that you have heard from me among many witnesses, commit these to faithful men who will be able to teach others also."*

"Be strong in the grace that is in Christ Jesus." To become strong in the grace here means that we have to strengthen our faith in the gospel of the water and the Spirit by believing in Him and holding on to Him. Jesus Christ came into this world to accept all our sins through His baptism, died on the Cross, was resurrected and became our Savior. This means that we should be strong in the grace of God and be thankful to Him. God saved us and therefore we should accept salvation through faith as a gift of God. This is salvation of the remission of sins. It has nothing to do with offering early morning daily prayers or donating money for the construction of a church. All of these things do more harm than good for receiving salvation.

Our salvation through the forgiveness of sin means that Jesus Christ, regardless of our deeds, was baptized to bear all our sins, then died on the Cross to blot out all our transgressions. He was resurrected in order to save us from all our sins. Pastors are forgiven for their sins by believing this gospel of truth, as are laymen. Anyone who believes in Jesus Christ like this with all his heart receives the forgiveness of sin. We can therefore have confidence in the grace of salvation and strengthen our faith.

If we want a life full of the Holy Spirit, we must become strong in our faith in the gospel of the water and the Spirit. There are areas in our lives where we fail to measure up, and have our share of weaknesses. That is why we should become strong in the grace of salvation. Every time our failings appear, we have to meditate on our faith by saying to ourselves, "God saved me through the gospel of the water and the Spirit. Jesus forgave all my sins through the water and the Spirit." We become righteous by believing in this gospel and strengthen ourselves by having the indwelling of the Holy Spirit. We were saved from all our sins and became strong by believing in the gospel of the water and the Spirit. We became blessed people through our faith.

Paul said, *"Whether you eat or drink, or whatever you do, do all to the glory of God" (1 Corinthians 10:31).* This is a very important. It means that we must dedicate our lives to God. *"Whether you eat or drink."* We should eat, drink and be strong for God in order to do His work. We should eat good things for our health in order to preach the gospel.

"No one engaged in warfare entangles himself with the affairs of this life, that he may please him who enlisted him as a soldier" (2 Timothy 2:4). You should lead a life full of the Holy Spirit in order to preach the gospel. We can live a faithful life when we lead life for the sake of preaching the gospel. All who live a faithful life like this is full of the Holy Spirit. We should all strive for lives full of the Holy Spirit. Even the offerings, which you earned through your hard work, should be used for the gospel.

If you want to maintain a life full of the Holy Spirit, you have to dedicate yourself to the Lord, be at His service, use your money for the gospel and share all your joys and sorrows with God. If we want to lead this kind of life, we must live in faith with strong will to serve the gospel.

Many people have led a life for themselves until now. They have put up walls and accumulated their property for themselves by being their own master. However, now we have to live for God. We must take God as our one and only Master. The Lord says, *"No one engaged in warfare entangles himself with the affairs of this life, that he may please him who enlisted him as a soldier."* Living the life of a good soldier means following the rules. The Lord solves our problems for us, protects and leads us if we live for Him as His faithful soldiers. He tells us to seek first the Kingdom of God and His righteousness (Matthew 6:33).

There is nothing false in the word of God. If we follow Him, we will experience the truthfulness of His word. But remember that first you must have the indwelling of the Holy Spirit in your heart. A person without the indwelling of the Holy Spirit cannot hand his own throne over to God. However, a person with the indwelling of the Holy Spirit can give the throne of his heart to God and thereby experience the fullness of the Holy Spirit and have happiness and peace in his heart.

The indwelling of the Holy Spirit will come true to you if you only understand and believe in the beautiful gospel of the water and the Spirit. If you want to have the fullness of the Holy Spirit and want to live a blessed life, you should serve God as the King and live for the good of His kingdom. Then you will be filled with the Holy Spirit and your heart will then become abundant and your prosperous life will be maintained as you win the blessings of being children in God's Kingdom.

I have delivered the message that people who have received salvation from sin and the indwelling of the Holy Spirit by believing in the Lord should lead a life full of the Holy Spirit. I have defined the life filled with the Holy Spirit and explained how this kind of life can be maintained. I have also explained that by faith you must hand over your thrones to the Lord and by faith you must serve Him and maintain a life filled with the Holy Spirit.

Once again, to someone who has the indwelling of the Holy Spirit, to be born again is not the end. He has to continue leading a life full of the Holy Spirit. We should certainly know and believe that our spirits and flesh can only be blessed if we lead such a life.

This kind of life doesn't happen spontaneously. It only happens when we believe in the Lord as our Master and place Him in the foremost position in our hearts. God saved us and has already given us a life full of the Holy Spirit, a life of serving the gospel. He also gave us His work and position to do His work so we could maintain a life full of the Holy Spirit.

You should dedicate yourself to Him and live life for Him. Serve Him by preaching this beautiful gospel. Your heart will then become full of the Holy Spirit, and happiness and grace will flow from you. On the day of His return, you will be blessed, proudly standing before God and winning His reward. You and I should admire the life full of the Holy Spirit. We should strive to live this kind of life through faith. This is how a life full of the Holy Spirit is maintained.

Have you abdicated the throne in your hearts in order to live a life full of the Holy Spirit? I hope you will let Him hold the foremost position in your heart. You must have the will to live a life full of the Holy Spirit. It is then that He will bless you so that you can lead a life full of the Holy Spirit. ✉

SERMON 12

To live the life full of
the Holy Spirit

To live the life full of the Holy Spirit

<Titus 3:1-8>
"Remind them to be subject to rulers and authorities, to obey, to be ready for every good work, to speak evil of no one, to be peaceable, gentle, showing all humility to all men. For we ourselves were also once foolish, disobedient, deceived, serving various lusts and pleasures, living in malice and envy, hateful and hating one another. But when the kindness and the love of God our Savior toward man appeared, not by works of righteousness which we have done, but according to His mercy He saved us, through the washing of regeneration and renewing of the Holy Spirit, whom He poured out on us abundantly through Jesus Christ our Savior, that having been justified by His grace we should become heirs according to the hope of eternal life.

This is a faithful saying, and these things I want you to affirm constantly, that those who have believed in God should be careful to maintain good works. These things are good and profitable to men."

How can we live the life full of the Holy Spirit?

We should understand the will of God and preach the gospel according to it.

Those who believe in Jesus and have the indwelling of the Holy Spirit must live a life full of the Holy Spirit. For Christians, a life full of the Holy Spirit is what God requires. We must follow His orders. Then how can we live a life full of the Holy Spirit? We must pay attention to what the apostle Paul said about this.

What is needed to live a life full of the Holy Spirit?

In Titus 3:1 Paul said, *"Remind them to be subject to rulers and authorities, to obey, to be ready for every good work."* First of all, he told us to be subject to rulers and authorities, to obey and be ready to do good works. What he meant was that we cannot live a life full of the Holy Spirit if we disobey the laws of the world. Of course, if the rulers of the world and the laws run counter to the truth, we ought not to obey them. But if the laws do not violate our faith, we must obey them to serve the gospel in peace.

We are the ones who received the indwelling of the Holy Spirit. How would we be able to live a life full of the Holy Spirit if we broke secular laws? Therefore, in order to live a life full of the Holy Spirit, we must follow the laws of the world. Those who receive the indwelling of the Holy Spirit must obey the social norms. We can walk with God only when we keep the laws of the world.

Suppose one of us had committed a crime on the way to the church. Would he be able to serve the Lord with comfort? How on earth would he be able to live according to the Lord's teachings if he lived outside the law? We must not violate social norms while walking in the Spirit. Nothing good comes of violating the law. We must keep the peace by obeying the law. We must strive to live upright lives while preaching the gospel. To live with the fullness of the Holy Spirit, it is wise for the saints to abide by the laws of society.

We must keep humility within our hearts

Paul said, *"To speak evil of no one, to be peaceable, gentle, showing all humility to all men."* To live a life full of the Holy Spirit, we must speak evil of no one, be peaceable, gentle and show humility to all men.

In the hearts of those who are born again, there is humility, self-control and gentleness. This is possible because of the Holy Spirit that dwells in us. Paul told us that we must not undermine the gospel by fighting with each other. Of course, we must fight when the social law goes against the gospel. But when it does not do so, we must live peacefully. We must cause others to think of us, "Although he seems wild as a lion at times, he is really peaceful as a pigeon. His belief in Christianity perhaps makes him polite and a man of sense."

There is no gentleness or humility in the lusts of the flesh. But through the indwelling of the Holy Spirit and through the Lord who saved us from our sins, we can be gentle to others. Forgiving someone who has done a terrible wrong to me is real "forgiveness" and treating him with humility from deep inside myself is real "humility." It is not humility for me to pretend to be kind for someone when I really have a hatred for him. Having a heart full of humility and forgiveness is the inward morality of the born again Christians.

We must also have gentleness when people do us wrong.

As long as they don't attempt to hinder the gospel, we must be gentle to everyone. But if they do, we must replace the light of gentleness with the light of the truth. Gentleness is found only in the truth of God, so those who oppose, interfere with or slander the word of God don't deserve to be treated with gentleness.

God does not forgive those who oppose Him but makes them pay the price. God told Abraham, *"I will bless those who bless you, and I will curse him who curses you" (Genesis 12:3).* People who oppose the gospel of the truth have no way to be saved. They will not be able to avoid the disaster that will ruin not only their lives but also up to third generations of their descendents.

Why do we have to be tolerant and humble? As it is written in Titus 3:3, *"We ourselves were also once foolish disobedient, deceived, serving various lusts and pleasures, living in malice and envy, hateful and hating one another."* We were just like these people before we were born again. So we must tolerate and forgive them because we were once like them.

In Titus 3:4-8, it says, *"But when the kindness and the love of God our Savior toward man appeared, not by works of righteousness which we have done, but according to His mercy He saved us, through the washing of regeneration and renewing of the Holy Spirit, whom He poured out on us abundantly through Jesus Christ our Savior, that having been justified by His grace we should become heirs according to the hope of eternal life. This is a faithful saying, and these things I want you to affirm constantly, that those who have believed in God should be careful to maintain good works. These things are good and profitable to men."*

According to the Bible, God did not save us from our sins because we did good works. He gave us the blessing of being born again because He loved and pitied us. In other words, Jesus Christ came to this world, was baptized, died on the Cross, was resurrected, and thus washed away all our sins. Jesus was resurrected and now sits at the right hand of God. By rising again among the dead, all of the uncompleted things in the world were perfected.

God blessed us with the Holy Spirit through Jesus Christ our Savior. Jesus Christ was baptized by John to take away all the sins of the world and died on the Cross so that all our sins could be forgiven. We were saved and have become righteous.

The Bible also says, *"We should become heirs according to the hope of eternal life."* This means that we, as the heirs of God, are the ones that inherited all His wealth and glory. To lead this kind of blessed life, we must live life in the fullness of the Holy Spirit. You must believe in the gospel of the water and the Spirit, be forgiven for all your sins and preach the gospel to others.

Therefore, having been forgiven for our sins, we must work for the benefit of others, we must keep the laws of the world and preach the gospel to those who are looking for God. And we must forgive people who do us wrong and treat them with goodness and humility so that they cannot interfere with the preaching of the beautiful gospel. *"These things are good and profitable to men."* If you long for the fullness of the Holy Spirit, you must remember what Paul said to us. This might not sound like anything special, but these are very important words.

Since we are living in this world, we cannot be filled with the Holy Spirit if we are in conflict with others by disobeying the rules of this world. Therefore we must obey the law unless it conflicts with the word of God. We must obey the laws of this world. Even if we have faith, obeying the law is the better choice if we wish to live lives that are full of the Holy Spirit. For us to do good works, we must obey the laws of the world and get along with our neighbors.

Do you want to live a life full of the Holy Spirit?

Ephesians 5:8-11 says, *"For you were once in darkness, but now you are light in the Lord. Walk as children of light (for the fruit of the Spirit is in all goodness, righteousness, and truth), finding out what is acceptable to the Lord. And have no fellowship with the unfruitful works of darkness, but rather expose them."* This passage tells us to walk as children of light and bear the fruits of the Spirit.

Then Ephesians 5:12-13 says, *"For it is shameful even to speak of those things which are done by them in secret. But all things that are exposed are made manifest by the light, for whatever makes manifest is light."* Paul says here that all things that are exposed are made manifest by the light. If a righteous person cannot live righteously, he will be exposed either by God or himself. What happens when a person is found to be doing the work of darkness, and then is rebuked by the light? After admitting his mistakes, his heart is lightened when he faces God again. *"All things that are exposed are made manifest by the light, for whatever makes manifest is light."* It is good to be exposed to the light. Then we can admit our transgressions and return to God.

If we really want to live a life full of the Holy Spirit, we must have kindness in our hearts. Even if someone has no sin in his heart, it does not mean that he doesn't have to be kind.

We must live with goodness and kindness in our hearts. We must preach with wisdom and pray for people who do not know the gospel of the water and the Spirit so that they can understand it and be forgiven for their sins. And we must not harm others either. We must eat, sleep and live the gospel and serve others as well.

To live a life full of the Holy Spirit, we must think of the importance of time and serve the beautiful gospel like men of wisdom. When we love the world, we are subject to the trickery of darkness and can be negligent in doing the work of God. Therefore, we must fix our eyes on the Lord and do what He wants. While believing in the salvation that God gave us, we also must be watchful at all times. A man of wisdom of the Spirit should be devoted to preach the beautiful gospel worldwide before the world becomes filled with darkness.

Understand the will of the Lord

We must try to find out what pleases God. We must learn what He wants us to do through His church and words. We should know what we can do to please God and figure out His will for us.

People who are forgiven for their sins are the ones who are born again and those who are born again are the ones that have the indwelling of the Holy Spirit. Those who have the Holy Spirit within are truly holy people and children of God. They must live a life full of the Holy Spirit. This is the duty of all the saints. We should not waste our abilities and energies on ourselves, indifferent to the needs of others. We ought not to hinder the works of God by going along with the stream of the times.

If we have been sanctified and received regeneration through the love of God, we must become a good person in order to continue and carry out His work. If we have become children of God by believing in him, it is right for us to be people of goodness.

The flesh of God's children is far from perfect but it pleases God; provided we are concerned about the will of God and do good things. But even the ones who are born again are apt to do evil to others if they live only for themselves. *"Do not be drunk with wine, in which is dissipation; but be filled with the Spirit" (Ephesians 5:18)* means that we must not become drunk with the lusts of the flesh but must do the works of goodness.

Paul said in Ephesians 5:19-21, *"Speaking to one another in psalms and hymns and spiritual songs, singing and making melody in your heart to the Lord, giving thanks always for all things to God the Father in the name of our Lord Jesus Christ, submitting to one another in the fear of God."* If we want to live a life full of the Holy Spirit, we must believe in and preach the gospel of salvation and reveal what God has done for us.

God blesses us whenever we pray and He has recorded all these blessings in psalms and hymns and spiritual songs for us to praise Him in one voice. We must commend, thank and praise Him. We can live blessed lives full of the Holy Spirit when we pray for those who are not yet saved and for each other. We must thank God from deep inside our hearts and respect Jesus Christ, who saved us. With these thoughts in our hearts, we must be able to admit our wrongs, express our appreciation for the cleansing of our sins and obey Him. This is what it means to live a live full of the Holy Spirit.

We must serve the beautiful gospel for the rest of our lives

We must plan good works and pursue them for the greater glory of the beautiful gospel. Being joined to God's church, we should pray together and call on God to save the souls of everyone. There are still many people who couldn't be born again because they do not know the beautiful gospel even though they have looked for God. We must pray for these people, saying "God, please save them too." And we must not pursue selfish things but offer our properties in serving the gospel to save the lost. Living for the souls of others and for the expansion of God's Kingdom is doing good work.

Doing this kind of work means living a life full of the Holy Spirit. Living with the fullness of the Holy Spirit does not mean having the ability to speak in tongues and perform miracles, rather learning how to please God. It means believing in the salvation God gave us, praising and glorifying God with poems and psalms. To thank, praise and glorify God with all our heart, and to serve Him with our bodies as instruments of righteousness is the will of God. Following His orders means living a life full of the Holy Spirit.

To live a life full of the Spirit, we must obey one another. If someone gives us advice, we must listen to what he says. In the same way, if I give advice to him, he should listen even if he does not agree with me. Likewise, we must live a life full of the Spirit by obeying each other and doing the work of God.

Living a life full of the Spirit means glorifying Jesus Christ

Living a life full of the Spirit means keeping the commandments of Jesus Christ. Let's find out what this means by reading Ephesians 6:10-13. *"Finally, my brethren, be strong in the Lord and in the power of His might. Put on the whole armor of God, that you may be able to stand against the wiles of the devil. For we do not wrestle against flesh and blood, but against principalities, against powers, against the rulers of the darkness of this age, against spiritual hosts of wickedness in the heavenly places. Therefore take up the whole armor of God, that you may be able to withstand in the evil day, and having done all, to stand."*

What does it mean to live a life full of the Spirit? It means being strong in the Lord and having faith in His power. It means living by the power of the Holy Spirit that dwells within us and not by our own will alone. Moreover, it means living a life of prayer. By praying, we can live a vigorous life receiving the various abilities and blessings God gives. Living this kind of life means putting on the armor of God. We are so weak that even if we try to walk with Him, to serve and obey God, we cannot live a life full of the Spirit unless we hold on to His words.

Belief in God's words is essential to boosting our spiritual power. Even if we have faith, we must put on the whole armor of God by saying, "I am sure it will be as it is recorded in the words of God." This is the faith that enables us to live a life full of the Holy Spirit.

Are any of you having problems living this kind of life? Then remember the words of the Scriptures and put on the whole armor of God. God told us to put on His whole armor. By taking words deep inside your heart, you will learn what it means to put on the whole armor of God. Regardless of our environment and what other people say, we must hold on to the words of God. In this way, we will live a life full of the Holy Spirit.

Where can we get this belief? Revelation 3:22 says, *"He who has an ear, let him hear what the Spirit says to the churches."* We should listen to what the Spirit says to the church. In other words, we couldn't hear the words of God nor live a life full of the Holy Spirit but for the servants of God. Through whom does the Holy Spirit speak? God speaks to the saints and all the people of the world through His servants in His church.

That is to say, you should believe that the teachings of God's church are surely based on the words of God. You need to accept the teachings of the church with this faith in mind. If the Holy Spirit didn't dwell in a preacher, it would be possible for him to teach his own thoughts. The preacher who has the indwelling of the Holy Spirit preaches God's words under the control of the Holy Spirit. If he does not do so but preaches biblically groundless words, the Holy Spirit stops him because He dwells in his heart.

The Holy Spirit is God. The authority of God's servant is exceedingly great because God dwells in him. In the New Testament, Jesus Christ said to Peter *"I will give you the keys of the kingdom of Heaven" (Matthew 16:19).* The keys to Heaven are the gospel of the water and the Spirit. In other words, this gospel is the key to entering Heaven. God gave the authority to preach the word of God not only to Peter but also to every servant of God and all the saints, as long as they are born again and have the indwelling of the Holy Spirit.

To live a life full of the Holy Spirit, we must put on the whole armor of God. If we don't have faith, we must keep the teachings of the church in mind every day by believing in the authority of the church and of the servants of God. Even if the sermon that you hear today is of no use and not directly related to your life, you must listen to it anyway and take it into your heart. Find the words in the Bible that are needed in your everyday life. Hold on to them. In this way, you will be a person of faith. Then you will be able to live a life full of the Holy Spirit, walk with God and win the battle against the principalities and rulers of darkness in the world.

You may have been confused because you were told that you should obey the rulers of the world but now I say that you should fight against the rulers of darkness of the world. In Roman times, the Roman Emperor called himself God and the law required all people to treat him as a God. But this was something the Christians could not do because it was against the word of God. So Christians during that time had no choice but to fight the Roman Emperor, who made people bow to him as if he was a God.

In order to win the fight with the devil, we must believe in and hold on to the word of God. If we live according to God's word, we will obtain His blessing and be able to beat the devil. Even if we are saved, we will lose the war against Satan unless we hold on to the word of God. God alerts us, *"Your enemy the devil prowls around like a roaring lion looking for someone to devour" (1 Peter 5:8)*. A person who does not believe in the word of God can be easily attacked by the devil.

Even Jesus couldn't have fought off Satan if it were not for the word of God. *"It is written, 'Man shall not live by bread alone, but by every word that proceeds from the mouth of God'" (Matthew 4:4)*. He drove away the devil through faith in what is written. And what about us? We have a lack of wisdom and are incomparable to Jesus. Therefore, we must believe in and hold on even more strongly to the word of God.

We should not just say, "I think the words are right but I can't believe in it entirely." We must hold on to the words. "I believe everything will turn out to be true as it is written." This is the proper faith and allows us to put on the whole armor of God. People who say, "Everything will be exactly realized as our Lord said" will be blessed. If one holds on to God's word and rely on it, things will turn out well according to his faith. Even if the devil tries to tempt us, he will certainly go away if we say, "I believe in the word of God. I believe His word is the right answers." This is the way to win the war against the devil.

We must hold on to the word of God

"Therefore take up the whole armor of God, that you may be able to withstand in the evil day, and having done all, to stand. Stand therefore, having girded your waist with truth, having put on the breastplate of righteousness, and having shod your feet with the preparation of the gospel of peace; above all, taking the shield of faith with which you will be able to quench all the fiery darts of the wicked one. And take the helmet of salvation, and the sword of the Spirit, which is the word of God" (Ephesians 6:13-17).

In the passage, *"Stand therefore, having girded your waist with truth,"* the word of God is compared to a belt girding one's waist. This means that we must gird our minds with the word of God. He is telling us to follow the words of truth so that we can be at one in mind with God. But as this belt fits tightly around the body, we must also tightly attach ourselves to the word of God. When we are at one in mind with God, we naturally become able to believe and say, "I believe everything will turn out well. I am sure everything will be realized just as God said."

Next, we have to put on the breastplate of righteousness. We must put on the breastplate of the gospel of the water and the Spirit that says God has saved us. We must gird our waists with truth, having put on the breastplate of righteousness. We must put on the breastplate of precious jewels. We must put them on in the belief that God has forgiven all our sins. We must believe the word of God with all our heart. We must also preach the gospel of salvation that gives peace.

After holding all the words above, we should shoe our feet with the preparation of the gospel of peace, and go preaching the gospel of salvation that gives God's peace to all the people. If we have been saved from our sins, we come to confess the belief through our mouth. And every time our sin and evil are revealed, we must wipe them away by ruminating on the truth that God has already forgiven all our sins. He did so through Jesus' baptism and His blood on the Cross. We must live a life of glory by thanking God. We must preach the gospel of the water and the Spirit, which gives peace to everyone who has not been delivered from his sins.

Above all, we must fight the wicked with the shield of faith. When Satan attacks, we must drive him away with the shield of faith in one hand and the words of truth in the other.

Then we must put on the helmet of salvation. We have to accept the words of salvation, saying, "I was saved from all my sins through the gospel of the water and the Spirit. God forgave my sins in this way." We should recognize the truth in our head. We must make the word of God, the helmet of salvation and the sword of the Spirit our weapons against the devil.

If Satan attacks us, we must draw the sword out and beat him down. "God said this! And I believe it is so!" We drive Satan away through faith in God's words. If we believe in the words of God and draw your spiritual sword, Satan will flee screaming "Ouch! How it hurts." We can beat off any kind of Satan's attack if we only believe in the word of God.

You should live such a religious life confessing, "My flesh is far from perfect but I am a person of God who has received redemption. I live by faith, holding on to the words that God has told me." If we have this kind of faith, we can drive Satan away with the sword of truth every time he comes to harass and interrupt our faithful lives. Satan does not even blink if we counterattack with mere earthly words. Thus we must fight him by saying, "This is what God said." Then Satan will surrender before the authority of God's word.

If we want to live a life full of the Holy Spirit, we must pray to God that the church, all the saints and the servants of God would devote themselves to preaching the gospel. By saying a prayer like, "Let me boldly reveal the secrets of the gospel," we will live a life aimed at serving the gospel. This is a life full of the Holy Spirit. Living a life full of the Holy Spirit is essential to all the saints. If we are to be true saints, we must live a life full of the Holy Spirit. Living such a life is essential to all the saints, just as receiving the remission of sins is essential to every soul. This is God's order.

Those who have been saved from their sins but do not know how to lead a faithful life must know that they have to live a life full of the Holy Spirit. This is what God wants. Saints must live a life full of the Holy Spirit, which is the will of God. A life full of the Holy Spirit promotes the saints to preach the gospel by doing good works. They love to preach the gospel, pray to God, and to believe in and hold on to the words of God. We must put on the helmet of salvation and the breastplate of righteousness and drive Satan away by saying, "I am righteous all the time."

Since the saints have the indwelling of the Holy Spirit, they walk in the Spirit and are able to receive the power of the Holy Spirit. They are doing His work with the blessings of God earned by the prayer of faith. And they should walk in the Spirit until they defeat Satan and stand before God. The people who can put on the whole armor of God are only the born again Christians who can live a life full of the Holy Spirit.

"For we do not wrestle against flesh and blood, but against principalities, against powers, against the rulers of the darkness of this age, against spiritual hosts of wickedness in the heavenly places" (Ephesians 6:12). The battle of those who are born again is not the battle of flesh and blood. However, the battle of those who have the indwelling of the Holy Spirit is against the spiritual hosts of wickedness and against those who interrupt our faithful lives, do not serve the gospel and disturb us.

When we go out to fight the spiritual war for the gospel of the Lord, we must put on the helmet and the armor of the Spirit. If we just wear ordinary clothes in this war, we will be wounded. Thus, we must put on the armor. We need swords, shields and helmets. To win the war, we must be perfectly prepared before battle. We must put on the breastplate, gird our waists and wear shoes on both feet. Then, with sword and shield in either hand, we must defeat our enemies. This is a life full of the Holy Spirit.

We must keep the beautiful gospel

Paul told us, *"That good thing which was committed to you, keep by the Holy Spirit who dwells in us"* *(2 Timothy 1:14)*. What is the good deposit? It is the gospel of the water and the Spirit that saved us from our sins. In Titus 3:5 it says, *"He saved us through the washing of regeneration and renewing of the Holy Spirit."* Our Lord washed away all the sins that we had committed in this world, died on the Cross and was resurrected. We must keep this beautiful gospel. We must put on the helmet of salvation and the breastplate of righteousness and gird our waists with truth. We must believe in the gospel of the water and the Spirit.

After arming ourselves in this way, we must win the battle against Satan. Only then will we be able to achieve victory and share it with others. We will have to fight many spiritual battles against Satan and take many trophies away from him until the day we will enter the Lord's Kingdom, which is our inheritance. The more battles we win against our opponent, the easier the next fight will be. We must all pray for His Kingdom to prosper and flourish. Then we will have gained a life full of the Holy Spirit.

We must not be satisfied with being forgiven for our sins but must live a life full of the Holy Spirit. For the gospel and our good works, we must believe in the word of God. We must be led by the Holy Spirit and live by keeping God's word and believing in it, so as not to lose the fight against Satan and be ruined.

Do you understand me? Only then will we have lives full of the Holy Spirit. I hope that you will also serve the gospel of the water and the Spirit and depend on and follow the word of God. Let's all do the work of saving souls from Satan. We can lead lives full of the Holy Spirit until the Lord comes again. To receive the fullness of the Holy Spirit is the second commandment that God gave us. Thank Him. We can have the indwelling of the Holy Spirit due to the remission of sins in our hearts. And if it were not for the indwelling of the Holy Spirit, I couldn't begin a life full of the Holy Spirit. I thank God for letting us lead lives full of the Holy Spirit.

Do you believe that you can have the indwelling of the Holy Spirit? To those of us who have been forgiven for our sins, we have the indwelling of the Holy Spirit. But those who haven't erased their sins do not yet have the indwelling of the Holy Spirit. Those who do not know or do not believe in the gospel of the water and the Spirit do not have the indwelling of the Holy Spirit. All the people in the world will be cast down to Hell if they do not have the indwelling of the Holy Spirit.

Since we have no sin in our hearts, we have the indwelling of the Holy Spirit. And because the Holy Spirit dwells in our hearts, we can live a life full of the Holy Spirit. We, who have the indwelling of the Holy Spirit, must obey the desire of the Spirit in order to be filled with the Holy Spirit. The more we obey the desire of the Spirit, the stronger our faith is becomes like a warrior of full uniform. But if we fail to obey the Spirit, it is the same for us as to be taken off our armor.

Let's grow through the words of the Holy Spirit and become a person of faith. When we hear the words of the Holy Spirit, our faith develops because God says *"Faith comes by hearing, and hearing by the word of God" (Romans 10:17).* Therefore even if Satan attacks us, we are protected by our faith in these words. Satan cannot attack those who have been armed with the shield of faith by believing in the gospel of the water and the Spirit. Faithful people have the power to fend off Satan's attacks with their faith.

Let's lead lives full of the Holy Spirit with faith. A life full of the Holy Spirit implies a life preaching the gospel of the water and the Spirit faithfully all over the world. Such is a life full of the Holy Spirit. ✉

SERMON 13

The works and gifts of
the Holy Spirit

The works and gifts of the Holy Spirit

<John 16:5-11>

"But now I go away to Him who sent Me, and none of you asks Me, 'Where are you going?' But because I have said these things to you, sorrow has filled your heart. Nevertheless I tell you the truth. It is to your advantage that I go away; for if I do not go away, the Helper will not come to you; but if I depart, I will send Him to you. And when He has come, He will convict the world of sin, and of righteousness, and of judgment: of sin, because they do not believe in Me; of righteousness, because I go to My Father and you see Me no more; of judgment, because the ruler of this world is judged."

What is the works of the Holy Spirit?

He convicts the world of sin, of righteousness, and of judgment.

In Genesis 1:2 it is written, *"The earth was without form, and void; and darkness was on the face of the deep. And the Spirit of God was hovering over the face of the waters."* We can see from this passage that the Holy Spirit doesn't dwell in hearts full of confusion and sin, but only lives in the hearts of those who believe in the beautiful gospel. However, many people in their confusion and emptiness fall under the influence of fanatical faiths, saying that they want to receive the indwelling of the Holy Spirit while having sin in their hearts.

The spirit received in a state of fanatic ecstasy is not the beautiful Spirit. The work of Satan rests on the lawless believers of fanaticism, and fanatical people are easily falling under the influence of his tricks and power. But the Holy Spirit is the Person God who is intelligent, emotional and has a definite will. He worked with God the Father and His Son Jesus Christ in creating this world. We will now learn about what kind of work the Holy Spirit has done in this world.

The Holy Spirit convicts the world of sin

What is the very first work the Holy Spirit does? He convicts the world of sin. The people who are convicted by Him are those who don't accept the beautiful gospel of Jesus' baptism by John and His blood on the Cross. He convicts all sinners and the sins of those who don't believe in the beautiful gospel of the water and the Spirit.

He convicts the world of God's righteousness

What is the second thing the Holy Spirit does? He bears witness to God's righteousness and Jesus' achievement in saving sinners from their sins. John 16:10 says, *"Of righteousness, because I go to My Father and you see Me no* more." We have to know what the righteousness of God in the Bible means. It means the truth that Jesus took away all the sins of the world through His baptism by John and that whoever believes in Him can become the righteous through God's grace. Jesus was baptized by John the Baptist and accepted all of the sins of the world, shed His blood on the Cross, was resurrected and became the Savior of all sinners. This is the beautiful gospel God gave us. Jesus took away all the sins of the world through the water and blood according to God's will and became the Master of our lives.

The Holy Spirit helps people believe in the gospel of Jesus' baptism by John and His blood on the Cross, thus helping them gain forgiveness for their sins. You should know that the works of God in the Trinity are complementary. The Holy Spirit works for the beautiful gospel, making people believe in the love of God. He also guarantees the true beautiful gospel of the water and the Spirit to be true.

He convicts the world of judgment

What is the Holy Spirit's third task? He destroys the works of Satan. Satan whispers into people's thoughts, saying, "You can believe in Jesus, but just think of Christianity as one of the many earthly religions." Satan tries to hinder people from believing in Jesus' baptism and His blood on the Cross so that they won't be able to obtain forgiveness for their sins even if they believe in Jesus. Because Satan reduces Christianity to an "ordinary" religion, many people fall victim to Satan's deception that the reason for believing in Jesus is to be good people. However, the real purpose of believing in Jesus is to be born again as righteous people.

You should not have false faith. False faith cannot make you sanctified no matter how much you believe in Jesus. If you have false faith, you won't know or see Jesus clearly due to Satan's lies. The Holy Spirit becomes the guarantee of salvation for those who have been saved by believing in the beautiful gospel of the water and the Spirit. All the beliefs of those who have sin in their hearts are useless.

The Holy Spirit testifies to the truth of the beautiful gospel. Jesus was baptized to take away all the sins of the world and He was crucified to pay off the wages of sin. The Holy Spirit testifies to this truth. The Holy Spirit advises all the people of the world to be forgiven for all their sins by believing in the true gospel. However, we should keep in mind that the Holy Spirit convicts and judges those who don't take the beautiful gospel into their hearts.

Everyone should have the blessed faith

What is the blessed faith? It is the faith that leads us to receive the indwelling of the Holy Spirit through the forgiveness of sin. However, we see many Christians throughout the world who still have sin in their hearts, even though they maintained their belief in Jesus over a long time. The longer they believe in Jesus, the more sinful they become. The biggest problem that hinders them from being delivered from their sins is that they think speaking in tongues and having visions is proof that they have received the Holy Spirit. They are unaware of God's judgment for their sins.

Many people in this world can't distinguish the work of the Holy Spirit from Satan's work. Satan's work leads people into a state of confusion by giving them false beliefs and then leading them on towards destruction. This is what Satan tries to achieve by turning against God. Satan causes people to fall under the influence of superstitious beliefs and takes them as his slaves. Satan instills in them a desire to experience supernatural miracles and wonders by causing them to think that such experiences are more valuable than receiving the indwelling of the Holy Spirit through the faith in the beautiful gospel.

However the Holy Spirit allows people to see God's world through the Word. Through the Holy Spirit, they come to know and believe that God created man, that God loves them, and that God wants to save them. His plan for sinners was for Jesus Christ to save them from their sins through the gospel of the water and the Spirit and to invite them to live in His love by faith.

1 Peter 3:21 says, *"There is also an antitype which now saves us — baptism."* Also, 1 Peter 1:23 says, *"Having been born again, not of corruptible seed but incorruptible, through the word of God which lives and abides forever."*

The work of the Holy Spirit is to enlighten man on the truth of sin, of righteousness, and of judgment, and to make them believe those truths. The Holy Spirit lets them know about God's judgment and that they can be delivered from their sins by believing in the beautiful gospel of Jesus' baptism and His blood on the Cross. The Holy Spirit gives them the knowledge that He is within them when they have faith in the gospel of the water and the Spirit.

So far we have looked at the deeds of the Holy Spirit. All the people in this world can have the indwelling of the Holy Spirit and God's love only when they have obtained the forgiveness of sins by believing in Jesus' beautiful gospel of the water and the Spirit.

The Personality of the Holy Spirit

The Holy Spirit is Almighty God. He possesses the essential characteristics of personality, namely, intellect, emotion, and will. Because the Holy Spirit possesses intellect, He even searches the deep things of God (1 Corinthians 2:10) and the hearts of men.

Because the Holy Spirit possesses emotion, He is pleased with those who believe in God's word, but sighs deeply against unbelievers. Also, the righteous can feel God's love through the Holy Spirit.

The Holy Spirit is also called "the Comforter." This means that the Holy Spirit helps the righteous in difficulties, and brings victory to them, fighting off their enemies. He possesses intellect, emotion, and will just as we humans do, and He dwells in those who believe in the beautiful gospel of the water and the Spirit.

The work of the Holy Spirit is as follows

The Holy Spirit allows people to realize the truth of the forgiveness of sin and dwells in the hearts of believers. His work is to testify to the truth that Jesus took away all the sins of mankind through His baptism and His blood (1 John 5:6-8). He also comforts His servants and saints in any trouble and strengthens them to stand again. He Himself intercedes for them when they don't know what they should pray for

(Romans 8:26). And He gives rest to the righteous in God's church and leads them to the abundance of His words (Psalm 23).

The work of the Holy Spirit related to the Bible

The Holy Spirit leads the righteous to recognize and believe in the truth in their hearts and to preach it to others. *"All Scripture is given by inspiration of God, and is profitable for doctrine, for reproof, for correction, for instruction in righteousness" (2 Timothy 3:16).*
"Search from the book of the Lord, and read: Not one of these shall fail; not one shall lack her mate. For My mouth has commanded it, and His Spirit has gathered them" (Isaiah 34:16).
   "Knowing this first, that no prophecy of Scripture is of any private interpretation, for prophecy never came by the will of man, but holy men of God spoke as they were moved by the Holy Spirit" (2 Peter 1:20-21).
The Holy Spirit had inspired the servants of God to write God's word so that we could read it. He introduces people to the gospel of the water and the Spirit and leads us to preach it to the world. Therefore even though the righteous may suffer many trials in their lives, they are able to overcome them thanks to the power of the Holy Spirit.

The gifts and fruit of the Holy Spirit

The gifts of the Holy Spirit means the abilities He gives to the saints to spread the beautiful gospel of God to others. The saints therefore devote themselves to God's work with the gifts He gives, and the Holy Spirit helps them give glory to the Lord. *"But the manifestation of the Spirit is given to each one for the profit of all" (1 Corinthians 12:7).*

The purpose of the gifts of the Holy Spirit was to equip the saints with faith and help them run the race that was ahead of them (Ephesians 4:11-12). The Holy Spirit gives capabilities to God's servants and the saints to help them in spreading the gospel. The church of God is a community of the saints who are sanctified in Christ Jesus (1 Corinthians 1:2).

Each Christian who has received the Holy Spirit should behave according to his given position and duties, since Jesus Christ is head of the church. The Holy Spirit gives spiritual perceptiveness and ability to the saints so that they can work for the Kingdom of God. He does everything in order to manifest the glory of the gospel that God gave us. He says, *"Therefore, whether you eat or drink, or whatever you do, do all to the glory of God" (1 Corinthians 10:31).*

The different kinds of gifts of the Spirit

There are 12 different kinds of gifts of the Holy Spirit. We can see in the Bible that these gifts appear in a variety of forms to different people. A lengthy list of the gifts appears in Romans 12:6-8, 1 Corinthians 12:8-10, and Ephesians 4:11. The following are the nine Spiritual gifts that are spoken of in 1

Corinthians chapter 12.

1) **The word of knowledge:** This gives us the Spiritual inspiration to understand the gospel of the water and the Spirit and lets us preach this beautiful gospel.

2) **The word of wisdom:** This is the ability to settle the numerous problems that come up in the life of the righteous through the written words of God.

3) **Faith:** The Holy Spirit gives strong faith and confidence to saints so that they can perform the miracle of saving souls from their sins and Satan. A righteous person can have their sins forgiven and heal their spiritual disorders through the power of faith.

4) **Healings**: The Holy Spirit gives the ability to heal the righteous people through their faith in God's word.

5) **The working of miracles:** This is the surprising gift that allows the saint to do work of God by believing in God's word. A miracle is something that happens supernaturally through faith, exceeding the bounds of human knowledge of natural law.

6) **Prophecy:** At this time, only those who believe in and obey the word of God can prophesy according to what is written. The words of someone who has beliefs that are not based on what is written in the Bible cannot be true prophecy. God's servants, who have the indwelling of the Holy Spirit, preach God's word and thereby edify and exhort them to do His work through the church, which is God's body. The Holy Spirit gave this ability to God's servants and the saints.

7) **Discerning of spirits:** This is the ability to determine whether someone has had his sins forgiven. It is possible for us to be led astray by Satan if we don't possess this gift. Because the world is under Satan's control, we can only possess this gift by believing in the beautiful gospel that God gave us and thus

overcome the trials, burdens and evils in this world. A righteous person receives this gift by believing in the true gospel. He can thus tell whether someone has sin in his heart.

8) **Speaking in tongues:** The Bible tells us about speaking in tongues: *"I would rather speak five words with my understanding, that I may teach others also, than ten thousand words in a tongue" (1Corithians 14:19).* A saint should know that it's much more important to understand God's word of truth than to speak in tongues that he himself is unable to understand. He should therefore abstain from speaking in tongues.

9) **Interpreting other tongues:** This gift was given to the disciples to allow them to preach the gospel in the time of the early church. Nowadays the Holy Spirit spreads the gospel through the ministry of translation and interpretation of messages into various languages. There is no need for an interpreter when the person who preaches the gospel can speak all other languages. However, when we are faced with language barriers, God always allows us interpreters to fulfill His work. God does not work in disorder or in states of ecstasy. The Holy Spirit works in the beautiful gospel and also leads the saints to translate the gospel into various languages.

What are the fruits of the Holy Spirit?

Regarding the fruits of the Holy Spirit, the Bible tells us, *"But the fruit of the Holy Spirit is love, joy, peace, longsuffering, kindness, goodness, faithfulness, gentleness, self-control. Against such there is not law" (Galatians 5:22-23).*

1) **Love:** True love is for the righteous to save all sinners from their sins by preaching the beautiful gospel of the water and the Spirit. Because righteous people possess the beautiful gospel that is the true love of Jesus, they preach the gospel of true love and possess true love for other souls.

2) **Joy:** This is the indescribably glorious happiness gushing out from deep down in our hearts when we are born again. The righteous person who has been forgiven for all of his sins has joy in his heart (Philippians 4:4). Because there is joy in the hearts of the righteous, they have the ability to share their joy with other people.

3) **Peace:** This is the heart of comfort that is given to the righteous person who has been forgiven for his sins by having faith in the gospel of the water and the Spirit. The Holy Spirit causes the righteous to preach the beautiful gospel of peace. People who have heard this beautiful gospel of peace are able to lead others to overcome the sins of the world and to have a powerful sense of faith and confidence in the gift of salvation. The righteous people that make peace between God and mankind are called sons of God (Matthew 5:9) and lead others to receive the forgiveness of sin (Proverbs 12:20). The Holy Spirit causes the righteous to lead righteous lives and bless others with peace by spreading the beautiful gospel.

4) **Longsuffering:** The fruits of longsuffering are in the hearts of the righteous, who have been delivered from their sins by believing in the true gospel. We can possess this fruit by fostering a long-lasting sense of fellowship with the Holy Spirit. There is a heart of longsuffering and patience in the righteous.

5) **Kindness:** God had mercy on us when we were full of sin and delivered us from all our sins through Jesus' baptism and His blood on the Cross. We can love and have mercy on others because Jesus had mercy on us and blotted out all our

sins, and because we believed in Him and received His grace. The righteous have hearts full of kindness and the fruits of the beautiful gospel.

6) **Goodness:** Goodness here means "virtue." Righteous people have goodness and faith in the Lord deep in their hearts.

7) **Faithfulness:** Faithfulness means a heart full of faith in God. The faithfulness in a saint comes from being loyal to Jesus.

8) **Gentleness:** This means having the ability to fully understand others and hold them warmly and tenderly in our heart. The righteous have hearts to love their enemies and pray for their deliverance.

9) **Self-control:** Self-control is the ability to regulate oneself, to avoid leading a dissolute life and instead to live one of self-control and temperance.

Being filled with the Holy Spirit

What is the result of being filled with the Holy Spirit? Receiving this blessing allows saints to live as Jesus Christ's disciples, joining themselves to the church of God. The Holy Spirit enables the righteous to become instruments of righteousness and to dedicate themselves to fulfilling Christ's will. The will of the righteous is controlled by the Lord's will, and they willingly dedicate all their possessions and talents to Him. The Holy Spirit causes the righteous to lead lives devoted to overcoming the sins of the world with a sense of victory, joy and confidence, not spiritual poverty, defeat or frustration (Romans chapter 7).

"But you shall receive power when the Holy Spirit has

come upon you; and you shall be witnesses to Me in Jerusalem, and in all Judea and Samaria, and to the end of the earth" *(Acts 1:8).* The fullness of the Holy Spirit leads the righteous to preach the gospel.

The Lord gave a powerful sense of faith to those in whom the Holy Spirit dwells. And God gave the right to become His children to those whose sins are forgiven by their faith in the beautiful gospel of Jesus (John 1:12). The righteous people who have become God's children through faith can preach the beautiful gospel in this world.

Righteous people have the ability to defeat Satan through the gospel for the forgiveness of sins. They also have the power to heal spiritual illness (Mark 16:18), to trample on Satan's powers (Luke 10:19), and to enter the Kingdom of Heaven (Revelation 22:14). Righteous people live with the same authority as kings by believing in God's words of promise (2 Corinthians 6:17-18).

The Holy Spirit causes righteous people to cast off all their worldly lusts. He also leads us to preach the true gospel (Galatians 5:6).

The Holy Spirit causes the righteous to read and believe in the beautiful gospel and to teach it to others (1 Timothy 4:13).

The Holy Spirit assembles the righteous at God's church every day (Hebrews 10:25).

The Holy Spirit causes the righteous to confess their sins (1 John 1:9) in order to make their hearts manifest by the light of the truth (Ephesians 5:13).

The Holy Spirit guides the righteous to the right path in their lives (Psalm 23).

The Holy Spirit tells the righteous not to quench His gifts (1 Thessalonians 5:19).

The Holy Spirit does great works through the wonderful

gospel (Mark 16:17-18).

The Holy Spirit leads the righteous to live as the Lord's disciples by joining them to God's church. He leads the righteous to live spiritual lives of preaching the beautiful gospel and to be filled with the Holy Spirit. This is the work of the Holy Spirit through the wonderful gospel (1 Peter 2:9).

He is working in the hearts of the saints at this very moment. Hallelujah! ⊠

SERMON 14

What is true repentance
for the receiving of
the Holy Spirit?

What is true repentance for the receiving of the Holy Spirit?

<Acts 2:38>
"Then Peter said to them, 'Repent, and let every one of you be baptized in the name of Jesus Christ for the remission of sins; and you shall receive the gift of the Holy Spirit.'"

What is the true repentance needed to receive the Holy Spirit?

It is to return to the beautiful gospel of the water and the Spirit and to believe in Jesus' baptism and His blood on the Cross.

The Bible says in Acts 2 that Peter's sermon moved people deeply and caused them to repent for their sins. They were cut to the heart and said to Peter and the rest of the apostles, *"What shall we do?"* Then Peter answered, *"Repent, and let every one of you be baptized in the name of Jesus Christ for the remission of sins; and you shall receive the gift of the Holy Spirit"* (Acts 2:38).

Peter's sermon clearly shows us that faith in the beautiful

gospel of the water and the Spirit is indispensable to receiving the Holy Spirit and it also shows us what true repentance is. We should know that we can receive the Holy Spirit along with the remission of sins by looking closely at the Scriptures and believing in the beautiful gospel of the water and the Spirit.

The first thing we need to have in order to receive the indwelling of the Holy Spirit is the belief in biblical repentance. However, we should be careful not to define this repentance as regret. Repentance here means faith in Jesus Christ. We can see in the Bible that the people already regretted crucifying the Lord. They regretted asking Peter what they should do and admitted their sins even before Peter told them to repent. We can see by this that the repentance Peter was talking about was not regretting sin or admitting it, but taking Jesus Christ into one's heart as his Savior and having faith in the beautiful gospel He gave us. This is the true nature of repentance.

The love of Jesus Christ came to us before there was any self-regret for the sins in our hearts. This means that Jesus took away our sins when He was baptized in the Jordan River, died on the Cross, and then rose again from the dead. In this way, He cleansed us of all our sins and iniquities.

True repentance means believing in this truth. Do you think our sins will be gone forever, simply if we regret our sins and beg for pardon? This is not true repentance. True repentance means receiving the remission of our sins by believing in the beautiful gospel of Jesus' baptism and His blood. The Bible says that we should be forgiven for our sins by repentance. Likewise, we have to believe in the gospel of Jesus' baptism and His blood in order to receive complete remission of our sins.

Peter administered baptism "in the name of Jesus Christ" to those who believed in Jesus. Jesus was baptized to take on the sins of all mankind. His baptism and death on the Cross was the completion of the beautiful gospel that enables believers to receive the indwelling of the Holy Spirit (Matthew 3:15-17). Mankind can be sanctified by believing in Jesus' baptism and His blood on the Cross. In short, those who have received the remission of sins by believing in the gospel have received the Holy Spirit.

Can prayer bring the indwelling of the Holy Spirit?

People can't receive the forgiveness of sins and the indwelling of the Holy Spirit no matter how hard they pray to receive it. In order to have the indwelling of the Holy Spirit, it is necessary to believe in the beautiful gospel accomplished by Jesus' baptism and His blood on the Cross. God's Holy Spirit is granted only to those whose sins have been completely washed away.

Faith in the gospel means acknowledging Jesus Christ as the true Savior. Acts 2:38 says, *"Repent, and let every one of you be baptized in the name of Jesus Christ for the remission of sins; and you shall receive the gift of the Holy Spirit."* The apostle Peter said that the indwelling of the Holy Spirit is given to those who are forgiven for their sins through faith by correct repentance. The forgiveness of sins and receiving the indwelling of the Holy Spirit are intertwined.

The Bible says, *"Repent, and let every one of you be baptized in the name of Jesus Christ for the remission of sins; and you shall receive the gift of the Holy Spirit. For the promise is to you and to your children and to all who are afar off, as many as the Lord our God will call" (Acts 2:38-39).*

One can receive the Holy Spirit only on condition that his heart is sanctified and without sin. Therefore, we should believe in the gospel that Jesus Christ gave us. We must become sanctified after obtaining forgiveness for our sins by believing in the wonderful gospel that says all the sins of the world were washed away when Jesus Christ was baptized. Only then can we receive the Holy Spirit. It is the will of God that the Holy Spirit dwells in humanity. *"For this is the will of God, your sanctification" (Thessalonians 4:2).*

True forgiveness is given not through people's efforts, sacrifices or inherent goodness, but only by believing in the beautiful gospel of what God, the Holy Trinity, accomplished through John the Baptist. God, the Holy Trinity, grants the indwelling of the Holy Spirit to those who are forgiven by believing in the beautiful gospel.

A crowd of people were pierced to the heart when they heard what Peter said on the Day of Pentecost. They cried out, *"What shall we do?" (Acts 2:37)* This indicates that they had changed their minds and now believed in Jesus as their Savior. They were also saved from their sins by believing in the true repentance preached by Peter. The forgiveness of sins was given to all of humanity depending on their faith in the beautiful Gospel of Jesus' baptism and His blood on the Cross.

The purpose of Jesus' baptism was to permit Him to bear the sins of the world. Belief in this is the essential condition for receiving the Holy Spirit. God grants the indwelling of the Holy Spirit to those who believe in the gospel of the truth based on Jesus' baptism. *"Then He had been baptized, Jesus came up immediately from the water; and behold, the havens were opened to Him, and He saw the Spirit of God descending like a dove and alighting upon Him" (Matthew 3:16).* The coming of the Holy Spirit on the Day of Pentecost has a special relationship with the apostles' faith in the beautiful gospel: Jesus' baptism, His death on the Cross and resurrection.

Acts says that people were baptized in the name of Jesus and received the Holy Spirit. We should believe that receiving the indwelling of the Holy Spirit is a special gift from God. In order to receive the gift of the Holy Spirit, all our sins have to be washed away through faith in Jesus' baptism and death on the Cross.

According to Acts, all those who heard Peter's sermon, in which he said, *"Be saved from this perverse generation" (Acts 2:40),* heeded his advice and were baptized. What we learn from the Bible is that the apostles in the days of the early church received the Holy Spirit on the basis of their faith in Jesus Christ's baptism and His blood on the Cross. This is the essential condition for receiving the Holy Spirit. Belief in the baptism of Jesus and His blood on the Cross are indispensable if one seeks the forgiveness of sin.

The belief that leads us to receive the Holy Spirit through true repentance

Let's look at Acts 3:19. *"Repent therefore and be converted, that your sins may be blotted out, so that times of refreshing may come from the presence of the Lord."* How should we define repentance? Let's think about it again.

In the Bible, repentance means returning to a belief in redemption. In those days, people behaved as they wished and worshipped things that God had created. But after they realized that Jesus Christ saved them from their sins with the water and

His blood, they were converted. This is biblical repentance. True repentance is to return to the beautiful gospel of the water and the Spirit.

What is the true repentance needed to receive the Holy Spirit? It is to believe in Jesus' baptism and His blood on the Cross. *"Times of refreshing may come from the presence of the Lord."* If people have this belief, they are forgiven for their sins and receive the Holy Spirit. Because Jesus sanctified all the sinners in the world through His baptism and blood on the Cross, we must believe in this beautiful Gospel, obtain redemption and receive the Holy Spirit.

In order to believe in Jesus and receive the indwelling of the Holy Spirit, one's sin must be passed on to Jesus through faith in His baptism and death on the Cross. We should believe that Jesus took away all our sins and died on the Cross in order to be judged for our sins. This is correct faith and true repentance, which enables us to have the indwelling of the Holy Spirit.

The Holy Spirit comes upon those who have the forgiveness of all their sins. Why does God give the Holy Spirit as a gift to those who have redemption? Because the Holy Spirit, being holy, wants to dwell within them and to seal them as His children.

The Holy Spirit is God. The Father, the Son, and the Holy Spirit are one God. They are three Persons, but they are the same God to those who believe in Jesus. The Father had a plan to save us from our sins and so Jesus the Son came into this world, was baptized by John in order to take away the sins of the world, died on the Cross, rose again from the dead on the third day and was taken up to heaven. The Holy Spirit leads us to believe in this beautiful gospel by testifying to Jesus' baptism and His blood on the Cross.

God seals those who have been saved through the Holy Spirit. The Lord grants the Holy Spirit to those who believe in the gospel that Jesus took away the sins of the world. God gives them the Holy Spirit as a pledge to seal them as His children. The Holy Spirit is the final evidence of salvation from sin to those who believe in the beautiful gospel.

Those who have the Holy Spirit are children of the Lord. Those who have the indwelling of the Holy Spirit always feel refreshed. They have a firm belief in the words of God, in Jesus' baptism and the blood on the Cross. They are truly happy. Those who repent in the proper way have no sin in their hearts and have the indwelling of the Holy Spirit.

The Bible says that there is repentance which brings the forgiveness of sins. Have you gone through such repentance? If you repent and adopt the true beliefs, you too can receive the beautiful gospel. I advise you to repent for your sins and receive the Holy Spirit. Are you ready to repent and believe in the beautiful gospel that leads to the indwelling of the Holy Spirit? ⊠

SERMON 15

You can receive the indwelling of the Holy Spirit only when you know the truth

You can receive the indwelling of the Holy Spirit only when you know the truth

<John 8:31-36>

"Then Jesus said to those Jews who believed Him, 'If you abide in My word, you are My disciples indeed. And you shall know the truth, and the truth shall make you free.' They answered Him, 'We are Abraham's descendants, and have never been in bondage to anyone. How can You say, 'You will be made free'?' Jesus answered them, 'Most assuredly, I say to you, whoever commits sin is a slave of sin. And a slave does not abide in the house forever, but a son abides forever. Therefore if the Son makes you free, you shall be free indeed.'"

What do we have to do in order to receive the indwelling of the Holy Spirit?

We must believe in the beautiful gospel of the water and the Spirit and live by faith.

Do you know what the truth is? Jesus said, *"I am the*

truth" (John 14:6). So knowing Jesus is to know the truth. Does the Holy Spirit dwell within you thanks to your belief in the beautiful gospel? You should recognize that Jesus' baptism and His blood on the Cross are the personification of the beautiful gospel and believe in it.

People today frequently use the expression 'born again.' "People should be born again. Politics should be born again. Religion should be born again." They use the phrase as a synonym for 'improvement.' However, being born again does not mean the improvement of the nature of flesh. To be born again means to receive the indwelling of the Holy Spirit by hearing and believing in the beautiful gospel of the water and the Spirit.

What are the words of truth that allow us to be born again?

Why should man be born again? Man is incomplete so he must receive the indwelling of the Holy Spirit in order to be born again as a child of God. We can see many people who believe in Jesus but don't have the indwelling of the Holy Spirit. Nicodemus was a ruler of the Jews. Nicodemus, who appears in John chapter 3, was a leader of Judaism who tried to keep the law handed down by God. However, he was working as a leader of a religion of the people, unaware of the indwelling of the Holy Spirit.

In order to receive the indwelling of the Holy Spirit, we must believe in the beautiful gospel of the water and the Holy Spirit and live by faith. Man can receive the indwelling of the Holy Spirit only when he comes to believe in the words of truth in the beautiful gospel of the water and the Holy Spirit. Jesus said, *"If I have told you earthly things and you do not believe, how will you believe if I tell you heavenly things?" (John 3:12)*

The beautiful gospel of the water and the Spirit is as follows. Our Lord was born in this world, was baptized by John at age 30, died on the Cross three years later, was resurrected and thus delivered us from all our sins. He became the Savior for those who believe that Jesus was baptized by John and rose again from the dead. He granted the remission of sins and the indwelling of the Holy Spirit to those who believed in this beautiful gospel.

Those who still have sin in their hearts must be forgiven for their sins by believing in Jesus' baptism and His blood. Man can't help committing sins before God and so must be saved by accepting Jesus as his Savior. Jesus washed away all the sins of the world with the beautiful gospel of the water and the Spirit. All sinners can be saved by listening to and believing in the beautiful gospel of the water and the Spirit. Those who believe in this beautiful gospel are blessed with the indwelling of the Holy Spirit.

"And as Moses lifted up the serpent in the wilderness, even so must the Son of Man be lifted up" (John 3:14). In the Old Testament, even though the people of Israel committed sins, were bitten by fiery serpents in the wilderness, and were dying desperately, many managed to live by looking at the bronze serpent set on a standard.

Likewise, we have got the indwelling of the Holy Spirit. Jesus gives the indwelling of the Holy Spirit to those who believe in the beautiful gospel. Satan hinders us from knowing the beautiful gospel of the water and the Spirit and tries to block us from receiving the Spirit of truth. However, God blessed us with the forgiveness of sins and the indwelling of the Holy Spirit through our faith in the gospel of Jesus' baptism and His blood.

You can also receive the indwelling of the Holy Spirit if you believe in this beautiful gospel. Do you acknowledge this beautiful gospel as true before God? Do you believe that you are able to receive the indwelling of the Holy Spirit by believing in this, the true gospel?

The Lord told us to know the truth that saves us from all our sins. *"And you shall know the truth, and the truth shall make you free" (John 8:32).* Do you know the truth of the beautiful gospel that saves us and blesses us with the indwelling of the Holy Spirit? If you accept this gospel, you will surely receive the indwelling of the Holy Spirit. ✉

SERMON 16

The mission of those who
receive the Holy Spirit

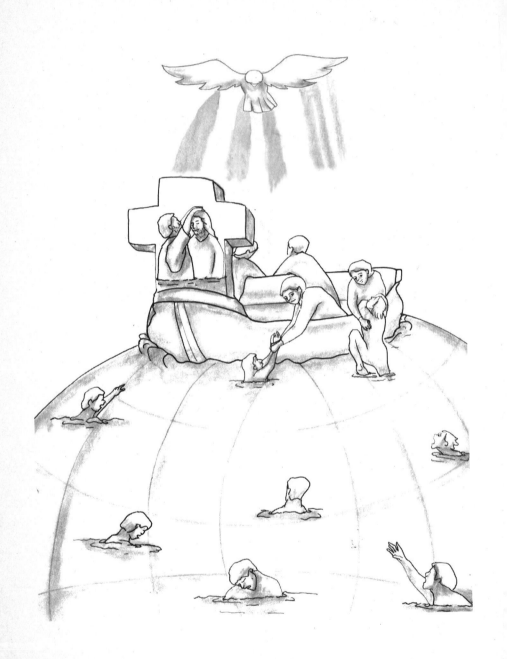

The mission of those who receive the Holy Spirit

<Isaiah 61:1-11>
"The Spirit of the Lord God is upon Me, because the Lord has anointed Me to preach good tidings to the poor; He has sent Me to heal the brokenhearted, to proclaim liberty to the captives, and the opening of the prison to those who are bound; to proclaim the acceptable year of the Lord, and the day of vengeance of our God; to comfort all who mourn, to console those who mourn in Zion, to give them beauty for ashes, the oil of joy for mourning, the garment of praise for the spirit of heaviness; that they may be called trees of righteousness, the planting of the Lord, that He may be glorified. And they shall rebuild the old ruins, they shall raise up the former desolations, and they shall repair the ruined cities, the desolations of many generations. Strangers shall stand and feed your flocks, and the sons of the foreigner shall be your plowmen and your vinedressers. But you shall be named the priests of the Lord, they shall call you the servants of our God. You shall eat the riches of the Gentiles, and in their glory you shall boast. Instead of your shame you shall have double honor, and instead of confusion they shall rejoice in their portion. Therefore in their land they shall possess double; everlasting joy shall be theirs. For I, the Lord, love justice; I hate robbery for burnt offering; I will direct their work in truth, and will make with them an everlasting covenant. Their descendants shall be known among the Gentiles, and

their offspring among the people. All who see them shall acknowledge them, that they are the posterity whom the Lord has blessed. I will greatly rejoice in the Lord, my soul shall be joyful in my God; for He has clothed me with the garments of salvation, he has covered me with the robe of righteousness, as a bridegroom decks himself with ornaments, and as a bride adorns herself with her jewels. For as the earth brings forth its bud, as the garden causes the things that are sown in it to spring forth, so the Lord God will cause righteousness and praise to spring forth before all the nations."

What is the mission of those who receive the Holy Spirit?

It is to preach the gospel of the water and the Spirit to all the people of the world.

What should a person who has received the Holy Spirit do? He should preach the gospel of the water and the Spirit to all people. God entrusted the beautiful gospel of being born again of water and the Spirit to those who have received the indwelling of the Holy Spirit. Those who were forgiven for their sins before God receive the Holy Spirit. Then why do you think God grant the gift of the Holy Spirit to them?

To give them the final guarantee that He has made them His children, He gifts them the Holy Spirit. He also wishes to help them overcome Satan. He makes those who have been forgiven for their sins and who have received the indwelling of the Holy Spirit do the following:

He makes them preach good tidings to the poor

What is the good news for the poor? It is the gospel of the water and the Spirit. God ordered those who received the indwelling of the Holy Spirit to preach the beautiful gospel to the poor. Those who received the Holy Spirit, since they have the hope of Heaven, are never satisfied with things on earth.

God granted the gospel of the water and the Spirit to the poor and forgave them for their sins. He then granted the indwelling of the Holy Spirit to them and let them into the eternal world. God commanded the righteous to preach the gospel of the water and the Spirit to the poor. He also persuaded them to spread the belief in God and Jesus. The reason that God gave us the Holy Spirit was to preach the beautiful news abundantly to the poor of the world.

He sends us to heal the brokenhearted

How does our Lord heal our minds? He heals the brokenhearted with the gospel of the water and the Spirit. There are many people with broken hearts. To them, life is worthless, and their own righteousness is wrecked. They have humble and painful lives because of their sins. Therefore, they are occasionally tormented by their doubts about life. All men wish to live gracefully and want to enjoy prosperity in their body and soul, but this does not happen easily in the same way as when people have been robbed of all their possessions by burglars.

Likewise, those with sin in their heart are continuously

robbed of all their righteousness, and at last, go to hell because of their sins. That's why the Lord, pitying the brokenhearted, commanded us to preach the beautiful gospel to them. With what words did God heal them? He did so with the beautiful gospel of the water and the Spirit. He healed the brokenhearted and also granted them eternal life.

He proclaims liberty to the captives of sin

He grants freedom to the captives. What does this mean? It means that God has freed the souls of people from all the sins of the world. He has given this mission only to those who received the Holy Spirit, and they can free others from their sins.

Man has a body and a soul. And his body and soul lives, being bound by the curse of sin and the law. He can't do anything but to live as a captive of sin, regardless of whether or not he believes in God. Born with sin, he can't help but sin. Thus, he is destined to live as a captive of sin throughout his life. He lives in this way and is destined to destroy in the end.

This is why he lives this unavoidable life while indulging in self-pity regarding his weakness which has put him in this position. God sent the Holy Spirit to those who can't but sin and are destined to die, so that they could preach the beautiful gospel to the inmates of sin, and give the captives the freedom from all their sin.

He comforts all who mourn

What did God give to those who mourn? Giving them the gospel of forgiveness, God comforts all the people of the world who mourn. He sent Jesus Christ into this world to forgive mankind for their sins. And to pass all the sins of the world onto Him, He had Him baptized by John and die on the Cross. That's how God purified us of our sins. Thus God saved us from all the sins of the world.

Our Lord comforts all who mourn by informing them of the beautiful gospel of the water and the Spirit. By doing so, He blesses those who suffer from an incomplete faith. He leads only those who have the Holy Spirit to preach this beautiful gospel, to heal the brokenhearted and to free the captives to sin.

The purpose of our existence in this world is to be forgiven by our Lord and then to preach the beautiful gospel to those who are bound to sin and need comfort to be freed from sin. God tells us that though our lives are short, they are not worthless at all. That God prepared the remission of sin and marvelous blessings for mankind is proof of this fact.

Our Lord also bequeathed all who mourn with a crown of glory. This means that sinners are forgiven for their sins thanks to Jesus' baptism and can thus enter the Kingdom of Heaven. If one is forgiven for his sins, he is refreshed in his mind and comes to appreciate this marvelous blessing. Our Lord crowns him with glory. He gave sinners the gospel of the water and the Spirit and made those who believe in it His children. Those who believe in this beautiful gospel are made to feel joy instead of sadness.

Just as all men are born and die with a cry, joy is momentary, and their minds are mostly full of sadness. However, God met them and caused them to be born again with hope and delight. Likewise, those who are born again by believing in the beautiful gospel live a new life and have new work. In addition, they are able to do what God wants, and that is to preach the gospel of the water and the Spirit to all the sinners of the world, drive out all sadness from their hearts and let them enjoy all manner of delights and happiness instead.

Those who are forgiven for their sins by God give glory to Him. He told the righteous to preach the beautiful gospel. He told them to preach who He is, what gospel He gave us, and how glorious is the Kingdom of Heaven He prepared for us. We can see the glory of God in those forgiven by Him. Those who mourned in their life before being filled with the Holy Spirit now delight in happiness, those who were bound to sin now feel the pleasure of freedom, and those who lived a worthless life now live a righteous life. These all reflect the glory of God. God referred to the righteous as those who would rebuild the old ruins, raise the former desolations, and repair the ruined cities.

In fact, this beautiful gospel of the water and the Spirit was the gospel preached by the Apostles in the days of the early church. Jesus was sent into the world about two thousand years ago. The beautiful gospel of the water and the Spirit had been preached in this world until AD 300. The gospel preached by the righteous today is the same gospel of the Holy Spirit, which the Apostles preached at that time. However, in the days of the early 4th century Roman Empire, when Rome made Christianity a state religion and gave its citizens freedom of religion, the gospel of Jesus' baptism was tarnished and gradually disappeared. It was after this, when Christianity as the established religion became more and more prosperous, that the very people who preached the true gospel vanished.

Why was the faith of those who believed and preached the

true Christianity and the true gospel changed? After Christianity had become a state religion of Roman Empire, Christians became liberated from various restrictions and came to enjoy the same privileges as the Roman citizen. Christians were then able to marry Roman nobles, and could also enter government service. Because of this privilege, their faith was reduced from a faith of resurrection to a mere religion. From then on, the beautiful gospel of the water and the Spirit disappeared, and a diminished form of the secularized Christianity began to flourish.

God commands us the last Christians at the time of His immanent return to preach the beautiful gospel of the water and the Spirit which was cast into ruin for such a long time, and thus save mankind from their sins. He will revive the beautiful gospel of the water and the Spirit that was preached in the days of the Apostles. The gospel in the days of the Apostles was the beautiful gospel of Jesus' baptism and His blood on the Cross. He calls us the men who repair ruined cities. He made us learn and believe in the gospel of the water and the Spirit, and made us farmers of His vineyard.

God gave us the same mission He did through the Apostles. He made you and me preach this original gospel of the water and the Spirit. *"The Spirit of the Lord GOD is upon Me, because the LORD has anointed Me to preach good tidings to the poor."* God made those who had already received the Holy Spirit preach the gospel and gave us the Holy Spirit.

God crowned us with flowers, removed all sadness, and put the garment of praise on us by inspiring delight in us. Those who have the Holy Spirit in their hearts sow the seeds of this beautiful gospel for others to receive Him. Then they will also accept the gospel given by our Lord, be forgiven, and at last receive the Holy Spirit.

We have become God's workers. You and I are blessed with glory of the Kingdom of Heaven. However, God made those who don't have the Holy Spirit blind so that they cannot know, see, or understand this beautiful gospel. They may be able to make others believe in Jesus nominally, but can never make them receive the Holy Spirit.

The Lord has done the following things through those who have the Holy Spirit. He made them preach the beautiful news to the poor and heal the brokenhearted with the gospel of the water and the Spirit. He also presented the captives to sin with the true freedom of salvation and comforted all those who mourn with the beautiful gospel of the water and the Spirit. He set free those who are bound to sin because of their weaknesses, presented them with joy and hope and then ascended to Heaven.

Following this, the Holy Spirit who dwells in us made us preach the gospel of the water and the Spirit to all people. Jesus Christ told those who are forgiven and have the Holy Spirit within them to save all sinners from their sins. The Lord empowered those who have the indwelling of the Holy Spirit to be in charge of what He planned to do. He made all righteous people do His work. We are His workers, the ones who were appointed as stewards in His vineyard, God's church. We are His servants. God has given us these amazing blessings.

We realize our weaknesses when we look at our flesh, but since God works with us, we believe in Him and have become His servants by faith. We believe God will do many great works through us and spread His dominion over us.

God decided to rebuild the desolate fortress of the gospel in the ruined cities. He promised that He would raise the former desolations, and repair the ruined cities. I believe there will be a revival of the gospel once again throughout the world!

This however is not my will. I believe it because God said it would be so. Our Lord made those who have the Holy Spirit preach this beautiful gospel to the whole world. He sent His son into this world and fulfilled the gospel, and I believe He is achieving His will again through those of us who have the Holy Spirit. Those who believe in this beautiful gospel will see the glory of God. Hallelujah! ⊠

SERMON 17

We must possess belief and hope in the Holy Spirit

The Kingdom
of Heaven

We must possess belief and hope in the Holy Spirit

<Romans 8:16-25>

"The Spirit Himself bears witness with our spirit that we are children of God, and if children, then heirs — heirs of God and joint heirs with Christ, if indeed we suffer with Him, that we may also be glorified together. For I consider that the sufferings of this present time are not worthy to be compared with the glory which shall be revealed in us. For the earnest expectation of the creation eagerly waits for the revelations of the sons of God. For the creation was subjected to futility, not willingly, but because of Him who subjected it in hope; because the creation itself also will be delivered from the bondage of corruption into the glorious liberty of the children of God. For we know that the whole creation groans and labors with birth pangs together until now. Not only that, but we also who have the firstfruits of the Spirit, even we ourselves groan with ourselves, eagerly waiting for the adoption, the redemption of our body. For we were saved in this hope, but hope that is seen is not hope; for why does one still hope for what he sees? But if we hope for what we do not see, we eagerly wait for it with perseverance."

*Why do the righteous possess
hope in the Holy Spirit?*

*Because we born again Christians will possess
the new heaven and earth even though those
who are not born again will perish
with the fall of this world.*

Now is a time without hope

Is there real hope now in the world? No, there isn't. It exists only with Jesus. Now is a time of uncertainty and hopelessness. Everything changes daily and rapidly, and people are trying very hard to keep up with these rapid changes. They neither seek spiritual truth nor have any concern for spiritual happiness. Instead they struggle to avoid failure and live as servants of this world.

New jobs emerge and old jobs die. Likewise, people are also undergoing dramatic change. Therefore they live very busy and anxious lives. And gradually, their hope for this world vanishes. One of the reasons for this is because they are leading lives without any certain guarantee for the future. We are living in such an unstable world.

We must hope for eternal life in the Holy Spirit

How can we obtain real hope? We can obtain it by

believing in the gospel of the water and the Spirit. The hope of those who received the Holy Spirit is not on earth, but in Heaven. The apostle Paul spoke of the true hope of Heaven. We who have already received the indwelling of the Holy Spirit hope for heavenly things. We do so because we believe that Jesus Christ came to take away all our sins and saved us sinners through His baptism by John and His blood on the Cross. The Lord granted heavenly hope to those who believe in the gospel of the forgiveness of sin.

Romans 8:19-21 says, *"For the earnest expectation of the creation eagerly waits for the revealing of the sons of God. For the creation was subjected to futility, not willingly, but because of Him who subjected it in hope; because the creation itself also will be delivered from the bondage of corruption into the glorious liberty of the children of God."* All creation hopes to be delivered from the bondage of corruption and death.

All things in this world are imperfect, so they groan and wait for the sons of God to be revealed. In addition, they also wish to be freed from the bondage of corruption and to live eternally. All creation waits for the day when they never decay nor fade away but instead live forever.

Someday all creations made by God will be renewed. Although a flower withers and decays in this world, it will always blossom and live forever in a new world. We who have the indwelling of the Holy Spirit will also see this new world.

Jesus Christ promised that He would come again, raise those who have the indwelling of the Holy Spirit, give a new body which is both incorruptible and immortal to each of them, and give them eternal life. He also promised them that they would live forever in Heaven together with God. All creations in the world are waiting for that day. They will also live forever with us, the sons of God, when that day comes.

This world seen through hope

When does this dream come true for the righteous? It comes true when our Lord returns. We must be in hope when looking at this world. Jesus says that there will be famines, pestilences, earthquakes and wars in various places (Matthew 24:7). But the end has not yet arrived. On the last day of this world, our Lord will come again, renew all worldly things and bequeath the spiritual body of immortality to us. This means plants and animals will also receive immortality. By believing this, we must see the world with renewed hope.

In this world, even those who have the indwelling of the Holy Spirit groan within themselves with all creation, eagerly awaiting the glory of redemption of our bodies as His children. We see the world with hope because the Lord will make us His children, who will never decay nor die when He returns.

Although the world will be destroyed someday, all things will be renewed when the Lord comes again. We must live with hope by believing that. The renewed world will be as joyful and wonderful as any fantastic world you have read of in fairy tales. Think about living in such a world for a thousand years. And we will also have eternal life as His children when we enter the Kingdom of Heaven. We must live with such hope.

Do you see any hope in this world? No. People live in a happy go-lucky way, because they don't have any hope for this world. But our Lord has given the hope of Heaven to those who have been forgiven and made righteous. *"For we were saved in this hope, but hope that is seen is not hope; for why does one still hope for what he sees? But if we hope for what we do not see, we eagerly wait for it with perseverance."* This means we must be patient enough to wait for Jesus' return because we were saved by our belief in God's words.

We have the indwelling of the Holy Spirit in our soul because we were saved from our sins. That is, those forgiven by Jesus have the Holy Spirit in their hearts instead of sin. What then of our bodies? Our weak bodies will also be resurrected, receive new life and immortality. We will live forever together with God when Jesus returns. Only those born again are privileged to do so in hope, and therefore our spirit and flesh will become perfect. Our flesh will become eternal and we will never become sick. Our worldly bodies are weak, therefore, it's impossible for us to live a perfect life. But then we will live a perfect life. Let's look forward to the Second Coming of the Lord. Only those who have the indwelling of the Holy Spirit can have that kind of hope and life.

The hope of the righteous is not only in Heaven but also come true in this world. The Bible says that our Lord will come again when this world is fallen after the Great Tribulation. He will surely come. When He came for the first time, He was baptized for the sake of sinners, died on the Cross to make them righteous, and finally ascended to Heaven. Now is the time when the Lord is about to come again.

At that time He will wake all the sleeping saints who believed in Jesus and received the indwelling of the Holy Spirit and will free them from the bondage of corruption. He will give them new heavenly bodies that never decay nor get sick. In addition, they will be caught up in the clouds to meet Him in the air and He will make all things new.

After that, we, together with Jesus our Lord, will live and reign with Him in the new world for a millennium in compensation for serving the gospel. This is a rehearsal for those who are to go to Heaven. This is the hope of Heaven and reality. At that time, all the imperfect things will turn perfect, and things that are to decay will never decay. The words, *"The body is sown in corruption, it is raised in incorruption" (1 Corinthians 15:42),* will be fulfilled at the time through Jesus Christ.

Let us who have the indwelling of the Holy Spirit have hope! You should remember that although all things weaken and die, this is not the end. We must have the belief of hope that our Lord will make the whole world new again. We must live in the hope of the new heaven and earth. Having this hope, we are able to preach the gospel.

We have the indwelling of the Holy Spirit because we were saved from the sins of the world. Likewise, the Holy Spirit within us is looking forward to the Lord's return. He makes intercessions to God the Father on behalf of us to live with hope and faith without disappointment in our hearts.

We should live in hope in the Holy Spirit

Where is the place of the righteous? It will be in **[5]the Millennium** that the Lord will rebuild by renewing this earth when He comes again and also the Kingdom of Heaven. Therefore, we should be patient enough to wait for that Day to come. We must believe that our Lord will make our bodies

---

[5] When the Lord Jesus comes down to this world for the second time according to His promise, He will descend from Heaven, and raise the dead in Christ first. Following this, He will change all the saints, the alive and the risen, into eternal bodies incorruptible and immortal, and He will catch up all the saints in the clouds to meet the Lord in the air (1 Thessalonians 4:16-17, 1 Corinthians 15:51-53).

Then He will make all things new after pouring the seven bowls of His wrath on to the remaining sinners. He will establish His Kingdom on the renewed earth, and will reign a thousand years with those who have part in the first resurrection (Revolution 20:4-5). After the Millennium, He will judge all the dead, and cast them into the lake of fire (Revolution 20:11-15). Then He will lead all His people into the heavenly City, the New Jerusalem, and will dwell with them forever (Revolution 21:1-4).

perfect when this world has fallen. We must have hope for a glorious tomorrow.

Having the indwelling of the Holy Spirit, Paul had the same hope that we have. We live with the same hope in our minds, waiting for the Millennium and the Kingdom of Heaven. Those who are not born again will perish with the fall of this world, but we born again Christians will possess the new heaven and earth. This hope will really come true. Our bodies will become perfect and we will live and reign with Jesus for one thousand years in the new world. Looking forward to that day, we can have hope and live without fear in the world.

Let us be patient and wait. Though our life is exhausting, our hopes will come true because we believe in God. Those without hope are nothing more than dead people already. Please have hope and maintain your dreams by believing in God's words.

Just as our forgiveness was real, the changes in our bodies will be real and it is real for all creatures to earn eternal life. Our hope is also real. Have faith in what you believe. Those who have hope can be beautiful and happy. People become unhappy if they do not have hope. Those without any dreams have no happiness. We can lead happy lives because we have hope for the Millennium and the Kingdom of Heaven, the new heaven and earth.

The righteous must have hope and preach this hope in the Holy Spirit. We must hope that our gospel spreads throughout the whole world. If you have firm faith, you will realize that the world is not that big. Though our beginning was insignificant, we will be able to preach the gospel throughout the world if we have hope and supplication. Just as Paul did, we must believe.

Those with hope are faithful in their work of preaching this beautiful gospel. We must hope for the gospel to spread in this age of hopelessness. We must preach the beautiful gospel to the exhausted, hopeless, poor and humble. We must deliver them from the darkness by preaching the hope about the Kingdom of Heaven, where only those who have been forgiven for their sins by believing the gospel of the water and the Spirit can enter. We must inspire them to have hope that the world of God will suddenly come like a thief after this time of hardship.

Servants and saints who are born again, please preach this gospel to the ends of this world, maintaining firmly your hope for Heaven. No matter how fast this world falls, those with hope never perish because they have something eternal beyond this earthly life. They surely have a second life given to them by the Lord. ✉

SERMON 18

The truth that leads believers to the indwelling of the Holy Spirit

The sin of the world

The truth that leads believers to the indwelling of the Holy Spirit

<Joshua 4:23>
"For the LORD your God dried up the waters of the Jordan before you until you had crossed over, as the LORD your God did to the Red Sea, which He dried up before us until we had crossed over."

What does the event of the Jordan River teach us?

It teaches us that Jesus Christ had completely eliminated death caused by sin and subsequent judgment from mankind.

I would now like to speak about the beautiful gospel of the truth that lets us receive the indwelling of the Holy Spirit. After the death of Moses, God appointed Joshua as the leader of Israel. Moses was the representative of the law in the Old Testament. If Moses had crossed the Jordan River with the people of Israel and arrived at Canaan, it would not have been necessary for Joshua to become the leader of the people. However, God made Moses reach the area just in front of the land of Canaan and prevented him from entering it.

Our Lord gave us Moses and Joshua

Moses, the representative of the law in the Old Testament, couldn't take the people of Israel into Canaan. If he had done so while being led by the law, it would have been against God's plan for our salvation. No one can be free from his sins before the law of God because nobody can keep the law. Because the law is only for the knowledge of sin (Romans 3:20).

The reason why God gave man the law is to give him the knowledge of sin, to make the law his tutor and lead him to Christ so that he could be justified by faith (Galatians 3:24). Since the law was nothing more than a guide to finding Jesus, people needed Jesus, and this is why Jesus had to come into this world. What God directed Joshua to do was to order the people of Israel to cross the Jordan River and enter the land of Canaan.

God led them to enter the land of Canaan with their new leader, Joshua, after the death of Moses. Joshua commanded the officers of the people, saying, *"Pass through the camp and command the people, saying, 'Prepare provisions for yourselves, for within three days you will cross over this Jordan, to go in to possess the land which the LORD your God is giving you to possess'"* (Joshua 1:11).

God ordered Joshua to enter Canaan after it had proven impossible through Moses. God commanded Joshua, saying, *"You shall command the priests who bear the Ark of the Covenant, saying, 'When you have come to the edge of the water of the Jordan, you shall stand in the Jordan.' So Joshua said to the children of Israel, 'Come here, and hear the words of the LORD your God.' And Joshua said, 'By this you shall know that the living God is among you, and that He will without fail drive out from before you the Canaanites and the*

Hittites and the Hivites and the Perizzites and the Girgashites and the Amorites and the Jebusites'" (Joshua 3:8-10).

After the death of Moses, God appointed Joshua the leader of Israel and ordered him to enter the land of Canaan with the people of Israel. The name Joshua means "the Savior," synonymous with "Jesus" or "Hosea." A servant of God, Joshua ordered the priests to bear the Ark of the Covenant and to cross the Jordan River while leading the people. When the priests bearing the Ark dipped their feet in the water (for the Jordan overflows its banks during the time of the harvest), the waters that came from upstream stood still and rose very far away at Adam, the city that is beside Zaretan. So the waters that went down into the Sea of Arabah, the Salt Sea, were cut off and the people could cross over opposite Jericho (Joshua 3:15-16).

Through this incident, God teaches us that He had completely eliminated death caused by sin and subsequent judgment from mankind. In other words, Jesus Christ our Savior took away all the sins of mankind when He was baptized by John the Baptist and was crucified. In this way, He saved mankind from their sins by leading them into the land of Canaan, which stands for the Kingdom of Heaven.

The Jordan River is the place where mankind was purified

The historical events surrounding the crossing of the Jordan river, as recorded in the Old and the New Testaments, were tremendously important events which were to lead to eventual salvation from the curses and judgments arising from the sins of mankind.

The Jordan River was referred to as the river of death, and the terminus of the river is the Dead Sea. The word Jordan means "a river that only flows downward, toward death" or "be immersed, suppress, to force down, fall out." This clearly indicates the history of humanity's sins. In this river, Jesus, through His baptism, received all the flow of sins that cannot be ceased by any human being, and later died on the Cross and thereby accepting judgment in humanities' place for these sins.

Where are we, the descendants of Adam and Eve, headed for? Since all creatures are born with sin, they commit sins, and as the wages of those sins, they march toward death. Throughout the history of humanity, all creatures are heading for destruction from their birth. Even though they try hard to control their sinful nature, they can't, and that's why they are moving toward a final judgment for their sins.

However, God cut off the flow of sin and judgment. God led Joshua to take the people of Israel into the land of Canaan by crossing the Jordan River. This was God's will for Joshua. This story suggests that in order to be freed from sin, we must pay the wages of sins, which is death, and that through this price, we are purified of all our sins and enter Heaven.

In the Old Testament, the flow of the river was stopped and it was changed into a dry land when the priests who bore the Ark of the Covenant dipped their feet in the water. This allowed the people of Israel to cross the river. This was the remission of sin that was given only to those who believed in the beautiful gospel. It was the gospel of the water and the Spirit that paid the wages of sin for mankind, and we have come to receive the indwelling of the Holy Spirit by believing in this beautiful gospel.

General Naaman

Naaman, who appears in chapter 5 of 2 Kings, was a great and honorable commander of the army of Syria who had saved his country from its enemies. He was also a leper who was destined to lose everything because of the curse. But he later heard the beautiful news that he could be rescued from this curse. It was said that he could be cured if he went to see a servant of God who lived in Israel. It was a small girl servant who delivered this news. She said, *"If only my master were with the prophet who is in Samaria! For he would heal him of his leprosy" (2 Kings 5:3).*

He believed this news and went to Israel. When he arrived at the front of the house of Elisha, Elisha sent a messenger to him, saying, *"Go wash in the Jordan seven times, and your flesh shall be restored to you, and you shall be clean." (2 Kings 5:10).* Having expected a miraculous cure, Naaman became furious and decided to return to his home country. However, because of his servant's eager request, he obeyed Elisha and went down and dipped his whole body seven times in the Jordan. There, his flesh was restored, becoming once more like the skin of a young child.

In the same way, we have come to know that in order to be forgiven for all our sins, we must forsake our own thoughts and accept what is written in the Bible. Then we will be given beautiful blessings. Whoever wants to be saved must obey God's words and wholly believe in them.

The Bible says that all the sins of the world were washed away by the gospel of Jesus' baptism and blood. We must not think in the same way as the disobedient Naaman. We can't be cleansed of our sins without the gospel of the water and the Spirit. Therefore, in order to be forgiven for all our sins, we must believe in the beautiful gospel of the water and the Spirit. Just as Naaman became clean by dipping his body seven times in the water, we believe that we can be cleansed of our sins by believing in the beautiful gospel of Jesus' baptism, crucifixion and resurrection. We must believe in this beautiful gospel as it is.

This miracle in the Jordan River presented all descendants of Adam with a blessing that cut off the flow of all sins and ended the judgment. All of humanity was expelled from the Garden of Eden because Adam and Eve sinned after being tempted by Satan. However, the incident in the Jordan was the beautiful gospel that leads all mankind to return to the Garden of Eden.

The event of the Jordan River

The Bible records the beautiful news that Jesus took away all sin in the Jordan. *"Permit it to be so now, for thus it is fitting for us to fulfill all righteousness" (Matthew 3:15).* The Bible states that all sins were passed on to Jesus when He was baptized in the Jordan River. In other words, Jesus' baptism was the event that cut the chain of sin that bound all of mankind. This is how Jesus put an end to sin and later offered us salvation with His blood on the Cross.

The Jordan was the river of baptism that cleansed all our sins. We were able to fulfill God's law, *"The wages of sin is death" (Romans 6:23),* because Jesus paid the wages by being baptized in the Jordan River and dying on the Cross. This is the beautiful gospel that our Lord gave mankind.

All the sins of mankind continued from Adam, but stopped utterly with Jesus' baptism in the Jordan River and His blood on the Cross. No sin has remained thanks to Jesus' baptism. What blessed and beautiful news it is. We, by believing in this beautiful gospel, are saved from the swirling flow of sins, are purified of all our sins and become sanctified in the redemptive law of God. As such, Jesus' baptism and blood on the Cross is the gospel that saves all mankind. We should truly believe in this. *"Whatever is not from faith is sin" (Romans 14:23),* says the Lord. Likewise, we are blessed only when we believe in this beautiful gospel.

Do you still have sin in your heart despite the fact that all sin was passed on to Jesus when He was baptized by John? Jesus took away all the sins of the world. You should accept what is written in the Bible. Only the gospel of Jesus' baptism and His blood on the Cross can blot out your sin and avert you from death and all other curses. To baptize means "to be washed, to be immersed, to be buried, to pass on to, and to be transferred."

All mankind can be forgiven for their sins by believing in the beautiful gospel given by Jesus. That's why Jesus called Himself 'the way to Heaven.' We can enter Heaven and have eternal life by believing in Him. He is our Lord, who gave us the indwelling of the Holy Spirit. We are exempted from all judgment for our sins by believing in His baptism and blood.

The curse ended and the river turned into dry land because the priests who bore the Ark of the Covenant dipped their feet in the water by faith. This was what God had planned, and Jesus' baptism and His blood accomplished this plan. What a beautiful gospel this is. This was the law of salvation and without this our salvation was impossible. Those who believe in this beautiful gospel can now cross the Jordan River and enter the land of Canaan. That the water dried completely means all the sins of the world were transferred to Jesus and He was judged for us. This is the gospel that gives us the indwelling of the Holy Spirit.

God, who created mankind, knows that the average person's IQ is only about 110 to 130 points. Therefore, He can't complicate this truth of receiving the Holy Spirit. God took away all their sins with Jesus' baptism and His blood on the Cross. He made it possible to receive the Holy Spirit by believing in the gospel of the water and the Holy Spirit so that all of them would know it. You will also come to realize the indwelling of the Holy Spirit by believing in this beautiful gospel.

According to what is written in the Bible, we can't receive the Holy Spirit just by praying in repentance. People think that the Holy Spirit is something given when they offer many kinds of prayers. But, this is simply not true. The Holy Spirit is given to those who believe in the beautiful gospel, and it is needed to make them God's children. That is to say, the indwelling of the Holy Spirit was a guarantee that a person had become a child of God. God gives the Holy Spirit to those who believe in the beautiful gospel to make sure they are His children.

If people believe in Jesus but don't know or believe in this gospel, they can't be confident in the fact that all their sins were passed on to Him. Therefore, all people must know and believe that Jesus' baptism and His blood on the Cross is the beautiful gospel that blotted out their sins.

Who testifies that Jesus took away all the sins of the world? John the Baptist does. That He was baptized by John and took away all the sins of the world is what God our Father had planned (Leviticus 4:13-21, 16:1-30). Who carried out His plan? Jesus did. Who finally guarantees the fulfillment of this plan? The Holy Spirit does. God in Trinity completed the remission of sin with Jesus' baptism and His blood on the

Cross to make us His children. The Holy Spirit dwells within us and guarantees that we were saved from all our sins when Jesus fulfilled God's plan.

Do things in this world appear to be breathtakingly complicated? And how confused are your thoughts? One can't believe in this beautiful gospel unless he gives up his own thoughts. The doctrine of today's Christianity that many people believe in is that 'original sin passed away, but actual sins are forgiven when one prays in repentance.' However, this is far from being the complete truth; it is in fact false gospel. If you believe it, you can't understand the Bible from the beginning to the end, and as time passes you will experience more and more difficulties in following Jesus. That's why among Christians there are those who believe in different gospels and a different God.

Some people say that they receive the indwelling of the Holy Spirit by 'praying.' It seems plausible, but the Bible states that the Holy Spirit descended on Jesus like a dove when He was baptized and came out of the water. This is the true gospel and the Holy Spirit comes on those who believe in this gospel.

In addition, some people say they receive the Holy Spirit by offering prayers in repentance. Is the Holy Spirit given when people simply beg for forgiveness? God is righteous. The Holy Spirit doesn't come just because He takes pity on them. No matter how hard people cry or pray, the Holy Spirit cannot come upon them. He comes upon those who believe that God fulfilled His plan to save them. You must keep in mind that you cannot receive the Holy Spirit no matter how long you cry for God or how hard you pray. The Holy Spirit is independent of man's will.

Even the historical decisions of mankind in this world can be changed, but the beautiful gospel and the law of the indwelling of the Holy Spirit are immutable; that is they can never change. If people don't understand the beautiful gospel, it's very hard for them to return to the true practice of faith. It is for this reason that many people can't receive the indwelling of the Holy Spirit. How chagrined would you feel if you believed in Jesus but were destroyed just because you didn't know of the beautiful gospel? The Bible says that for some people the beautiful gospel of Jesus is a stumbling block and a rock of offense.

If you have come to understand the mystery of Jesus' baptism by John, you can also be forgiven for your sins and have the indwelling of the Holy Spirit. He saved all sinners by being baptized, dying on the Cross and being resurrected. The redemption Jesus gave us was a righteous method of salvation. He became the true Savior of all sinners, and confirmed the indwelling of the Holy Spirit.

Only if you believe in it!

It is recorded in the Old Testament that when the priests dipped their feet in the Jordan, the river turned into dry land. It is miraculous enough that the water stopped, but more miracles were to follow. What is more incredible is that the river turned into dry land. This incident served as a guarantee of God's salvation, which led to the remission of sin through Jesus' baptism and His blood on the Cross. The dry land represented the way that all the sins of the world would be forgiven thanks to Jesus' baptism and His blood on the Cross. All sins went forth from Adam out to all mankind, but the curse of judgment ended with Jesus' baptism. Now, all we need to do is to be forgiven for our sins by having faith and receiving the indwelling of the Holy Spirit. Do you believe in the beautiful truth that Jesus took away all your sins through His baptism in the Jordan River?

You should believe that Jesus Christ was baptized to take away all the sins of the world. In addition, you should also know, understand and believe how important His baptism was. If the priests hadn't entered the Jordan, the people of Israel wouldn't have been able to make a successful entry into the land of Canaan. The very first step for entering Canaan was the crossing of the Jordan River. Therefore, only when we cross the river with the Ark of the Covenant can we enter the land of Canaan. This teaches us that one can be forgiven for his sins by believing in the gospel of the water and the Spirit.

The Bible says that Jesus' baptism was the work of God. This also happened in relation to the priests. Just as the water of the Jordan River stopped when the priests dipped their feet in the water, the people of the world are saved from their sins by believing in this gospel.

The indwelling of the Holy Spirit is granted based on faith in this beautiful gospel. Jesus' baptism and His blood on the Cross will lead you to receive the forgiveness of sin and the Holy Spirit. This beautiful gospel of the water and the Spirit is indispensable to obtaining the indwelling of the Holy Spirit. ✉

SERMON 19

The beautiful gospel that tore the veil of the Temple

The beautiful gospel that tore the veil of the Temple

<Matthew 27:45-54>
"Now from the sixth hour until the ninth hour there was darkness over all the land. And about the ninth hour Jesus cried out with a loud voice, saying, 'Eli, Eli, lama sabachthani?' that is, 'My God, My God, why have You forsaken Me?' Some of those who stood there, when they heard that, said, 'This Man is calling for Elijah!' Immediately one of them ran and took a sponge, filled it with sour wine and put it on a reed, and offered it to Him to drink. The rest said, 'Let Him alone; let us see if Elijah will come to save Him.' And Jesus cried out again with a loud voice, and yielded up His spirit. Then, behold, the veil of the temple was torn in two from top to bottom; and the earth quaked, and the rocks were split, and the graves were opened; and many bodies of the saints who had fallen asleep were raised; and coming out of the graves after His resurrection, they went into the holy city and appeared to many. So when the centurion and those with him, who were guarding Jesus, saw the earthquake and the things that had happened, they feared greatly, saying, 'Truly this was the Son of God!'"

Why was the veil of the Temple of God torn when Jesus gave up His spirit on the Cross?

Because the Kingdom of God came to be opened to those who believe in His baptism and crucifixion.

In order to understand the truth of this beautiful gospel, one must first know and understand the sacrificial system performed to forgive people's sins before God in the Old Testament. You must know and believe the following truth.

According to the ancient sacrifice of atonement, as recorded in Leviticus chapter 16 in the Old Testament, the high priest laid his hands on a live goat and transferred to it all the sins accumulated by the people over the course a year. Then on behalf of the Israelites, the sacrifice was killed and the high priest sprinkled its blood on the mercy seat. This atoned for all the sins of the Israelites. Likewise, only those who believed in the laying on of hands, the blood and the words of God could enter the Holy sanctuary.

The priests always went into the first part of the tabernacle, performing the services. But into the second part, the Most Holy Place, the high priest could enter alone once a year, not without blood, which he offered for himself and for the people's sins committed in ignorance (Hebrews 9:6-7). Likewise, even the high priest couldn't enter the Most Holy Place without the blood of the sacrifice prepared through the laying hands on by faith.

As told in the New Testament, Jesus Christ was sacrificed for us

In the New Testament, we are told that one could enter the Kingdom of God through his belief in Jesus' baptism and His blood on the Cross. When was the veil of the Temple of God torn in two from top to bottom? It was when Jesus was crucified after He came into this world and was baptized by John.

What was the reason given for this? Jesus came to this world as a sacrifice, namely as the Lamb of God, took away the sins of the world by being baptized by John, and so cleansed mankind of all their sins when He was crucified. The tearing of the veil is a symbol that all the sins of mankind that separated us from God were purged through His baptism and blood on the Cross.

Jesus Himself broke down this barrier by paying the wages of sin, which is death. Jesus was baptized and crucified to take away the sins of the world. This was the reason that the veil of the Temple of God was torn in two. Just as priests could enter the tabernacle with the belief in the laying on of hands, now we can enter the Kingdom of Heaven thanks to our belief in Jesus' baptism and blood.

When Jesus was crucified, He cried out in a loud voice, saying, *"Eli, Eli, lama sabachthani?"* that is, *"My God, My God, why have You forsaken Me?" (Matthew 27:46)* When He finally gave up His spirit, He said, *"It is finished!" (John 19:30)* Jesus was forsaken by His Father at the Cross for a moment because He bore all the sins of the world since His baptism by John in the Jordan River.

He died for the salvation of all mankind. As a result of

Jesus' baptism and His death on the Cross, all who had faith in Him were saved. Because we are born sinners and are destined for condemnation, Jesus was baptized to take away all our sins.

The gate to the Kingdom of Heaven was firmly closed until Jesus purged us of all our sins. When Jesus was baptized by John and died on the Cross, the veil of the Temple of God was torn in two from top to bottom so that anyone who believes in the beautiful gospel could enter the heavenly Temple of God.

I am thankful to the Lord that I have faith in the gospel of the water and the Spirit. I can now enter the Kingdom of Heaven through my belief in the beautiful gospel that Jesus accomplished through His baptism and blood. I could not have achieved salvation through my own powers, achievements and efforts.

The blessing that leads us into the Kingdom of Heaven is not attained through mere prayers, donations and devotions. One can be saved from sin only by believing in Jesus' baptism and His blood on the Cross. One can enter the Kingdom of Heaven only by having faith in this beautiful gospel. Jesus is the gate to Heaven. No other beliefs are necessary to those who believe in Jesus. Entrance to Heaven is not granted as compensation for one's devoted donations, worldly efforts or other good deeds. The one truly necessary thing for believers to enter the Kingdom is faith in the gospel of Jesus' baptism in the Jordan River and His blood on the Cross.

Believing in the water (Jesus' baptism in the Jordan River) and His blood (the Cross) will lead you to the Kingdom of Heaven. The person who still has sin in his heart, even though he believes in Jesus, needs to believe in one thing: the gospel of the water and the Spirit. *"And you shall know the truth, and the truth shall make you free"* (John 8:32).

We never know the exact time of our death but Jesus

knows all. Since He knew our sinful nature so well, He washed away all our sins through His baptism and the blood on the Cross about two thousand years ago.

We must believe in this beautiful gospel that tore the veil of the Temple of God

The Savior was born to a virgin to save mankind from their sins. It was through His baptism at the age of 30 in the Jordan River, that Jesus took away all the sins of the world. All the sins of mankind resulting from their weaknesses and shortcomings were forgiven thanks to Jesus. His baptism and blood are the eternal keys to the salvation of all mankind. Jesus was baptized and bled on the Cross and now all those who have faith in this gospel can enter the Kingdom of Heaven.

The veil of the Temple of God was torn when Jesus gave up His spirit on the Cross. How could the veil of the Temple of God be torn in two when Jesus died on the Cross? The reason is that the salvation of mankind was achieved by Him in the beautiful gospel.

In the Old Testament, we learn about the tabernacle of Israel. There lay the altar of the burnt offering and the laver. Past this laver, was the tabernacle and inside the tabernacle behind the veil lay the ark, where God's presence and glory resided. The veil was so firmly woven that four horses pulling from the four directions could not tear its fabric. Even though King Solomon replaced the tabernacle with the Temple, the basic form was not changed, and the veil was still there blocking the way to the Most Holy Place. However, it was torn in two from top to bottom when Jesus died bleeding on the

Cross. This testifies to the fact that how beautiful and perfect the gospel that was completed with Jesus' baptism and His blood is.

God blessed all mankind with the forgiveness of sin and everlasting life, embracing them in the beautiful gospel. Jesus, as the sacrifice, paid off the wages of sin when He was baptized by John and died on the Cross. The Bible says, *"The wages of sin is death" (Romans 6:23)*. Just as in the time of the Old Testament, one could enter the Temple of God with the blood of the sacrifice and receive atonement for sin, so we could come to God with our sacrifice, which was Jesus, and be forgiven for our transgressions. This is the truth. And the words, *"The wages of sin is death"* shows us how perfect the beautiful gospel is.

The way to Heaven is to believe in the beautiful gospel. The tearing of the veil in two represents the opening of the Kingdom of God. When we come to know and believe in this gospel, saying, "Oh, Jesus took away all my sins. Oh, Jesus paid all the wages of sin on the Cross!" the gate to Heaven will open up before us. Heaven is now open to those who have achieved redemption through their faith in Jesus' baptism and His blood. The blood of Jesus saved sinners from death and His baptism was a means to take on the sins of all mankind.

The earth shook and rocks split open when the Lord gave up His spirit on the Cross. Just then, His blood dripped to the earth and began flowing toward the lower grounds. When Jesus died on the Cross, all the sins of mankind were purged, the beautiful gospel was completed and all believers became eligible to enter the Kingdom of Heaven. This is the very truth of being born again.

There are many scholars who have conducted research seeking to deny the existence of Jesus Christ as a real person.

But they could not persist in their hypothesis against the numerous historical evidences of His existence. Among them, many have given in and have come to believe in the gospel of Jesus' baptism and blood. They came to realize that the evidence of Jesus was too substantial to deny His existence. They accepted Jesus as their Savior when they came to know and believe in this beautiful gospel, namely, His birth, baptism, death, resurrection, ascension and the Second Advent.

We did not witness Jesus' baptism. Our eyes did not see what took place about 2,000 years ago. However, through what is written, anyone can come in contact with this beautiful gospel. Jesus broke down the barrier of sin between God and man through His baptism and blood, and thus the veil of the Kingdom of God was torn in two from top to bottom.

Now anyone who believes in this beautiful gospel, which was completed by Jesus' baptism and His blood, can enter the Kingdom of Heaven. Do you have faith in the fact that Jesus' baptism and His blood, namely this beautiful gospel, is the key to the Kingdom of Heaven?

I once was a sinner myself, who trusted Jesus to be my Savior but wasn't aware of the beautiful gospel. However, one day I came to read about His unconditional love for me in the Bible. I came to know that He was baptized for me, died on the Cross for me and was resurrected for me. Jesus saved us by being baptized in the Jordan River and crucified to pay the wages of sin because of His love for us. We are able to enter the Kingdom of Heaven by believing in this beautiful gospel.

This is God's greatest righteousness for mankind and the epoch-making event of history. All His ministry – His birth, baptism in the Jordan River, death on the Cross, and resurrection – was to save us from all our sins. We were destined for hell after our deaths, but Jesus spared our souls from eternity in hell and granted us the beautiful gospel as the way to enter the Kingdom of Heaven.

Dear brethren, when Jesus was dead on the Cross, a soldier pierced His side with a spear, and immediately blood and water came out. This is as it is written in the Bible. This testifies to the truth of the beautiful gospel of Jesus' baptism and His blood.

Do you consider that your faith in Jesus' blood on the Cross is sufficient to free you from all your sins? Is Jesus' baptism less significant or only incidental to your salvation? If you believe so, please repent. We now have to believe in the gospel of Jesus' baptism and blood and recognize it as God's truth.

Do you want to be cleansed of all your sins?

Just as we need to pay to get out of debt, we must have faith in the beautiful gospel of Jesus' baptism and blood in order to be cleansed of all our sins. We should not commit the sin of disbelief in the gospel of Jesus' baptism and blood. Although we did not directly pass on our sins to Jesus, a mediator called John the Baptist did the task for us.

When Jesus died on the Cross, some tombs of the saints in Jerusalem opened and three days later He was resurrected and went into Galilee. This wonderful event really did take place, but there were many people who did not believe it.

Our Lord granted the Kingdom of Heaven to us, the righteous, who received the remission of sin. We were saved and born again, not through our own physical power or religious efforts, but through our faith in the beautiful gospel. This gospel is not a fictional story. All the sins of the world were passed on to Jesus when He was baptized. There was no sin in Him, but He had to die on the Cross to atone the very sins He took on at His baptism.

When Jesus gave up His spirit, the earth quaked and the rocks split open. When the centurion and those with him who were guarding Jesus' body felt the earthquake and the things that had happened, they felt tremendous fear, testifying, *"Truly this was the Son of God" (Matthew 27:54).*

Joseph a rich man from Arimathea took the body of Jesus, wrapped it in a clean linen cloth and laid it in his own tomb. The high priest and the Pharisees gave orders for the grave to be made secure until the third day.

However, Jesus was resurrected to give new life to those who believe in the beautiful gospel. He went into Galilee, where He had promised to meet His disciples before He was crucified. All these things – His birth, baptism, crucifixion, resurrection, ascension and the Second Advent – were aimed at those who believe in the beautiful gospel. I have also become a testifier who testifies that Jesus is the Son of the living God and my Savior.

By whom is the true gospel preached?

The believers in Jesus' baptism and blood testify to the beautiful gospel of the truth. The beautiful gospel is spread through the testimony of these people saved from all their sins. When a person is freed from his sins by believing in the gospel, the Spirit of God begins to govern him, and He changes him regardless of his own will. The soul winning words of God continuously transforms a righteous man and gives him even stronger faith. In turn, he comes to praise the Lord. The word of God abides in him, and as a result he experiences the renewal of his inner being day by day. Seeing him thus transformed, people testify, "He is really a delivered man. He became a genuine Christian and a child of God."

Even the devil accepts and succumbs to this beautiful gospel. "I'm mortified!" he says. "But it's true that there is no sin in the world. No one has sin in his heart." Therefore the devil works in the thoughts of people, interfering with their faithful lives. The work of the devil is to prevent them from receiving the spiritual blessings of the gospel.

Satan lost the battle with Jesus absolutely. Satan succeeded in having Jesus crucified by controlling people's minds. However, Jesus had already taken away the sins of the world when He was baptized, and when He died on the Cross to pay off the wages of the sin. For this reason He completely saved all the believers in the gospel.

The devil was unable to obstruct God's plan to save mankind from their sins. Jesus paid for the sins of mankind through His baptism and blood to complete the beautiful gospel. Now there is no sin in this world. Jesus took away all sin through His baptism and put an end to all sin through His death on the Cross, saying, *"It is finished!"(John 19:30)* Satan was deprived of the power to accuse those who have faith in the beautiful gospel. Jesus defeated the devil through His birth, baptism, crucifixion and resurrection.

Do you still have sin in your hearts? No. Christians can confidently say, "I have no sin in my heart" on the basis of their faith in the beautiful gospel of truth. The person who believes in the beautiful gospel of Jesus' baptism and blood doesn't have even an ounce of sin in his heart.

Now the beautiful gospel has been engraved in our hearts. We now stand free of any compunction in the presence of God. Do all of you believe that Jesus took away all your sins through His baptism in the Jordan River? If so, your gratefulness to God and joy will be made full. By having faith in the beautiful gospel, we have been sanctified and freed from our sins in this world. We thank God.

"He has delivered us from the power of darkness and conveyed us into the kingdom of the Son of His Love, in whom we have redemption through His blood, the forgiveness of sins" (Colossians 1:13-14). Hallelujah, praise the Lord.

Jesus opened up the gate to salvation through the beautiful gospel. You also must break down the barrier in your heart all at once with the power of the beautiful gospel, just as the veil of the Temple was torn in two. The beautiful gospel was made for you and me. We can enter the Kingdom of Heaven by believing in this gospel, and it is the ultimate truth that allows us to achieve the indwelling of the Holy Spirit. ✉

SERMON 20

The person who has the indwelling of the Holy Spirit guides others to receiving the Holy Spirit

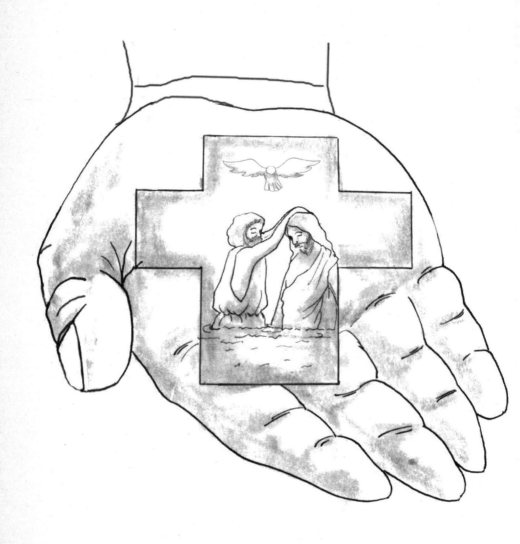

The person who has the indwelling of the Holy Spirit guides others to receiving the Holy Spirit

<John 20:21-23>

"So Jesus said to them again, 'Peace to you! As the Father has sent me, I also send you.' And when He had said this, He breathed on them, and said to them, 'Receive the Holy Spirit. If you forgive the sins of any, they are forgiven them; if you retain the sins of any, they are retained.'"

What authority did the Lord give to the righteous?

He gave them the authority to forgive the sins of any through the gospel of the water and the Spirit.

John Chapter 20 contains a record of Jesus' resurrection. Our Lord rose again from the dead and told His disciples, *"Receive the Holy Spirit."* The disciples of Jesus received the indwelling of the Holy Spirit as a gift from Him. Jesus gave the indwelling of the Holy Spirit and eternal life to those who believed that His baptism and blood washed away all their sins.

The Bible says the baptism of Jesus is the antitype of salvation, which means that His baptism saved all mankind from their sins (1 Peter 3:21).

Why was Jesus baptized?

Why was Jesus baptized by John? The answer to this question can be clearly seen from what Jesus said in Matthew 3:15, *"Thus it is fitting for us to fulfill all righteousness."* Here, *"thus"* means that Jesus took away all the sins of the world when He was baptized. His baptism was carried out in the same way that the laying on of hands was conducted in Old Testament times. The purpose of His baptism was to pass on the sins of the world to Jesus.

What is the meaning of "all righteousness?" What does the word "fitting" imply? "All righteousness" means that it was fitting for Jesus to take away the sins of the world through His baptism. And "fitting" implies that all this was the most appropriate and just way in the eyes of God.

Jesus took away all the sins of mankind through His baptism and purged them for all those who believed in Him. Jesus was baptized and crucified in judgment for their sins. This is the gospel of the remission of sin. The righteousness of God is the remission of sin that blotted out all the sins of sinners.

If people perceive the mystery of Jesus' baptism as it is written in Matthew 3:13-17, they will be able to receive the remission of sins and also the Holy Spirit. What Jesus did in His public ministry — His baptism, crucifixion and resurrection — was to provide us with the righteous way toward salvation, as predestined by God. In this way, Jesus became the true Savior of all sinners. The gospel of His baptism and blood is that of salvation, which washed away all our sins.

People can receive the Holy Spirit only when they know and believe in the gospel of Jesus' baptism and blood. Because the baptism of Jesus took away all the sins of the world, our sins were passed on to Him. His death on the Cross on behalf of mankind was my own death, and His resurrection my own resurrection. As such, Jesus' baptism and blood on the Cross is the gospel of the remission of sin and of receiving the Holy Spirit.

I hope you learn the reason for Jesus' baptism and have faith in the gospel. Then, your sins will be blotted out and you will receive the Holy Spirit. Why was Jesus baptized? It was to take away all the sins of the world. *"Thus it is fitting for us to fulfill all righteousness" (Matthew 3:15).* Amen, Hallelujah!

Today, some believe that speaking in tongues is evidence of receiving the Holy Spirit. However, the true evidence of it is the precious faith in the beautiful gospel engraved in the hearts of those who have truly received the Holy Spirit.

The Lord gave the authority to forgive sin to all righteous people

The Lord gave His disciples the authority to forgive sin, saying, *"If you forgive the sins of any, they are forgiven them; if you retain the sins of any, they are retained" (John 20:23).* This implies that when the disciples preached the gospel of the water and the Spirit, the sins of all who listened and believed were forgiven. However, this does not mean they could forgive the sins of anyone, regardless of their belief in gospel of the water and the Spirit.

The disciples of Jesus have the authority to forgive the sins of any through the gospel of the water and the Spirit. Therefore, if they teach what is written, we must believe in it. You must believe that Jesus Christ gave you the gospel of the water and the Spirit in order to purge all your sins. Only then can you obtain the remission of sin and receive the indwelling of the Holy Spirit. Jesus also gave us the power to save all people from their sins by preaching the gospel of the water and the Spirit.

The power of the ruler of the world

In the past, where I used to live, we had to take the bus over an unpaved road. People had to get off the bus at one point and push it up a hill. Once, the president of Korea came to the opening ceremony for a thermal power plant on that road. People welcomed the president by sweeping the road and placing trees along its side when they heard the news. When the day arrived, motorcycles guided the way and behind them came the president's car. Crowds of people came out to greet him with national flags in their hands. It was said that the president remarked, "This road is too bumpy, it needs to be paved." A few days later, the road was paved with asphalt.

What happened here? One passing remark from the president was enough to cause this drastic change in the road's condition. A president's command has such a great power. However, we are well aware that the gospel of the water and the Spirit granted to us by Christ is far more powerful. We must believe that this gospel has the power to free us from all our sins throughout our lives.

The true authority to forgive sins

"If you forgive the sins of any, they are forgiven them; if you retain the sins of any, they are retained." The disciples of Jesus preached the gospel that all their sins were forgiven. They told the people, "Jesus blotted out all the sins of the world with His baptism and blood. There is nothing to worry about. Although you are destined to sin in the future, Jesus already took away all your daily sins and bled for you on the Cross after being baptized by John. Jesus saved you! You must believe it!"

Sinners were given redemption by hearing and believing the gospel of the water and the Spirit through Jesus' disciples. Jesus granted His disciples the authority to forgive sin through the gospel of the water and the Spirit. Because Jesus' disciples preached the gospel of the water and the Spirit to all the people of the world, believers could receive the remission of sin. Jesus granted them this gift along with the authority to forgive sin.

Many people have read the books I have previously published, and they have been saved from their sins after reading them. Some admitted their realization that the reason Jesus died on the Cross was the result of His baptism to take away all the sins of the world, quoting, *"He was wounded for our transgressions, He was bruised for our iniquities" (Isaiah 53:5).*

After His resurrection, Jesus said to His disciples, *"Receive the Holy Spirit. If you forgive the sins of any, they are forgiven them; if you retain the sins of any, they are retained" (John 20:22-23).* Jesus granted them the authority to forgive people's sins.

We were bound by confusion, emptiness and sin before we believed in this truth. However, now that we have faith in Jesus' baptism and blood, and are free from sin, we are the ones to preach this gospel to others. Furthermore, our Lord gave His disciples peace. Our Lord also gave us peace and the blessing of Holy Spirit, too. In order to receive peace and the Holy Spirit from God, we must receive the remission of sins by believing in Jesus' baptism and blood on the Cross.

What frees us from sin is faith in the gospel of the water and the Spirit. This is the spiritual faith that brings us heavenly blessings. But arbitrary faith based on man's own thoughts leads him to destruction. We must obtain redemption by believing in the gospel of the water and the Spirit and thus receive the Holy Spirit. In order to have such faith, we must forsake our earthly thoughts and turn our faith to the gospel of the water and the Spirit.

In order to have the faith needed to receive the Holy Spirit, one should accept the gospel that Jesus was baptized and crucified for us. The Lord provided us with the remission of sin, peace and the indwelling of the Holy Spirit because we believe in the gospel of the water and the Spirit. He gave His disciples the indwelling of the Holy Spirit and the authority to forgive the sins of anyone who believed in the gospel of the water and the Spirit.

We also received the Holy Spirit by believing in this gospel. The gospel of the water and the Spirit has helped many others do the same. When we preach the gospel to our neighbors and to the world, those who take it to heart are granted the Holy Spirit. If the gospel that we preach cannot enable people to receive the Holy Spirit, it is not the true gospel. On the other hand, if the gospel we preach can lead them to receive the Holy Spirit, that gospel is genuine.

How blessed and thankful we should be to have such a gospel. The gospel that has been preached by you and me is such a perfect and elevated one. But unfortunately, it is hard to find a person who truly knows and believes in this gospel today. Therefore we must preach the gospel all over the world. We must help people receive the Holy Spirit.

Those who are deluded by Satan into denying the gospel of the water and the Spirit

We are helping even those who already believe in Jesus. Many of them still haven't received the Holy Spirit even though they believe in Jesus. So we help them by preaching the gospel and thus helping them receive the Holy Spirit.

If a man hasn't received the Holy Spirit even though he believes in Jesus, there might be some problems in his belief. Only those who have received the Holy Spirit through their belief in Jesus can be regarded as people who possess the true faith. Therefore we must all keep the faith that leads us to receive the Holy Spirit. We must know the gospel of the water and the Spirit, because only the truth of this gospel is what enables us to receive the Holy Spirit.

We preach the gospel of the water and the Spirit so that others can receive the Holy Spirit. However, those who preach the gospel are bound to encounter many difficulties. Some Christians think they can receive the Holy Spirit by making efforts over an extended period of time. They have many confusing experiences that are irrelevant to receiving the Holy

Spirit. A lot of time and sacrifice is thus needed to enlighten
them with the gospel of the water and the Spirit.

Who would not believe in the gospel of the water and the
Spirit if everyone thought that one could receive the Holy
Spirit through faith in this gospel? Satan deceived people with
a different gospel before the true gospel came. Such people
wonder what more there is to believe in when they already
consider themselves to believe in the gospel of Jesus. Therefore
they come to deny and refuse the gospel of the water and the
Spirit.

A lot of people in this day and age do not fully accept the
true gospel of the water and the Spirit, for Satan has already
blinded them. As a result, they think believing in Jesus is a
simple task. However, coming to fully understand the truth of
the gospel is not at all easy. The true gospel of the water and
the Spirit is veiled by a false gospel.

People think that anyone can enter the Kingdom of Heaven
if they attend church and profess that they believe in Jesus.
Many believe that the indwelling of the Holy Spirit is granted
through their own efforts, such as praying and fasting.
However, such beliefs are far from the truth of receiving the
Holy Spirit. They think that speaking in tongues and other
miracles are signs of receiving the Holy Spirit.

Thus they scarcely understand that in order to receive the
Holy Spirit, it is necessary to believe in the true gospel of the
water and the Spirit. However, the Bible says that one can
receive the Holy Spirit only by believing in the word of God.
God concealed the mystery of receiving the Holy Spirit in His
words.

Those who want the indwelling of the Holy Spirit

I once went to Taiwan with some of our workers. People there asked us for books on the Holy Spirit. The same thing happened in Japan and Russia. The reason so many people want books on the indwelling of the Spirit is that the people of today so eagerly want to receive the indwelling of the Holy Spirit. Many people believe in Jesus and are at times unsure whether they have truly received the Holy Spirit, because they don't have the indwelling of the Holy Spirit.

There are plenty of people who believe in Jesus and claim that they have received the Holy Spirit. However, people who have received the Holy Spirit permanently and for eternity are scarce. Many people are unable to do so despite their faith in Jesus, and that is why they yearn to do it now.

Among Christians of the world, there are many people who think they have experienced the Holy Spirit. Some say they have encountered Jesus in their dreams, and some claim they have the Holy Spirit within them because they have experienced the casting out of demons. As such, there are many people whose faith is based on personal experience. However, seldom have people like this truly received the indwelling of the Holy Spirit through faith in the gospel of the water and the Spirit.

I once thought it strange that there weren't books in this world on achieving the indwelling of the Holy Spirit through faith in the pure gospel of the water and the Spirit. Many people talk about their experiences with the Holy Spirit, but why aren't there books on the indwelling of the Holy Spirit? Such books are hard to find, even if you look far and wide throughout the world.

Those who incorrectly insist that they have received the Holy Spirit claim that they have even met Jesus in person and have visited the Kingdoms of Heaven and hell. They insist that Jesus said, "You have come ahead of time. You have much left to accomplish in your world, so hurry back to where you belong." Such an experience is not impossible. However, could the Jesus that they encountered be the real Jesus? Would Jesus have met them when they still had sin in their hearts? Does Jesus abide within a sinner?

It's true that most Christians today don't have the indwelling of the Holy Spirit even though they maintain a degree of faith in Jesus. Therefore we, the ones who have the Holy Spirit within us, must spread the gospel that will lead others to receive this gift. Everyone needs to receive the Holy Spirit, and in order to do so, faith in the gospel of the water and the Spirit is essential. For only by believing in the gospel can one receive the Holy Spirit. Through the gospel of the truth that we all know, we can receive the gift of the Holy Spirit from God.

We must all thank and praise the Lord for giving us the gospel of the water and the Spirit. I have experienced the joy of the Holy Spirit while He prevailed on me to write this book. When this book is published, many people will receive the indwelling of the Holy Spirit through their faith in the gospel of the water and the Spirit. *"Did you receive the Holy Spirit when you believed?" (Acts 19:2)* said Paul to the would-be disciples in Ephesus.

We all must receive the Holy Spirit. Christians worldwide are especially interested in receiving the Holy Spirit at this turbulent time in world history. I am preaching the biblical way to receive the Holy Spirit, just as the Holy Spirit guides me to do. To live a satisfactory life, you must believe in the truth of the indwelling of the Holy Spirit. For it is your last chance to receive the Holy Spirit deep in your heart.

I feel compelled to spread the gospel that helps everyone receive the Holy Spirit because Jesus Christ gave me the gospel of the water and the Spirit and bequeathed me with the gift of the Holy Spirit.

The Gentiles must also have faith in the gospel of the water and the Spirit

The Bible relates how Jesus' disciples let others receive the indwelling of the Holy Spirit. Even the Gentiles had to keep the same faith as the disciples in order to receive the Holy Spirit. Furthermore, the Gentiles in particular needed to have faith in the gospel of the water and the Spirit, which the disciples had, in order to enter the world of God. Therefore we, who are Gentiles, must also believe in the true gospel in order to receive the Holy Spirit. God sent Peter to Cornelius, who was a Gentile, in order that he would be enlightened with the gospel of the water and the Spirit, which is necessary for receiving the Holy Spirit.

The Jewish believers were astonished to hear that the gift of the Holy Spirit also had been poured out on the Gentiles. When Peter returned to the church of Jerusalem after preaching the gospel of the water and the Spirit, those who were circumcised criticized him. *"You went in to uncircumcised men and ate with them!" (Acts 11:3)* But Peter explained everything to them from the beginning.

His explanation is well contained in Acts 11:5-17. *"I was*

in the city of Joppa praying; and in a trance I saw a vision, an object descending like a great sheet, let down from heaven by four corners; and it came to me. When I observed it intently and considered, I saw four-footed animals of the earth, wild beasts, creeping things, and birds of the air. And I heard a voice saying to me, 'Rise, Peter; kill and eat.' But I said, 'Not so, Lord! For nothing common or unclean has at any time entered my mouth.' But the voice answered me again from heaven, 'What God has cleansed you must not call common.' Now this was done three times, and all were drawn up again into heaven. At that very moment, three men stood before the house where I was, having been sent to me from Caesarea. Then the Spirit told me to go with them, doubting nothing. Moreover these six brethren accompanied me, and we entered the man's house. And he told us how he had seen an angel standing in his house, who said to him, 'Send men to Joppa, and call for Simon whose surname is Peter, who will tell you words by which you and all your household will be saved.' And as I began to speak, the Holy Spirit fell upon them, as upon us at the beginning. Then I remembered the word of the Lord, how He said, 'John indeed baptized with water, but you shall be baptized with the Holy Spirit.' If therefore God gave them the same gift as He gave us when we believed on the Lord Jesus Christ, who was I that I could withstand God?"

Peter said that he did not only go in to uncircumcised men and eat with them, he also told them the gospel thanks to the guidance of the Holy Spirit. When they heard these things they became silent, and they glorified God, who granted repentance and life to all of them – Cornelius, his relatives and his close friends.

The apostolic gospel for receiving the Holy Spirit

*What is the grave
mission of apostles?*

*Preaching the gospel of the water
and the Spirit in order for them
to receive the Holy Spirit.*

Did the Apostles really preach the gospel of the water and the Spirit that? We must first confirm whether the apostle Peter believed in the gospel of the water and the Spirit. In the Bible, Peter said, *"There is also an antitype which now saves us – baptism" (1 Peter 3:21).* The apostle Peter truly believed that Jesus saved all sinners from their sins when He was baptized and died on the Cross. He also believed that when Jesus was baptized (Matthew 3:15), all sins were passed on to Him, that He was crucified and later resurrected to save us all.

These days there are people who have the same faith as Peter. Those who preach the gospel of the water and the Spirit are the ones who preach the same gospel as Peter did. This truth suffices to allow listeners to receive the indwelling of the Holy Spirit.

Just as many people received the Holy Spirit when Peter preached the gospel of the water and the Spirit, we also see people believe in the gospel and receive the Holy Spirit when we preach the same truth. A person does not receive the Holy Spirit by vaguely believing that one will go to heaven if he only believes in Jesus as his Lord, but rather by believing in the gospel of the water and the Spirit.

Peter once considered the Gentiles as little more than bugs

that creep on the ground. According to the law, they were like unclean animals before Jesus was baptized, died on the Cross and was resurrected. However, even the Gentiles could be blessed with the indwelling of the Holy Spirit by believing in the gospel of the water and the Spirit. So a voice spoke to Peter, saying, *"What God has cleansed you must not call common" (Acts 10:15).*

We, as Gentiles, were never able to receive the Holy Spirit but we can have the indwelling of the Holy Spirit by having faith in the gospel of the water and the Spirit. When we preach the gospel patiently to people full of their own thoughts, often we see them come to believe in the gospel and finally receive the Holy Spirit in the end. We may also see them confess that they have no sin in their hearts after coming to believe in Jesus' baptism and blood. Only then does the Holy Spirit dwell within them.

Our purpose in preaching this gospel is not merely to make others understand it, but to lead them to receive the Holy Spirit. The fact that those who believe in the gospel that we preach are forgiven for all their sins is very significant. And the fact that they receive the indwelling of the Holy Spirit at the same time is even more important. We not only preach the gospel to the people of the world, but also take it a step further and lead them to receive the Holy Spirit at the same time.

We must preach the gospel of the water and the Spirit in this context to those who are in need of it. If we were to cease after merely preaching the gospel, the whole meaning of our labors would be lost. We must be aware that this gospel leads people to have the indwelling of the Holy Spirit. When we preach the gospel bearing this in mind, the flames of the Holy Spirit will spread like wildfire over the whole world.

When an evangelist believes that this gospel can guide the

people of the world to receive the Holy Spirit, he comes to feel keenly aware that his ministry is not simply about persuading people to believe in Jesus Christ, but is about helping them receive the indwelling of the Holy Spirit. Therefore it is very important for us to preach the gospel of the water and the Spirit at this time.

One needs only listen with his ears and believe with his heart in the gospel that we preach in order to receive the Holy Spirit. Clearly, the gospel that we are preaching has a great influence over people's lives. The power of the gospel is the authority and blessing given by God.

Peter was an evangelist of the Jews, while Paul was that of the Gentiles. While Peter was praying on a housetop, he saw Heaven open and an object like a great sheet bound at the four corners descended on him. In it were all kinds of unclean animals that the Bible said were forbidden to eat.

Peter had never eaten anything common or unclean. However, God ordered him to kill and eat them. Peter refused, saying, *"Not so, Lord! For I have never eaten anything common or unclean!"* And a voice spoke to him, *"What God have cleansed you must not call common."* What does this suggest? God is saying that Jesus washed away all the sins of the world, even of Gentiles, when He was baptized and died on the Cross.

The spiritual meaning of God's order for him to kill and eat unclean animals was to teach Peter that even the Gentiles can become children of God by believing that Jesus was sent into this world, baptized to take away all our sins and crucified to be judged for them.

Peter was still following the regulations of the law instead of seeing them with the spiritual eyes of faith, even after receiving the Spirit. But Peter repented and believed that God had already washed away even the sins of the Gentiles. Peter came to realize the riches of the beautiful gospel more deeply. He saw the Holy Spirit fall on his listeners when he preached God's words.

How could we discern whether the evangelists of today have received the Holy Spirit or not? It depends on whether they accept the gospel of the water and the Spirit. The person who believes in the beautiful gospel as it is when an evangelist preaches the words of God has received the indwelling of the Holy Spirit. The Holy Spirit that dwells in the heart of the evangelist also comes to dwell in him. The evangelist and the listener will come to have fellowship with one another like childhood friends. They will see the love of God abide in each other. The evangelist will see the listener become one of God's people by accepting the gospel of the water and the Spirit.

When we preach the gospel, we can see the Holy Spirit descend on believers as soon as they believe in the gospel of the water and the Spirit. It is not a separate experience from salvation. That is the primary reason why we must preach the gospel of the water and the Spirit. The gospel that we preach is one that leads others to receive the Holy Spirit.

Those who have the indwelling of the Holy Spirit are children of God. The gospel of the water and the Spirit is not a theoretical doctrine of a denomination, and therefore when we preach this to others, they come to have faith, receive the Holy Spirit and become children of God. How great a blessing this is! What an amazing gospel! And how marvelous His work is! Those who preach the gospel of the water and the Spirit help build the Kingdom of God. We merely preach the gospel, but they receive the Holy Spirit.

Some people think believing in Jesus is one thing and receiving the Holy Spirit is another. Therefore, Christians still pray for the Holy Spirit. However, the Bible says that the Holy Spirit comes upon those when they listen and believe in the gospel preached by His servants. People all around the world are craving the Holy Spirit. The gospel that we preach leads them to satisfy their desire. That is why we have the responsibility to spread the gospel all over the world. We are children of the Father and His heirs, who are faithful to His Great Commission.

We must preach the gospel with faith while keeping in mind that our mission is to allow people to receive the Holy Spirit. The gospel of the water and the Spirit is something evangelists must truly believe in before preaching it to others. Then their listeners will receive the Holy Spirit through their faith in the gospel. In this way, we can breathe the eternal life into all those who believe in the gospel. Our goal is to have them delivered from the power of darkness and conveyed into the Kingdom of God. Evangelists transfer sinners destined to die under the power of darkness into the Kingdom of the Son of God. It is a very important work to transform sinners into children of God.

Many people do not know the key to receiving the Holy Spirit and try to receive Him with their own effort. However, this will prove to be in vain. Only the faith in the gospel is needed, for the faith frees one from all sins.

How did you receive the Holy Spirit? Through prayer? Or perhaps through the laying on of hands? No, that is not the way. We receive the Holy Spirit only when we believe in the gospel of the water and the Spirit. We must pray and preach the gospel so that all the people of the world can receive the Holy Spirit.

The word "apostle" means "one who is sent by God." What do apostles do? They preach the gospel of the water and the Spirit so that people can receive the Holy Spirit. Wouldn't you like to take up this job as well along with us? We all must have the indwelling of the Holy Spirit and preach it to all people. Hallelujah! Praise the absolute truth of the gospel that the Lord gave us to receive the Holy Spirit! ✉

APPENDIX 1

Testimonies of Salvation

Testimonies of Salvation

Sister Joyce Meyer, USA

I started attending church due to the emptiness I felt in my heart and the lack of satisfaction I felt with my life. I used to think that if I got married, I'd find satisfaction in having adorable children, a loving husband, and an economically stable kind of life. So I got married and although my life wasn't luxurious, I led the kind of life that I'd wanted. Some say that my family life was an enviable one, but my heart was still empty and gloomy. I thought if I went to church, believed in God, mingled with a lot of people and took part in various church activities my heart and my life would change. Therefore, I used to attend church earnestly.

At the church that I attended, we held an all-night prayer meeting every Friday. In these sessions, we were told of the importance of speaking in tongues and that we could only receive the Holy Spirit in this way. Therefore, I earnestly gave my prayers of repentance in hopes that I could speak in tongues. When they conducted the laying on of hands, the elders of the church told me to repeat "Hallelujah, hallelujah, la-la-la" and so I did as I was told.

There were others who spoke in tongues, prophesied, saw illusions, and earned the Holy gift of clairvoyance. These people were objects of astonishment and envy to me and so I attended every church meeting in hopes of being like them. I did just as the people told me to do and repeated "Hallelujah, hallelujah" faster and faster but I couldn't achieve my goal. Someone told me I couldn't do it because I didn't say enough prayers of repentance. So I thought, I had sinned so much that my prayers of repentance were not sufficient for Him to send me the Holy Spirit. I then gave my prayer of repentance more fervently.

In passing, I came to receive the gift of tongues, and then I went to church more earnestly. My husband too became an ardent Christian believing that God had healed his wife's back, because I had testified that God healed my chronic backache miraculously.

One of the sisters who prayed with me could prophesy and I translated for her. And there was another sister who was barren for the first 7 years of her marriage. We prayed together often, and once during our prayers, I saw an image of her holding a newborn baby boy. So I told her, "Sister, by this time next year, you'll have a son." And exactly a year later, that sister gave birth to a baby boy.

Now, that sister too has been forgiven for her sins and has received the Spirit. Together we've been serving the gospel. Looking back, all that I did was play the role of a sorceress in the name of Jesus. But at that time, I believed that the Holy Spirit resided in me and so I laid my hands on the ill and I prayed for the demon-possessed saying, "I speak in the name of Jesus Christ of Nazareth, go away demons!"

I decided to live a life that would make Him happy. So for every Lent, I didn't have breakfast and instead gave the food to a poor old lady in my neighborhood. I went to hospitals and prisons to deliver God's words to the lost souls there. We took care of sick people and one of my fellow Christians who prayed with me actually adopted an orphan and sent him to school. I took care of a patient with a brain tumor and tried to look after him with the love of Jesus, however, I couldn't adequately look after these patients.

I therefore used to lament through my prayers of repentance. Whenever I thought of the verses in chapter 13 of 1 Corinthians, I cannot but condemn myself. "But it profits me with nothing. I visited the patient with a brain tumor every day and told him of Jesus and gave him food, but I felt guilty in my heart for I could not do all that I wanted to do with perfect love."

Then my backaches returned and I had to go to the hospital and undergo surgery. I was depressed and confused by my aches and pains because I couldn't seem to heal them myself. My heart and body was exhausted. I went mad and was almost taken to an asylum. I couldn't become sanctified however hard had I tried. Whenever I tried to pray, the sins in my heart made me cry and I was so exhausted with my belief in Jesus.

I gave numerous prayers that I might receive Jesus in my heart. But I was still unsure that I'd been forgiven for my sins. Jesus said that He had given us peace, which the world could not give, and that the river of spring water would flow from our hearts. But my heart was always anxious and oppressed. I wanted to give up believing in Jesus and just die. But then, God sent me His servant who had received the Holy Spirit. That pastor taught me the gospel that could help me receive the same Spirit.

In the Old Testament, when giving a sin offering, people were forgiven for their sins when they placed their hands on the head of the sacrificial animal. Likewise, Jesus was baptized by John and took away all the sins of the world and was judged for our sins on the Cross. This meant that those who believe in Him could receive the Holy Spirit.

As the pastor told me more about God's words, all my sins were passed onto Jesus. There was no longer any sin in my heart. When I heard His words, I didn't shiver or feel a burning sensation in my heart. Rather, my heart was filled with tranquil peace and joy and I was convinced then that I had received the Holy Spirit.

I heard that the baptism of Jesus was the truth of salvation. From then on, I am sure that there is no sin in my heart due to His words. People can receive the Holy Spirit only when they are sinless but I'd been saying that I had received the Holy Spirit when my heart was still full of sin. I could not have been more foolish.

After receiving the Holy Spirit, He guided me to live my life for the truth. I thank the Lord for giving me the gospel of the water and the Holy Spirit and helping me receive the Holy Spirit otherwise I would have gone to hell. I came to believe in the gospel of the water and the Holy Spirit and I received the Holy Spirit. I thank God for this truth. ⊠

Sister Anne Graham, New Zealand

When I look back on the time before I received forgiveness for my sins, I am embarrassed and ashamed of my behavior, but at that time, I was so fervent and serious. I thank the Lord for forgiving my sins.

I went to a church near our house from my infancy. However, all that I wanted was to speak in tongues, which I did for the first time when I attended a discipleship training meeting in the middle of my teenage years. I cried out "Lord" three times and prayed for the forgiveness of my sins. Then suddenly, I started speaking in a language quite similar to French. That was what they called speaking in tongues. I was jubilant. I was so proud that I had spoken in tongues prior to any of my friends.

When I was in college, I attended every all-night prayer meeting once a week, and went to all the church programs if possible. During that time, when I gave a prayer of repentance, I spoke in tongues that no one could understand. I repeatedly murmured "Jesus, I love you," and I used to pray with tears in my eyes, overwhelmed by my own emotions. I prayed for the more fluent tongues and the gift of translating prophesy. But my heart was filled with obscure emptiness and my faith felt equally void.

I thought if I were truly a child of God, I wouldn't have to feel lonely. But my relationship with Him was blocked by my sins and I couldn't stand the emptiness I felt when I wasn't doing anything for Him. I met many people who went through the same thing and so I believed that I would live like them and die like them.

But then, I heard about the gospel of the water and the Holy Spirit from my brother. The words in the gospel told me that human beings are born evil and therefore evil things come from within and defile them (Marks 7:20-23). The gospel says that even if people try not to do wrong, they cannot but commit sin and neither erase their sins for themselves. That's why Jesus came to this world to save us and it's why John, as the representative of all mankind, baptized Jesus to pass on to Him all the sins of the world (Matthews 3:13-17). Jesus was baptized to take away the sins of the world and was judged for them on the Cross.

This gospel was a shock to me. I was reading about His word every day but I'd never known the truth that we are born evil natured and that Jesus took away all our sins through His baptism. I had gone to church for more than 20 years but all that I'd learned was words about His death on the Cross, to live a good life, to repent every day and to serve God faithfully.

How I tried to follow the teachings of my church! But I realized by reading about the gospel of the water and the Holy Spirit that because we are born evil, we were unable to follow the commandments of God. But the gospel of the water and the Holy Spirit taught me that Jesus, the Son of God, came to this world and was baptized by John the Baptist to take away all the sins of the world.

I thought, 'Then was everything that I've done until now a waste?' But such doubts disappeared upon reading the Bible. I realized, *"By that will we have been sanctified through the offering of the body of Jesus Christ once for all"* (Hebrews 10:10). The forgiveness of our sin is not written in the future tense but in the past participle. While my faith had been in the future tense the day before. *"Their sins and their lawless deeds I will remember no more. Now where there is remission of these, there is no longer an offering for sin" (Hebrews 10:17-18).*

The Bible records that all my sins were forgiven about 2,000 years ago when Jesus was baptized by John and died on the Cross. This truth is so evident. People do not go to Heaven by giving prayers of repentance but by believing in the gospel of the water and the Holy Spirit, and by being forgiven for their sins. I finally know why my heart was so empty and what kept me from Jesus. It was sin in my heart.

I thought if I spoke in tongues, it would be the evidence of my receiving the Holy Spirit. But now I realize that believing that Jesus' baptism was to wash away all the sins of the world (Matthews 3:15) is the only way to receive God's Spirit. The Holy Spirit of God is a holy being and therefore cannot reside in the hearts of sinners, so people must believe in Jesus' baptism and His blood, and so should receive forgiveness for their sins. What I did before I came to believe in this was just witch's trickery. People believe that speaking in tongues is the external evidence of their receiving the Holy Spirit, but this is just one of Satan's tricks.

So many Christians have fallen for such tricks. They do not know that they've been deceived by Satan. I feel pity for them and so I would like to give them this testimony. I thank the Lord for saving me from such deception. *"God has given them a spirit of stupor, eyes that they should not see and ears that they should not hear, to this very day" (Romans 11:8).*

Only those who believe in the gospel of the water and the Holy Spirit can realize the truth and do as God wishes. I came to realize the truth and recognize Satan's deception through the gospel of the water and the Holy Spirit. God is the Spirit of truth. The Holy Spirit of God does not come on us like demons, instead He sends His servants to save us with His words and then sends His Spirit.

I thank the Lord for His grace, for saving me from Satan and spiritual chaos and helping me receive the Holy Spirit. I encountered His servant and believed in His words and He sent me His Spirit as a gift. I am truly happy because of the Holy Spirit who dwells in me. ✉

APPENDIX 2

Questions and Answers

Questions and Answers

Many people in this world have a great deal of interest in the indwelling of the Holy Spirit and have sent us questions through different kinds of media, including the Internet. Here we try to answer some questions, which we regard as either the most frequently asked or most important.

Question 1: I believe in Jesus, and I think I have received perfect remission of sins. I also believe that the Holy Spirit dwells within me. I know that a person who has been saved is a temple of God. Every time I go astray and commit a sin, the Holy Spirit restores my relationship with God anew, by accusing me and helping me to confess my sin to obtain forgiveness for it. I learned that if I didn't do this, God would punish me. Is it really true that the Holy Spirit does not dwell within us for a while unless we confess our sins and are forgiven for them?

Answer: This is definitely not the case. The indwelling of the Holy Spirit does not depend on us, whether we do something righteous or not. In other words, it doesn't depend on our will or wishes. Then how can it be achieved? The Holy Spirit doesn't dwell in a person because he or she confesses their sins and is pardoned for them; instead the Holy Spirit dwells within someone forever when he or she receives forgiveness for sins by believing in the gospel of the water and the Spirit. The Holy Spirit cannot dwell in a person who possesses even the slightest amount of sin.

However, many people think that the Holy Spirit dwells in

them only if they confess their sins and beg for forgiveness, and that if they don't, He won't dwell within them. This is definitely wrong. The Bible says that He came on the apostles on the Day of the Pentecost. But we should keep in mind that they received the indwelling of the Holy Spirit not through their prayers, but because they were forgiven for their sins by having come to believe in the gospel of the water and the Spirit.

The Holy Spirit is the Spirit of God, and He comes upon the righteous who have been sanctified by receiving forgiveness for their sins. What the Bible means by the word "holy" is to "be apart from sin." Taking away your sins by confessing and praying for forgiveness whenever you commit a transgression is not perfect forgiveness in the sight of God. How dare anyone say such that he can confess all his sin without omission before God?

Only those who believe that Jesus was baptized by John and shed His blood on the Cross according to God's plan for their salvation receive perfect forgiveness of their sins together with the indwelling of the Holy Spirit as a gift from God. However, the reason why many people try to receive the Holy Spirit through their own efforts is that because they haven't received perfect forgiveness for the sins in their hearts.

The true Holy Spirit doesn't come upon people through confession. He automatically comes upon them only when they are forgiven for all their sins by believing in the gospel of the water and the Spirit. This is an essential element of faith in order to receive the indwelling of the Holy Spirit before God.

The Holy Spirit doesn't come by any kind of effort or deed on our part. He comes upon a person if his sins are forgiven perfectly by believing in the gospel of the water and the Spirit. We are forgiven for all our sins by believing that Jesus took on the sins of the world through His baptism by John in the Jordan River almost 2,000 years ago. The Holy Spirit can only dwell in a person who exhibits this kind of faith.

He cannot dwell in a person who has sin in his heart. This is the truth. If a person asks for the indwelling of the Holy Spirit through confession every time he sins instead of faith in the true gospel, he can never receive the Holy Spirit. This only shows that he still has sin in his heart even though he believes in Jesus.

Satan is the one who condemns us. In Romans 8:1, it is written, *"There is therefore now no condemnation to those who are in Christ Jesus, who do not walk according to the flesh, but according to the Spirit."*

Even though one claims to have definitely received the forgiveness of sin and the indwelling of the Holy Spirit, if one hasn't been forgiven for all sins by believing in the gospel of the water and the Spirit, sin remains in the heart. This is why you have to have accurate knowledge of the gospel of the water and the Spirit in order to receive the indwelling of the Holy Spirit. If you want to learn about the gospel of the water and the Spirit in more detail, we cordially recommend you to read Paul C. Jong's first volume, "Have you truly been born again of water and the Spirit?"

Question 2: Does the Holy Spirit dwell within a born again person all of the time if he or she believe in the gospel of the water and the Spirit, or does the Holy Spirit hover around them and come into them whenever they asks for help?

Answer: The Holy Spirit is the Helper, in other words, the

Spirit of truth whom God has given to all righteous people who have been born again of water and the Spirit, ever since Jesus Christ was baptized by John the Baptist, died on the Cross and resurrected (John 15:26). Ephesians 1:13 says, *"In Him you also trusted, after you heard the word of truth, the gospel of your salvation; in whom also, having believed, you were sealed with the Holy Spirit of promise."* The Holy Spirit comes upon the righteous who have received forgiveness for their sins by believing in Jesus Christ and thereby seals them as children of God.

In John 14:16, the Lord said, *"And I will pray the Father, and He will give you another Helper, that He may abide with you forever."* Jesus' disciples received forgiveness for all their sin by believing that Jesus took on all the sins of the world through His baptism. This was why John the Baptist said, *"Behold! The Lamb of God who takes away the sin of the world!" (John 1:29)*

"The sins of the world" are all the sins that all the people of this world have been committing from the beginning until the end of the world. He accepted all the sins of the world at once, died on the Cross, was resurrected and thereby made us righteous forever. In Hebrews 10:12-14 it's written, *"But this Man, after He had offered one sacrifice for sins forever, sat down at the right hand of God, from that time waiting till His enemies are made His footstool. For by the offering He has perfected forever those who are being sanctified."*

The Lord was baptized by John, was crucified then resurrected, and thereby made us righteous forever. We were forgiven for all our sins at once and became God's children through Jesus, and this truth is immutable for all eternity. Those who have become righteous through faith don't have sin in their hearts. Even though people cannot help but sin due to their weaknesses, they have no sin forever because Jesus took away all their sins. Therefore, they can never become sinners again.

The Holy Spirit dwells eternally in the hearts of the righteous who have been sanctified. We cannot but sin due to our insufficiencies; but if we would became sinners every time we sin, then the gift of Jesus Christ, who made us righteous forever, would be wasted, and He would have to die for us again after accepting our sins. This is the sin of blaspheming the Holy Spirit (Hebrews 6:4-8, 10:26-29).

Accordingly, the Holy Spirit dwells within the righteous who have received forgiveness for their sins and have been born again by believing in the gospel of the water and the Spirit. Paul said, *"For you are the temple of the living God. As for God has said: 'I will dwell in them and walk among them. I will be their God, and they shall be My people'"* (2 Corinthians 6:16).

The Holy Spirit always dwells in God's children who have been sanctified forever. The word "dwell" here doesn't mean that He hovers around us then comes to us whenever we pray and call for Him; instead He "always abides in us." He always lives in those who have been born again of water and the Spirit, teaching them all things and leading them to know God's words (John 14:26).

Therefore, anyone who doesn't have the Holy Spirit of God is not His (Romans 8:9). The Holy Spirit dwells in those who are purified and sinless, teaching them all heavenly things and testifying that they are the children of God. It is not true that the Holy Spirit is near us, coming to us as a price for our own efforts; instead He always dwells in God's children who have been born again by the gospel of the water and the Spirit.

However, many people lack knowledge of this and try to

receive the indwelling of the Holy Spirit with their sinful hearts. As a result, they think that He comes upon them when they put effort into fervent prayers of repentance, but that He leaves when they sin. This is the faith of those who have not received the indwelling of the Holy Spirit. Those who have true faith believe that they receive the indwelling of the Holy Spirit as a gift through the forgiveness of sins. One should forsake one's own thoughts and return to the faith in God's word.

Question 3: **Both of my parents insisted that they were born again Christians even before they got married. Additionally, I have led a religious life from birth. I thought that the Holy Spirit had been within me from the time I was born. However, I am so confused because I don't have the biblical knowledge about the indwelling of the Holy Spirit. Does the Holy Spirit really come upon a person only if he is born again of water and the Spirit?**

Answer: Yes, this is true. Everyone needs to have his sins forgiven by believing in the gospel of the water and the Spirit in order to receive the Holy Spirit. The Bible tells us that "water" is the antitype of salvation (1 Peter 3:21). Here the water stands for the baptism Jesus received from John (Matthew 3:15).

First of all, everyone needs to be forgiven for all his sins by knowing the meaning of the baptism of Jesus in order to receive the Holy Spirit. Galatians 3:27 says, *"For as many of you as were baptized into Christ have put on Christ."* Here "being baptized into Christ" doesn't indicate our water baptism, but means receiving the forgiveness of sins by understanding and believing in the reason for Jesus' baptism by John.

Everyone is born in a sinful body. Romans 5:12 says, *"Therefore, just as through one man sin entered the world, and death through sin, and thus death spread to all men, because all sinned."* All the people in this world are born sinners, inheriting sin from Adam and Eve.

Therefore in Psalms 51:5 it is written, *"Behold, I was brought forth in iniquity, and in sin my mother conceived me."* In Isaiah 1:4 it's written, *"Alas, sinful nation, a people laden with iniquity, a brood of evildoers, children who are corrupters!"* People have the seeds of sin starting from the day they are born. All the people in this world inherit sins from their parents and are born into this world as sinners. In other words, our flesh is bound to bear the fruits of sin during our lifetime.

That is why thinking that if both of someone's physical parents are born again Christians, then their children will also receive the Holy Spirit, is merely a credulous and superstitious faith. He who has this kind of faith tries to receive the Holy Spirit through his own thoughts and the indwelling of the Holy Spirit cannot occur with this kind of faith.

Therefore, everyone should believe in the gospel of the water and the Spirit that Jesus gave us. This is the only way to receive the Holy Spirit, because He is a gift from God. Jesus Christ, the only begotten Son of God, took on all the sins of the world by being baptized by John, then was judged on the Cross and thereby made all believers of the truth righteous. This is God's plan and will toward mankind, and He has given the indwelling of the Holy Spirit to those who have faith in it according to His will.

Every one in this world is born with his own sin into this world. Therefore, he can receive the Holy Spirit as a gift only if he receives the forgiveness of sins and becomes sanctified by believing in the gospel of the water and the Spirit. Therefore everyone should keep it in mind and also believe that the Holy Spirit comes upon him only when he is born again of water and the Spirit.

He does not come upon us depending on some kind of condition or effort we make, but His indwelling is entirely up to the faithfulness of the One who made the promise. In other words, He doesn't come to dwell according to any human or spiritual achievement. The indwelling of the Holy Spirit can be received by faith according to God's will.

His will was to send Jesus Christ, His only begotten Son into this world in order to save all mankind from the sins of the world by having Him baptized by John, and having Him die on the Cross; thereby allowing the Holy Spirit to dwell in the hearts of believers. The righteous who are delivered from all their sins by obeying His will and by believing in the gospel of the water and the Spirit can receive the indwelling of the Holy Spirit.

Therefore, believing that one has received the Holy Spirit just because he was born of born again parents is a superstitious and credulous faith. This is just like trying to receive the Holy Spirit according to his own will regardless of God's will. There is no other way but to believe in the gospel of the water and the Spirit if one wants to receive the indwelling of the Holy Spirit.

Question 4: I think the Holy Spirit speaks to us every day. Even in the time of the early church, Jesus' disciples performed many miracles. I think the Holy Spirit who worked at that time is still working today in the same way. Therefore, many men of God perform miracles in Jesus' name, for example, casting out demons or healing diseases and doing other works aimed at returning people to Jesus. I think these works are done through the Holy Spirit. If this is not true, what is the difference between the Holy Spirit that strongly worked at the time of the early church and the One who performs miracles today? Is not God always the same yesterday, today and forever?

Answer: There is no real difference between the Holy Spirit who worked at the time of the early church and the One who works today. The only difference is whether the people who perform miracles at this time believe in the gospel of the water and the Spirit. The reason for this is that even though the Spirit of God is always the same regardless of time, the difference is whether one has accurate knowledge of the way to receive the Holy Spirit.

Many people nowadays perform wonders without having accurate biblical knowledge to receive the Holy Spirit. The Bible shows us in Acts 2:38, 1 John 5:2-8, and 1 Peter 3:21 that the only way to receive the Holy Spirit is to believe in the gospel of the water and the Spirit. *"There is also an antitype which now saves us — baptism."*

Of course, the Holy Spirit did things like healing diseases and casting out demons while dwelling within the Apostles at the time of the early church. However, they didn't receive money or cause uproar while using their spiritual gifts like some people nowadays tend to do. The Apostles demonstrated their abilities only as a means of delivering the gospel. Furthermore, healing disease and casting out demons were not all of the works of the Holy Spirit at the time of the early church. They were only a small part of it.

Therefore, it is very dangerous to think that all the wonders such as healing disease, casting out demons and speaking in tongues in today's Christianity are surely the works of the Holy Spirit. We should believe that all the peculiar phenomena we see with our eyes in Christianity today are not caused by the power of the Holy Spirit. Instead, we should discern the true servants of God who have received the indwelling of the Holy Spirit from the fraudulent servants who are possessed by evil spirits. Even if a person can cast out demons, heal disease and speak in tongues, if he has sin in his heart and does not believe in the true gospel, he is surely possessed by demons.

Jesus also said in Matthew 7:20-23, *"Therefore by their fruits you will know them. Not everyone who says to Me, 'Lord, Lord,' shall enter the kingdom of heaven, but he who does the will of My Father in heaven. Many will say to Me in that day, 'Lord, Lord, have we not prophesies in Your name, cast out demons in Your name, and done many wonders in Your name?' And then I will declare to them, 'I never knew you; depart from Me, you who practice lawlessness!'"*

We should not think that just because one performs miracles, he is doing it through the work of the Holy Spirit. Instead we should examine closely if he preaches the gospel of the water and the Spirit or if he is righteous by having received complete forgiveness for his sins. The Holy Spirit never dwells in a person who has sin in his heart. The Holy Spirit cannot be along with sin.

The forgiveness of sin at the time of the early church was the proof of the coming of the Holy Spirit and He was God's gift to those who were forgiven for all their sins.

However, many people still think that healing disease, speaking in tongues and casting out demons in Jesus' name is unconditionally the work of the Holy Spirit. This is a wrong and dangerous belief. We should be able to clearly tell if they are truly performing wonders. Even if a person is able to perform many wonders in Jesus' name, but if he doesn't know or believe in the true gospel of the water and the Spirit, then he must be a false teacher. Such people kill the souls of many people and demand money in order to satisfy their worldly greed.

Therefore, the work of the person who has sin in his heart is not truly the work of the Holy Spirit, but the work of demons. The Holy Spirit who worked at the time of the early church and the One working now is the same. However, there is a clear difference between the work of the Holy Spirit that appears to people who have really received the Holy Spirit and that of demons who appear through false prophets.

Question 5: What does the Holy Spirit do at this time?

Answer: The Holy Spirit at this time clearly does the work of discerning the true teachings from the false in the word of God. He preaches the gospel of the water and the Spirit, which the Lord gave us, to souls who are dying due to iniquity in this time of confusion, in order to save them.

We should know that there are many false prophets working inside Christianity today throughout the world. Even though they have sin in their hearts, they are still doing wrong: speaking in tongues, performing false wonders, and having visions. To the confused souls of this age, the Holy Spirit, "the

Helper" convicts the world of sin, and of righteousness, and of judgment (John 16:8).

First of all, the Spirit of truth convicts mankind of sin. Sin in the sight of God is not to believe in the gospel of the water and the Spirit that God gave us. He convicts those who don't believe in the beautiful gospel of Jesus' baptism by John the Baptist and His blood on the Cross, warning them that they are sinners destined for Hell.

He also bears witness to God's righteousness. Here the meaning of God's righteousness is that God sent Jesus into this world in the appearance of a man in order for Him to accept all the sins of the world. He helps people who believe in Jesus receive the forgiveness of sin by believing in the gospel of the water and the Spirit. He also warns that those who don't obey the true gospel despite knowing the will of God will later be judged for their sins.

In the beginning, when God created the world with His word, the Holy Spirit worked with Him and later shone the light of the truth on the empty and confused hearts of mankind in order to illuminate the gospel of the water and the Spirit (Genesis 1:2-3). Thus the Holy Spirit enlightens the confused souls of this age of their sins, on God's righteousness and on the judgment for their sins.

Question 6: Isn't speaking in tongues proof of the indwelling of the Holy Spirit? Otherwise how can we know if He dwells in us?

Answer: We can't assure that one has received the indwelling of the Holy Spirit just because they speak in tongues. Even demon-possessed people can speak in tongues.

You should know that devils could make people speak in strange tongues fluently under the name of Jesus Christ.

If we say that speaking in tongues is proof of the indwelling of the Holy Spirit, then this is definitely incorrect from a biblical standpoint and puts us into the sin of blaspheming against the Holy Spirit. 1 Corinthians 12:30 says, *"Do all have gifts of healings? Do all speak with tongues? Do all interpret?"* Because the Holy Spirit is God's Spirit, He can by no means be with sin and neither can He dwell in a person who has sin in his heart.

We should not believe that one has received the Holy Spirit just because he speaks in tongues, but should first examine if he has received the forgiveness of sin by believing in the gospel of the water and the Spirit. If someone thinks that he has received the Holy Spirit just because he has some kind of special experience, such as speaking in tongues, it could be that he is being tricked by a shrewd deception of Satan (2 Thessalonians 2:10). The Holy Spirit is a gift that is given by God to people who have received the forgiveness of sin through His words.

In answer to the second question, the Holy Spirit is God Himself and the Spirit of truth. Therefore, He works together with the gospel of the water and the Spirit. He does not work according to human will. He leads sinners to believe in the gospel of the water and the Spirit, teaches the truth to the righteous, and also quietly preaches the gospel, which is God's will, together with them. He doesn't come on people with fire-like emotions or irresistible vibration of bodies. God gave the Holy Spirit to the righteous, whose sins were blotted out by obeying the true gospel of the water and the Spirit. He taught them that they have become God's children. The Holy Spirit testifies in the hearts of the righteous that they have become sinless and completely righteous through the gospel of the water and the Spirit.

Therefore, if someone speaks in tongues but still has sin his heart, the spirit in him is definitely not the Holy Spirit, but the spirit of Satan. If you want to have the indwelling of the Holy Spirit in your heart, you should believe in the gospel of the water and the Spirit. Then the Lord will bless you with the indwelling of the Holy Spirit.

Question 7: Did Jesus' disciples receive the Holy Spirit by being delivered from their sins through the forgiveness of sin, or was it a separate experience without regard to the forgiveness of sin?

Answer: Receiving the Holy Spirit is not a separate experience from redemption. We can see in the Bible that Jesus' disciples already knew and believed that Jesus took all the sins of the world through His baptism by John even before they received the Holy Spirit (1 Peter 3:21 – *There is also an antitype which now saves us – baptism*).

The forgiveness of sins means salvation from sin, in other words it means all the sins in our hearts are washed away and gone. Nowadays, many Christians are often confused about the meaning of the forgiveness of sin that Jesus gave us. People do not know how they can receive the forgiveness of sin. They think they have been delivered from their sins simply because they believe in Jesus as their Lord.

Those who have received forgiveness for their sins have the witness in themselves. However, if someone doesn't have the witnessing word of his redemption, then he has not received the Holy Spirit nor was forgiven for all his sins. If he has spirit-filled feelings, it is only the result of being deceived by his own emotions. Satan transforms himself into an angel of light (2 Corinthians 11:14-15, Galatians 1:7-9), deceiving him into straying from the truth (Matthew 7:21-23).

Those who are forgiven for their sins have the witness in them because they believe in the gospel of the water and the Spirit. In 1 John 5:4-12, God bears witness to Jesus Christ who came by water and blood. Furthermore, He says if one preaches about a different spirit or a different gospel (2 Corinthians 11:4), then he has not received the forgiveness of sin nor the Holy Spirit. People can receive the forgiveness of sin only when they believe in Jesus Christ, who came by the gospel of the water and the Spirit. Receiving the Holy Spirit is crucial to the forgiveness of sin. The forgiveness of sin is crucial to the indwelling of the Holy Spirit.

Question 8: What does it mean to receive the baptism of the Holy Spirit?

Answer: We should know the reason for Jesus' baptism. Paul preached the gospel of Jesus' baptism to some Ephesians when he heard that they were only baptized into "John's baptism." They were baptized in the name of Jesus Christ and received the Holy Spirit in their hearts by believing what Paul said about Jesus' baptism. The nature of the baptism Jesus received from John and that of John's baptism of repentance were different. Jesus' baptism was to wash away sins, which was directly related to our receiving the Holy Spirit.

Then what was the nature of John's baptism? He shouted, "Repent, brood of vipers! Forsake foreign gods you were serving, and return to the true God." His baptism was that of repentance, which made people return to God. However, the baptism Jesus received from John was in order for Him to take over all the sins of the world. This is the difference between John's baptism and Jesus' baptism by John. Jesus' baptism was to fulfill all righteousness.

Then what is the baptism that has fulfilled all righteousness? It is the baptism through which Jesus took away all the sins of mankind starting from Adam to the last person in the world. In other words, Jesus' baptism by John was to fulfill all righteousness.

To fulfill all righteousness means that God let His Son be baptized by John to take all the sins of the world on to Him so that He could be judged for us by being crucified on the Cross. God raised Jesus from the dead and sanctified all believers.

This was done for all mankind. Jesus' baptism and His blood on the Cross brought us eternal salvation, forgiveness for all our sins and the chance to live together with God forever. This is God's righteousness, love, and salvation for all mankind. Here we can confirm that the baptism of the Holy Spirit was fulfilled through Jesus' baptism and His blood on the Cross.

In order to be baptized in the name of Jesus Christ, we need to have the witness of believing that all the sins of this world were passed on to Jesus through His baptism. Everyone who has received the forgiveness of sin by believing in Jesus' baptism and His blood on the Cross should be baptized in the name of Jesus Christ.

Therefore, we are baptized as the proof of our faith in Jesus' baptism and in line with His commandment saying, *"Go therefore and make disciples of all the nations, baptizing them in the name of the Father and of the Son and of the Holy Spirit" (Matthew 28:19)*. Jesus was baptized by John in order to take away all the sins of the world, and because this truth leads people to receive the Holy Spirit, so it is also called the baptism of the Holy Spirit.

Question 9: How does the Holy Spirit appear differently in the Old and New Testaments?

Answer: The Holy Spirit is the same God regardless of time. Therefore, His divine nature doesn't change no matter whether we read about Him in the Old or the New Testaments. However, it is true that He worked differently in the Old and the New Testaments by God's providence in order to save mankind from their sins.

In the Old Testament, God poured the Holy Spirit to men of God by special methods in order to speak His words, to show His will through wonders, and to do His work. For example, the Spirit of the Lord began to move upon Samson the Judge, thereby doing many mighty works through him (Judges 13:25, 14:19). In other words, the Holy Spirit came on elected people restrictively at the time of the Old Testament.

However, at the time of the New Testament, by designating the Day of Pentecost as the starting point for the coming of the Holy Spirit, God sent the Holy Spirit to every saint who has received the forgiveness of sins through their faith in the gospel of the water and the Spirit. And He permits the Holy Spirit dwells in them forever.

Therefore, after the coming of the Holy Spirit on the first Pentecost, all the righteous whose sins were forgiven by believing the gospel of truth can have the indwelling of the Holy Spirit (Acts 2:38). Peter went into the house of Cornelius, a Gentile and centurion of Rome, and preached the gospel of Jesus' baptism and His blood on the Cross. While Peter was speaking the gospel, the Holy Spirit fell upon everyone who heard the word (Acts 10:34-45). This proves that the moment one hears and believes in the gospel of Jesus' baptism and His Cross, which Jesus has fulfilled, he receives the Holy Spirit as a gift.

God caused the Holy Spirit to dwell in all the righteous who were forgiven for all their sins by believing in the true gospel. The Holy Spirit in the Old Testament played the role of leading people to Jesus Christ, and the Holy Spirit in the New Testament bears witness to God's righteousness and stands as the guarantee for it. God's righteousness means that Jesus forgave all the sins of the world through His baptism and His blood on the Cross. And the Holy Spirit stands as a guarantee of the gospel of salvation and helps everyone believe in it.

Question 10: **I spent many sad days after the doctor diagnosed my case as stomach cancer. One day, a Christian friend of mine visited me and told me that anyone attending a revival meeting at his church would be healed of any kind of disease. To me, an atheist at that time, the healing of disease by God's power seemed too good to be true. On the last of day of the meeting, everyone came up to the minister to receive the laying on of his hands. While he laid his hands on me, he told me to repeat some inapprehensible words and asked me if I believed in Jesus Christ's healing power. Even though I didn't truly believe in my heart, I was upset and answered yes. And right at that moment I felt something hot like electricity running through me. I could feel my whole body quivering and I felt that my cancer was cured. I decided to believe in the Lord on the spot and after that, a great happiness and peace came into my heart and I**

began a new life. I also devoted myself to spreading the gospel. I think that the Holy Spirit caused all these things and I believe that He dwells in me. Don't you think of it as the same way?

___Answer:___ You have really had an amazing experience. I have heard many confessions from people who dedicated their lives to the Lord after experiencing God's answers to their prayers. However, I would like to ask you if this amazing supernatural experience could be the definite proof that you received the Holy Spirit.

As a matter of fact, many Christians nowadays would answer "Yes" to the question above. When Western Christianity was in decline amid the growth of materialism, the so-called Pentecostal-Charismatic Movement arose and Christianity revived tremendously, especially in the under developed or developing countries.

As a result, many Christians fell under the influence of the Pentecostal-Charismatic Movement, which stresses the importance of supernatural experience. Those who lead revival meetings sometimes obtain worldwide fame as Evangelical revivalists. Furthermore, because they have surprising testimonies of their own and express their own faith through their experiences, their followers pursue experience-based faith like them.

However, the Bible says "No" to the question above. Of course, the Holy Spirit has the ability to give us supernatural experiences. However, because He is the Spirit of truth (John 15:26), we can receive the Holy Spirit only through the word of truth.

Peter received the Holy Spirit on the Day of Pentecost and confidently preached the gospel saying, *"God has made this*

Jesus, whom you crucified, both Lord and Christ." Then the Jews who heard this said to Peter and the other Apostles, *"Men and brethren, what shall we do?" (Acts 2:36-37)* He answered them, *"Repent, and let every one of you be baptized in the name of Jesus Christ for the remission of sins; and you shall receive the gift of the Holy Spirit. For the promise is to you and to your children, and to all who are afar off, as many as the Lord our God will call" (Acts 2:38-39).*

In other words, God clearly said that He would give the Holy Spirit as a gift to the righteous who received the remission of sin by believing in Jesus Christ's gospel. The only proof of the indwelling of the Holy Spirit in one's heart is the word of truth.

Have you received the remission of sin through the gospel of the water and the Spirit? If so, you can be assured that the indwelling of the Holy Spirit has already taken place in you.

However, no matter what amazing experiences you may have had or no matter how many wonders you have performed, you have definitely not received the Holy Spirit if you still have sin in your heart. The reason is that you don't have the witness of the remission of sin based on the word of truth. Just as darkness can't be found in the light, the Holy Spirit can neither come on a sinner nor dwell with sin.

Therefore, the true indwelling of the Holy Spirit only happens to people whose sins are completely washed away by the gospel of the water and the Spirit. God wants all people to hear the truth and to receive the indwelling of the Holy Spirit. Now you can receive the indwelling of the Holy Spirit by believing in the gospel of the water and the Spirit.

I have received numerous other questions besides these and you can find all the answers to them by having faith in Jesus' baptism by John and His blood on the Cross. Now everyone who believes in Jesus can receive the Holy Spirit, which God promised to pour out of on all in the last days. We give thanks to the Lord. Hallelujah!

This book contains a great deal of information on the Holy Spirit. This book will help you answer your questions. If you want to know more about the gospel of the water and the Spirit, please refer to the author's first two books of his Christian Book Series.

Have You Truly Been Born Again of Water and the Spirit? Seoul: Hephzibah, 1999.

Return to the Gospel of the Water and the Spirit. Seoul: Hephzibah, 1999.

God wants you to receive the indwelling of the Holy Spirit and wait for the Lord's Coming. If you believe in God's words together with the author, you will receive the indwelling of the Holy Spirit and give glory to the Lord. ⊠

HAVE YOU TRULY BEEN BORN AGAIN

OF WATER AND THE SPIRIT?

PAUL C. JONG

Among many Christian books written about being born again, this is the first book of our time to preach 'the gospel of the water and the Spirit' in strict accordance with the Scriptures. Man can't enter the kingdom of heaven without being born again of water and the Spirit. To be born again means that a sinner is saved from all his lifelong sins by believing in the baptism of Jesus and His blood on the Cross. Let's believe in the gospel of the water and the Spirit and enter the kingdom of heaven as the righteous who have no sin.

This book can be also purchased at world's largest online store like Amazon.com (www.amazon.com) or Barnes & Noble.com (www.bn.com).

♠ **Hephzibah Publishing House**
Website: www.pauljong.com

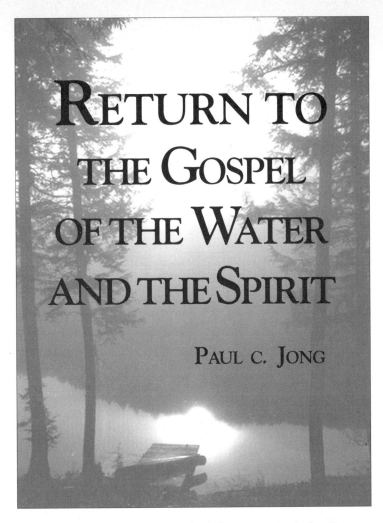

RETURN TO THE GOSPEL OF THE WATER AND THE SPIRIT

PAUL C. JONG

Let's return to the gospel of the water and the Spirit. Theology and doctrines themselves can't save us. Many Christians still follow them and are not born again. This book clearly tells us what mistakes theology and doctrines have made and how to believe in Jesus in the most proper way.

This book can be also purchased at world's largest online store like Amazon.com (www.amazon.com) or Barnes & Noble.com (www.bn.com).

♠ **Hephzibah Publishing House**
Website: www.pauljong.com